MIKE PHILLIPS
Half **TRUTHS**

MY TRIUMPHS, MY MISTAKES, MY UNTOLD STORY

WITH MATTHEW SOUTHCOMBE

Reach Sport

For my sons Elias and Zayn.

I love you both so much.

Remember, do as Daddy says, not as Daddy did!

Reach Sport

www.reachsport.com

Written with Matthew Southcombe

First published in Great Britain and Ireland in 2021 by
Reach Sport, a Reach PLC business.
www.reachsport.com
@Reach_Sport

Reach Sport is a part of Reach PLC.
One Canada Square, Canary Wharf, London, E15 5AP.

Hardback ISBN: 9781914197185
Paperback ISBN: 9781914197406
eBook ISBN: 9781914197192

Photographic acknowledgements:
Reach PLC, Alamy, Getty Images, Mike Phillips personal collection

Every effort has been made to trace copyright.
Any oversight will be rectified in future editions.

Typesetting by Danny Lyle

Printed and bound by CPI Group (UK) Ltd,
Croydon, CR0 4YY.

Contents

Acknowledgements

There is only one place to start, isn't there? Without my parents, I would never have achieved what I did. I had the perfect start in life, growing up on the farm just outside Bancyfelin, with all the values that instils in you. Ours was always a happy home and I couldn't have asked for anything more as a kid. I was never pushed to become a rugby player, there was never any pressure to do one thing or the other and for that I will always be grateful. I'm sure some of my misdemeanours frustrated them during my career but the love and support was always there. I know I did them proud and that means more to me than any medal. For better or worse, my brothers, Mark and Rob, had a profound impact on me growing up. Like most younger siblings, I wanted to be like my older brothers and help shape me into the man I became.

My wife might have missed the majority of my career but she was unbelievably supportive and understanding when I made the transition through retirement. She has strong values and is a fantastic mother to our boys. She continues to be a shoulder to lean on, somebody to share laughs with and I'm incredibly proud of everything that she has achieved and continues to achieve in her career.

There are simply too many team-mates to mention but the bonds you create in a professional rugby environment are so special. I've had the fortune of playing with some of the best players that have ever walked this earth and it is a privilege to call many of them friends. There is no doubt that I'd have struggled to get through certain moments in my career without the support of my team-mates, which is something that often gets overlooked. We lived out our dreams together and nobody can take that away from us.

Gareth Jenkins gave me my first shot at the professional level. He was also always there if I needed advice and I will be forever grateful to him for that. Dai Young and Lyn Jones were both excellent too. Both were outstanding man managers who had the respect of the dressing room and both have fantastic rugby brains.

Even though things did not end how I would have liked, it would be remiss of me not to mention Warren Gatland here. I repaid the faith he showed in me but he had to give me the opportunity to do so first. And I want to mention Rob Howley. Again, our relationship wasn't always great but, especially in the beginning, I thought Rob was a good coach who wasn't afraid to try new things. We were all in an elite environment and just wanted to do the best we could for Wales. Then there's Shaun Edwards. We always saw eye-to-eye and got on really well. He's a great bloke who always checked in on me. We continue to be good friends today.

These books do not happen by accident and I must mention Matthew Southcombe for bringing my words to life and helping me give you a little insight into what really went on in

Acknowledgements

my career. Thanks too must also go to Steve Hanrahan and Paul Dove, my publishers at Reach Sport, and Chris Brereton and Harri Aston for their editing.

Finally, I want to thank you, the fans. Throughout my career, you meant everything to me. Your roars made the hairs on the back of my neck stand up, I thrived in the arenas that you created. Without you, I don't think I would have been the player that I was because you lifted me, inspired me to reach new heights. I craved your adulation and I can't thank you enough for your support. I hope I repaid you.

Mike Phillips, September 2021

Foreword by
Paul O'Connell

My earliest memory of Mike Phillips dates back to 2005. I was part of a Munster side that travelled over to Stradey Park to face Llanelli Scarlets in the Celtic League. During the match, there was an injury and our players went into a huddle and so did theirs.

Suddenly we heard a load of commotion coming from their huddle and Robin McBryde had just had enough of Mike and the pair of them were getting into an argument. All I could hear was Robin, in his thick Welsh accent, repeatedly shouting: "I've had enough of it!" Then, when it was all over, there was a scrum and as it was being set, Mike was standing there throwing the ball up in the air as he looked at one of our players and said: "What is his problem?" He then nodded his head towards McBryde.

It turned out that Mike and Ronan O'Gara, our fly-half, had been sledging each other relentlessly during the game and this had wound McBryde up. He couldn't take any more of it. On another occasion we were playing against Wales in Cardiff and were going through the warm-ups. Obviously, each team takes a half of the pitch to go through their preparations and Mike was doing some box kicking when the ball landed near Ronan O' Gara in the Ireland half of the pitch.

Mike held his hands up for O'Gara to pass him the ball back but, instead, he just booted it into the stands. The pair of them then started abusing each other – and you've got to remember that this was before the game had even kicked off! Neither of them were going to back down because Ronan O'Gara enjoyed a bit of sledging too. Mike would actually respect that sort of stuff because he enjoyed giving as good as he got. I'm sure he likes to believe that we hated him over in Ireland but we didn't.

Whenever you're playing against a team, you're always creating an Us vs Them mentality. We're the good guys and they're the bad guys. That's just the way it is. Sometimes, it was easy to make Them out to be the bad guys when Mike was in their team because he liked the verbals and he was very confrontational. Once we went on a Lions tour with him, every single one of the Ireland lads got on with him and enjoyed his company. It was exactly how you might expect it to be.

I didn't get to know Mike when I played against him but he was very tough, very combative and very lippy. When you faced him, he was the kind of guy that you'd hate but every so often, he might pick you up off the floor, pat you on the back or compliment your tackle. Then you'd be thinking to yourself: 'Okay, maybe he isn't that bad!'

Then you go on tour with him and you find out what he's really like. I was lucky enough to travel with Mike on the Lions tours of 2009 and 2013.

I always compare him to my old Ireland and Munster team-mate Alan Quinlan in the sense that you loved playing with him but you'd hate to play against him. He was one of those guys where the more you got to know him, the more you loved him and the more you enjoyed playing with him.

He absolutely revelled in the physical side of the game. He's obviously a big man and he wanted to take people on. There was a cockiness about him but, really, he was just a confident person. The cockiness was just playful. If you didn't know him, you'd probably think he was arrogant but if you know him, you know he's just having fun. When you were playing with him, his confidence filtered through to you. He had genuine belief in his physical ability, in his skill level, he believed in the people around him and I think he made the people around him better through that.

You might see him on the TV now and he'll make the odd funny, cocky comment but that's just him having a laugh. The belief I'm talking about is how he prepared, how he trained, how he spoke during the week of a Test match, how he played – that's the lovely confidence that I enjoyed and felt we got value out of on the Lions tours.

I'd say he was good for the Welsh boys too. The Welsh are such incredible rugby players but a lot of them are quiet guys, they are very humble and don't raise their heads above the parapet too much. To have a guy that did that a little bit, a guy that stuck his chest out, particularly in such a pivotal position, is probably part of the reason Wales were so successful when Mike was there.

If you'd been on that 2005 tour to New Zealand, you dearly wanted the 2009 and 2013 tours to be a success. So people that were going to do everything in their power to make it a success, people who were going to empty the tank in every way possible – off the field and on the field – those were the guys that I was drawn to the most and Mike was certainly one of those guys.

You look at him and you think: 'We can win with this guy and we can have a whale of a time doing it.'

These days everyone talks about connections and relationships, they are real buzzwords, but it just puts a false narrative around becoming a good team-mate. It's referred to now like it's something you can learn out of a book but it's not. Mike built relationships with people due to his funny nature, his playfulness and his vulnerabilities. He'd get himself into trouble between arguing with people and wearing his heart on his sleeve, and having a night out. But because of all that, he built relationships really easily and it's almost impossible not to grow very fond of him very quickly. Besides him being this great guy, who people enjoy being around, you've also got this excellent rugby player that gives other people confidence. It's a great mixture when you're trying to create a team that wants to win things. The Lions need great players to win but they also need that glue, the friendships, when they come under pressure. Mike was fantastic at generating and building that.

All the Welsh boys have this legacy that they have to live up to when it comes to the Lions. For them, there seemed to be a sense that until you'd become a Welsh Lion, you couldn't live up to some of the greats that had gone before. So, to me, whilst a lot of the Welsh boys used to get more homesick than others, they absolutely adored the Lions.

Mike would be one of those that really loved playing for the Lions, the pressure, the big games and trying to live up to what it means to be a real Welsh legend on a Lions tour. That motivated Mike and he trained incredibly hard. He was the same in training as when he played; incredibly committed, very skilful, physical, vicious, competitive. He was the same in the gym and he prepared remarkably well. Then at the weekend, he always had a night out and that probably made him what he was. I'd say that if he didn't have a night out and a chance to blow off some steam, he probably wouldn't have been the same player. That really endears you to him because you see how committed he is as a player and you see how much he enjoys people's company. He loves sitting with people, talking to them and slagging them. If he finds out you have a nickname, he'll never call you by your first name again!

I was fortunate enough to captain Mike on the 2009 Lions tour to South Africa and he was fantastic. I liked a night out, so I wasn't one of those captains that was looking across at Mike worried about what he was going to do on Saturday night because I was generally there with him!

As a captain, you want people that have an opinion and are almost going to do the job for you as well. You want people that are aggressive, abrasive, that believe in themselves, that will make the environment fun and competitive, and drive high standards. Mike ticked all those boxes.

We had a particularly good relationship. I couldn't get enough of him because he made the environment such a fun place for everyone but operated at the highest of levels. Those guys are few and far between. Sometimes the guys who perform at the very top are reserved – they don't have a drink, they're very serious characters and they might not show any vulnerabilities. Whereas Mike was the best of both worlds. Whilst he might have enjoyed himself when he got the chance, he never let it affect his performance. He was incredibly committed to his training and he raised standards.

Some guys don't train very well but play very well and they can be frustrating. They're probably not as frustrating as the guys that train very well and don't play so well but Mike had it both. He was a ferocious, competitive trainer and there were plenty of barbs to make it fun. He took that onto the pitch as well. When you watched him train during the week, you knew you were going to get that and some more on top when it came to Saturday.

Mike has a great appetite for life as well as the Lions and that's why I think we got on so well. He was so determined to make the tours a success and gave every bit of himself to those trips. We were encouraged to socialise, have nights out and build relationships. He went at that hammer and tong but he never missed a training session unless he had a genuine injury. He trained hard, he pushed people hard. I enjoy those kind of personalities, those kind of guys who people think are incredibly cocky but they're not, they're just having fun. The joke's on you really if you don't get it. Mike must have a library of images on his phone of every time that he managed to beat a player. You mightn't hear from him for six months and suddenly he'll send you a photo of you missing a tackle on him with your face in the dirt. He won't even write a message, he'll just send you the picture. I enjoy that. He is keeping the connection in his own way. Checking in but also getting a dig in as well.

I've played with so many incredible players down the years but I rate Mike Philips massively highly. He was a dream of a team-mate because his standards never dropped. He was one of the best players in the world and is one of the best nines that has ever played the game. But at the same time he brings people together through his personality. Those kinds of guys are not as common as you think they are. Only a handful of players I've played with are like him in that regard.

Mike was an absolute nightmare to play against but it was a genuine pleasure to play alongside him. He's become a great friend. He's one of those friends that you meet through rugby and you may not spend a lot of time with them. But when you do meet up, you pick up where you left off. It's a friendship that comes from a good place. It comes from respect.

Paul O'Connell, September 2021

1

I'm Losing It

A bouncer is pressing my face against the floor in the centre of Cardiff and his mate has positioned himself right in the middle of my back.

There are a few different ways this could have gone but I find a moment of clarity, even after a pint or 10. The voice in my head is telling me one thing and one thing only; do not react.

The only thing that would have achieved is to escalate what I deem to be a relatively minor incident into something far more serious. I manage to turn my head, scraping it across the floor. As I look up, I find myself staring into a camera lens.

Great.

Now I'm starting to realise that the situation has taken a sinister turn for the worst. I know those pictures are not going to look good. I knew where this was heading. I don't think I've hit rock bottom but I'm not far off. I am, of course, describing the now infamous events of June 14, 2011, a night that, despite everything I achieved, will always be something that I'm remembered for.

It also took place less than a week before Wales' preparations for the 2011 Rugby World Cup were due to begin, so the timing wasn't the best. If you've read the newspaper reports, you'll have figured out that the chap pinning me to the concrete and his mate are both McDonald's bouncers. But you only know part of the story.

In order to fully understand the events that occurred that night, we need to rewind a little bit. Before we begin I want to make one thing clear: I'm not here to make excuses for my behaviour.

I look back now and I can't escape the stupidity of it all, arguing with a bouncer outside a fast food restaurant in the early hours of a Tuesday morning, especially so close to a huge moment in my career. I should have been tucked up in bed. But we all make stupid decisions from time to time.

In some ways, I was a ticking time bomb. It wasn't just an argument with a bouncer, it was a culmination of a lot of things. Shortly before the incident I'd ended a two-year relationship with Aimee Duffy, the incredibly successful singer from Bangor. I'd been commuting from our place in London down to Swansea to train with the Ospreys three days a week, which is a six-hour round trip and only added to the stresses I'd been wrestling with as a result of dating another person who is in the public eye.

Truthfully, it was no way to be living and I'm not sure how I managed to keep performing to a high level during that period, with all the travel. Things had come to a head and I decided to end it but that doesn't mean I was in a particularly happy place mentally.

On the rugby front, my relationship with the Ospreys had completely deteriorated after some disagreements and miscommunication during contract negotiations. Things turned sour for the final few months of the season and they stopped picking me altogether. Then they went on a trip to Dubai, which I didn't bother attending. The upshot of that situation was that the region pretty much discarded me and I was left looking for another club. All the while, I was trying to put my best foot forward on the pitch because the World Cup was around the corner. I didn't need all these distractions in my life but they are the kind of things that I was dealing with in the background and, quite frankly, I needed to blow off some steam.

I was out that night toasting the fact I'd agreed to join French club Bayonne that very same day. That was a big relief for me. Being left without a club is never a nice feeling, so to secure the move was a great moment. During the latter stages of my relationship with Aimee, I'd stopped going out entirely to spend more time with her and now I was more than happy to celebrate some much-needed good news.

Plus, there was no rugby going on at that particular moment and I was in the middle of having some time off. So into the city I went with one of my good mates. It was nothing too wild but we enjoyed ourselves. The drinks had been flowing at Tiger Tiger, one of the boys' favourite watering holes after a match.

At the end of the night, like a lot of people, I fancied some food to take home with me so, along with my mate, I headed to McDonald's. The incident that followed was a storm in a teacup. I wanted food. I was looking forward to a nice McChicken sandwich meal, a cheeseburger and a Coke to wash it all down. But the bouncer wouldn't let me in and a few words were exchanged as a result. He gave me a bit of stick and started having a bit of a go at the team in general, saying things like: "No wonder you boys are shit."

He was quite cheeky and an argument followed but I was ready to leave it. I'd actually started walking away but before I realised that the situation was about to spiral well out of control, one bouncer jumped on my back and wrestled me to the floor before two of them pinned me. It caused a bit of a scene and somebody was snapping pictures on their phone as events unfolded.

I'd had a terrible few months but things were about to get a whole lot worse. A number of people had gathered around but nobody was interested in helping me out or backing me up, they just whipped their phones out and started snapping pictures. I was more relieved than you might think to see the police arrive because I knew that it would de-escalate the situation. They took me away, put me in the back of the van and I just said to them: "Boys, check the CCTV. I've done nothing."

At that point, they just took me home. Which was obviously for the best. When you're in that position, face to the floor, people all around you taking pictures, knowing the damage it could do to your reputation, the impact it will have on your loved ones and how it all looks, you feel pretty helpless. But I don't blame anyone apart from myself. I put myself in that situation and I should have been smarter and more aware. I don't blame the bouncers or anything like that. I was really annoyed at myself for a long time afterwards, I really punished myself for what had happened.

In the days that followed, I had a series of difficult conversations with a number of people and they were tough for different reasons. One of the first I had was with my good mate Sonny Parker, the former Wales centre who I played with for years at the Ospreys.

The morning after the debacle, I was out on my speedboat with a friend of mine. We were just outside the Cardiff Bay barrage, chilling out and enjoying the sun. I was just trying to relax before the training camp started whilst also trying to forget about the night before. There was little chance of that happening. I wasn't on Twitter at the time, it was a relatively new phenomenon and I hadn't really picked up on it. These days, it's very rare that a high-profile sports person isn't on social media but people were still trying to feel their way into it back then, trying to figure out exactly what it was, how it should be used and what the pitfalls were. Sonny's text read: "Have you seen these pictures of you on Twitter? You'd better get on there and get them taken down."

That's when the penny really dropped and I realised that I was pretty fucked. I was devastated. But the real kicker was that whoever had posted the pictures had sent them to the *News of the World*. At that point, I knew it would have been a waste of time trying to get them removed. It took a couple of days to come out in the press, but it was in the *Western Mail*, the *Daily Mail*, *The Sun* and just about every other UK newspaper. The news was out and that's when things really started to get uncomfortable.

The next call was the toughest. I was sitting in my bedroom in Penarth. It felt like my career was collapsing around me and my mum was on the phone. To say she was displeased with me would be putting it mildly. I didn't get a word in. She was screaming down the phone: "What are you doing? Sort yourself out!" It was genuine anger. She wasn't disappointed, she was furious. She went on and I was trying to explain but I had to put the phone down on her in the end because we weren't getting anywhere and we didn't really speak again until after the World Cup.

I knew that I'd really upset her and that ate me up inside. That was the toughest part of the whole thing. Nobody wants to let their parents down and I knew that's exactly what I'd done. I was no saint, so this wasn't the first time, either. My parents are well thought of back in the village and the last thing you want is for people to think badly of them.

Then Wales got in touch, which I guess was inevitable really. I was a regular in the side and I'd just been named in the wider squad to train for the Rugby World Cup that was a few months away. Our training camp was due to start the following week. However, I would not be there.

A lot of people think that when you get dropped or selected that there is some big heart-to-heart with the coach and you talk it out in a very philosophical manner but that doesn't always happen. In this instance, I got a message from team manager Alan Phillips – known as 'Thumper' – to say that I was suspended from the squad for two weeks. That was it. We didn't speak on the phone and I didn't really have any more detail than that, although I figured they'd be looking into the matter to establish exactly what had happened.

Did I think I'd blown my chances of going to the World Cup? To be truthful, I didn't care. At that point in time, the last place I wanted to be was in a Wales squad going to a World Cup and I was ready to tell the management just that. I hope that doesn't come across as ungrateful because I cherish every cap I won for my country but I'd had enough.

Mentally, I was at a real low point and it just felt like there was always some issue that I had to deal with in Wales. A lot of the time people would make stuff up and there always seemed to be a complaint or a problem. There was constant aggravation following me everywhere I went. Looking back, I brought a lot of it on myself but I was under a lot of stress.

My life was 100mph on and off the field and I wasn't coping with it. I decided to get on the phone to Christian Gaijan. He was director of rugby at Bayonne at the time and he'd just signed me less than 24 hours before I ended up hitting the headlines. I felt I had to call him given that I had just signed for the club and I got a lot of stuff off my chest to him. I'd had enough of Welsh rugby, a total gut-full.

When I made that phone call, I had no intention of going to the World Cup, even if Wales wanted me back. I just felt like the whole thing was totally ridiculous. How could something so small be blown up into this massive incident? I just wanted to get out of Wales, go to France straight away and get away from all the nonsense. I said: "I just want to get away from it all, come to France and be anonymous, and get back to enjoying my rugby again." I told Christian all this and, to his credit, he said: "Mike, you have to go to the World Cup, it's a massive opportunity and you'll regret it if you don't go. Then, when it is all over, you can come to France."

He was a really good guy. He'd have been well within his rights to give me an earful as well because I was his latest big signing and within a matter of hours I was getting involved in this rubbish. The two weeks that followed were a pretty low point in my life. In all honesty, I feared I'd done permanent damage to my reputation and I wasn't sure it would blow over. These things always do eventually but when you're in the eye of the storm, sometimes it's difficult to see how things can end positively.

It frustrated the hell out of me as well because I didn't think it was all that bad. The pictures made it look horrendous and people were putting two and two together and getting five. Warren Gatland was great in fairness and he did reach out after the initial message came through from Thumper. He didn't say a lot but he just told me: "Get yourself sorted and be ready to come back in a few weeks."

He was usually quite good with stuff like this but he didn't always get it right. Sometimes he managed players well, other times he didn't. But I hadn't done anything particularly serious,

7

I hadn't hurt anyone. I think they did a bit of digging and probably found that out for themselves. I still wasn't entirely convinced that I wanted to go to New Zealand but, luckily, I hadn't let that slip to any of the management. Soon after the incident, my ex-girlfriend Aimee got in touch.

Our break-up had played a part in my behaviour at the time and, whether she knew that or not, she reached out after seeing my name – and the pictures – in the newspapers. I think she figured that I was in a pretty rough spot mentally and she wanted to check in on me. It was Aimee who talked me into going to a wellness centre in Kent, where I spent a week following the incident.

She sold it to me as this place where successful people from all walks of life – from celebrities to business people – go in order to gain that one or two percent that can make all the difference. It wasn't a rehabilitation facility and I wasn't dealing with those sorts of demons. But she thought it would be good for me to sort my head out a little bit because it was clear to those closest to me that I wasn't coping with what was going on around me at the time. Obviously, I disagreed. I wasn't convinced that I needed to spend time at some wellness centre but there was plenty of upside.

It would give me a chance to shut off from the world a little bit, which was going to be necessary because I knew I would be in for a fair bit of flak in the coming days. I also knew that it would help smooth things over with the Wales management. It would play well with them and help my case when it came to getting back into the set-up.

Even though I didn't think I needed it, I did find the whole experience worthwhile. I didn't really know what to think before I went but it was essentially a group of people sitting around just talking about life and all the stress that comes with it. More importantly, we explored how to deal with it all. Being able to open up like that, speak freely and discuss what was going on in my head was really quite beneficial. It felt like a weight was being lifted off my shoulders. I no longer felt suffocated.

When we weren't in sessions discussing life, there were other activities to keep us busy but I spent most of my time in the gym. While I was suspended from the Wales squad, I knew the rest of the players would be going through hell in training, getting plenty of fitness work done. Therefore, I had to make sure I was keeping myself ticking over physically, so that I was ready when the call came.

That week in the wellness centre helped get my mind right and process everything that was going on in my life. It also gave me a real appreciation of the benefits of focusing on your mental health. After that experience, I started using the sports psychologist that was on offer. It just makes sense. If you want to be a better sprinter, you do more sprint training. If you want to be more flexible, you do more yoga. Nobody ever talked about improving your mental strength but all the most successful people in the world put value on it. Why should rugby be any different?

By the time I was done in Kent, I felt recharged and was ready to throw myself into the World Cup campaign. I'd managed to shut off from the chaos of the last few months and was driven to turn recent events into a positive. I'd always been determined that no matter what I did in my spare time, it didn't impact my performance. I went on to play some of the best rugby of my career at the 2011 World Cup, so the trip to the centre must have had some impact.

Publicly, the Welsh Rugby Union had said that I was suspended 'indefinitely', which made it look like they'd taken a strong stance against what had happened. They also said there had been some meeting with the WRU's top brass. That never happened. I was told by Thumper that my suspension was always going to last a fortnight and that I should take the time to sort my head out. I didn't get fined for it, which may come as a surprise to some. I think they just realised that it was really much ado about nothing and that the two weeks were sufficient.

Again, I think the trip to the wellness centre helped smooth things over as well. Also, at the end of the day, I hadn't punched anyone and it's not a crime to have an argument. It did cost me a £15,000 deal with a watch manufacturer, though, so it stung me in the pocket. I was gutted when that went up in smoke. A rival fast food restaurant approached me to do a quirky advert taking the mick out of the whole situation but it didn't take me long to turn that one down! You've got to draw the line somewhere and it didn't take a genius to realise that would have been a terrible idea. I just wanted to get back to the rugby.

Once I'd decided that I wanted to go to the World Cup, I threw everything I had at the preparations. But before I could get to the training field, I had to face my team-mates. I wasn't thrilled about the idea of standing in a room full of players and pouring my heart out to them. I'm a pretty reserved bloke who likes to keep things to himself but Gats pulled me to one side at the indoor training centre after I'd returned to camp and pushed for it.

He thought it would be a good way of moving on from the whole incident and allow us to focus on the rugby. I saw his point but public speaking wasn't a strength of mine. Some players thrive in the team meetings, someone like Ryan Jones, the former Wales captain, used to be in his element. I don't mean that in a bad way but he loved it, that was his thing. I was the opposite, as were the majority of the boys. Most preferred to do their talking on the field. Gats wanted me to say to the squad that I had issues but I was like: "Hang on now! I haven't got issues!" There was no way I was going to stand there and say that but I knew I had to look them in the eye and let them know that I held myself accountable for what happened and acknowledged the consequences of my actions.

When you're a professional rugby player, the things that you do have implications not only for yourself, but also the people around you. It's a kind of butterfly effect and it can impact on the reputation of the squad as a whole. I knew that if the boys had played poorly at that World Cup, the press would have brought things back to the incident on Queen Street. I hadn't just dragged myself through the dirt, I'd dragged my team-mates through the dirt and the timing could hardly have been worse. There is always pressure on the Wales national team and I'd just dumped a little bit more on top. I'd harmed the boys' chances with Gats as well. If they wanted to go out and have a quiet beer as a squad during the upcoming camps and tournament, Gats could quite easily stop that from happening because I'd got into it with a McDonald's bouncer. That never transpired and the boys were able to enjoy a beer within reason, but I'd jeopardised that.

It didn't help that there were a lot of big characters around the squad at that time – Andy Powell and Gavin Henson were about – and I wasn't the only one getting myself in hot water, shall we say. The press were on our case about a string of incidents that had taken place, mine being the latest, but I don't think anybody in the squad held it against me at the time. We all realised from then on that we had to be squeaky clean. I think that might have been a factor in Sam Warburton being made captain. At the age of 22, Sam might have been young – I wasn't sure whether he was ready for it at the time – but he was a good captain and he had many qualities that made him perfect for the role. What will have probably helped his case is that you just knew he would do everything by the book and wouldn't get himself into any bother.

Warby always said the right things in the media and never put himself in compromising positions. Around that time, it felt like somebody was getting themselves in the papers for the wrong reasons all the time and I think we just needed that clean edge to lead the squad. He was exactly that. When I arrived back in camp, I stood up at a meeting, just after breakfast, in front of the entire squad. None of the backroom staff or management team were in the room, it was just the players but because it was the wider training squad, there must have been over 40 boys in there. That scenario is pretty much my worst nightmare, to be stood in front of everyone, explaining myself.

I was dreading it but I had to do it. I said the bare minimum to get through it as quickly as I possibly could. And behind it all, I didn't really feel like I deserved to be going through all this. I didn't hit anyone, I walked away from an argument. But here I was, standing in front of the team. I said: "Sorry for what I've done and for letting you boys down. I'm determined to put it right and I'll make it up to you." I told them I'd been in a bad place, changed my attitude and I vaguely alluded to the fact I'd been to the wellness centre, which was a huge deal for me. It was only 2011 but there was still a significant stigma attached to mental health, particularly in an environment bursting with testosterone, like rugby.

Don't get me wrong, I wasn't up there for half an hour, professing to be a changed man or pleading for forgiveness. I tried my best to open up to the point that I felt was necessary but the whole thing was over within about 40 seconds. That was it. Meeting over. Nobody really spoke after me, we just got on with it. Which was exactly what I was hoping for. A rugby team is a very matter-of-fact environment, most players are like-minded individuals and we learn to compartmentalise things, you have to know what is worth dwelling on and what you have to just forget about otherwise it can affect your performance.

There isn't enough time to sweat the small stuff and that really helped me here. I'd screwed up to some degree, I'd apologised to my mates and they moved on. It didn't fester like it might have in other environments. That's one of the many great things about being part of a rugby team. There was a bit of a split in how the squad reacted to the whole situation.

Lou Reed – one of Welsh rugby's great characters, a real joker and great fun to be around – was a bit bemused by it all. He was a bit older but hadn't been around too many Wales squads before and he couldn't believe that I'd had to stand up there and apologise like I did. He didn't really think it was necessary. Then we had quite a few younger players in that squad who went on to achieve great things – people like Warby, Taulupe Faletau, Rhys Priestland, Jonathan Davies, George North, Leigh Halfpenny. I don't think they really knew how to take it. For them, it was more of a realisation of the kind of scrutiny you are under as a Welsh rugby player and their profile was about to sky-rocket off the back of the 2011 World Cup and the Grand Slam that followed.

My incident really highlighted to them what could happen if you put yourself in a compromising position. Social media was always going to be a huge part of their lives as professional athletes and that has been the case. That's what Gats was trying to achieve by pushing me to speak to the boys as well, he used me as an example. Although he never actually said this, it was a case of: 'Look lads, this is what happens if you mess up!'

Those younger boys were realising that you do get spotted on the streets of Cardiff and people will recognise you and come up to you, which is quite hard to deal with sometimes, especially if you're a naturally shy person. Those younger lads came through a different system to me so, culturally, their experiences of rugby had been different. Everyone had to wise up because this sort of thing had never been around before.

I'd imagine that if camera phones and Twitter existed in the 1970s, a few of those boys would be a bit worried as well! I'd been naive to it all and it was a lesson to the newer boys on the scene. Fortunately, none of them have ever really gotten themselves into hot water like I did. I like to think they learned from my mistakes. Thank me later, boys.

This was a bit of a defining moment for me off the field because I'd started to realise that I had to protect myself a bit more whenever I was out in public. You just can't let your guard down and it's even more intense for the boys these days. I love Cardiff. It's a great city and there is genuinely no better place, let alone stadium, to play rugby in the world than our capital. However, on the whole, I rarely had any problems unless I was in Cardiff on a Saturday night and I was just putting myself in stupid positions.

That's exactly what happened with the McDonald's incident. Particularly on a match day but, in truth, on any given weekend, the city is this explosion of excitement, temptation and indulgence. At times it's like the Wild West! If a bunch of Martians landed in Cardiff on a Saturday night, they'd probably turn around straight away and go home! It's bedlam and it's also great fun. But for somebody who is in the public eye, it can be an absolute snake pit, there are far too many opportunities for shit to happen, especially if you lose sight of the fact that people will know who you are and there are some people out there who will try and get a reaction out of you.

You want to put yourself in the middle of it because 95 per cent of the fans are amazing and, as a player, you love to have the adulation. Any player who tells you they don't enjoy that kind of attention is lying. The boys are all normal blokes at the end of the day and they don't always want to be cooped up in the VIP section in the back of some bar, they like being amongst the fans. But there are always one or two snakes in the grass with their phones ready, waiting for you to slip up. I had to learn that I couldn't keep putting myself in those positions or I would run the risk of ruining my career.

My performance levels rarely dipped around the times that I got into a few scrapes so it meant that they were quickly forgotten. But I knew there was going to come a day when that would stop being the case. I had to be smarter. You have to make sure that you surround yourself with good people, use some common sense and know when you can let your hair down and when you really can't.

When I was going out with Aimee, I was very good at this. I wouldn't put myself anywhere near compromising situations. I wouldn't have any pictures and I certainly wasn't having pictures with fans who happened to be female because I was terrified of how that could be spun by a newspaper or somebody on social media, no matter how innocent it was.

I didn't want to do anything that would harm her reputation. I was largely in control of these things but after we broke up I totally forgot that I had to protect myself on nights out. It was a huge lesson for me but I should have learned it long ago, in all honesty.

It was a relief to get back onto the training field and get the ball in my hands. I was determined to play well after everything that had happened. Looking back, I realise that it shouldn't have had to come down to something like that to motivate me but that was the situation I found myself in. In a way, it was a really good thing. Upon leaving the wellness centre, my focus became about rugby and I was more determined than ever to prove people wrong. I had doubters and critics coming at me from all angles and nothing was going to stop me shoving it back in their faces.

I loved nothing more. I went into the World Cup camp and trained my arse off. When we eventually got to New Zealand, I played the best rugby of my career. I'd realised that, no matter how down I felt after the incident, that my career was not over. There are people out there who have done far worse than me. It was a bit of a launchpad, I had to have a look in the mirror and change my mindset. Try to turn it into a positive. I had to put it right.

2

Rugby or Nothing

Before we get started, there are a few things you need to know and understand about me. Some of it might surprise you but to accept why somebody makes certain decisions or behaves a certain way, you have to gain an appreciation of what is going on beneath the surface. Because there are two sides to me. There is the side I let you see for the 16 years that I was a professional rugby player and the side I'm about to reveal.

I grew up on a dairy farm just outside Bancyfelin in Carmarthenshire but I went to secondary school in Whitland and a lot of my mates were from there. My grandparents lived in St Clears, so I was always back and fore there as well. I have an association with all three places, so whenever I'm asked where I'm from I always say all three just to keep everyone happy!

My dad Trevor was a good looking chap when I was younger, he always wanted to make people laugh and was very warm and friendly. When I was playing rugby as a kid, I'd always run out onto the pitch and look for him and, when I spotted him, it would make my day. I just wanted to play well for him and do him proud. But he never put me down after games or put pressure on me. If he had, I would have probably turned away from rugby and looked for something else.

Back then he had about 100 milking cows and when I was a kid, I'd be out on the farm getting stuck in with odd jobs; mucking out, feeding and odd jobs around the farm. Strangely, though, I've never actually milked a cow properly. At the time I probably found growing up on a farm a little bit frustrating. I was a bit isolated. My mates could just pop down the park to kick a ball around but I was a bit more out of the way. However I was incredibly lucky to have that upbringing, with all that space to play in. Like most kids, I went through the sporting calendar.

When the Crucible was on, I'd be on the small pool table we had pretending to be Jimmy White for hours, genuinely thinking I was going to become a snooker player, smashing 147s. Wimbledon would come around and then I'm outside smacking a ball against the side of the cowshed, thinking I was Andre Agassi and that I was going to be Wimbledon champion one day. Then the rugby would be on and I'd just go and kick a ball around. Repeat the process when it was cricket season. I used to enjoy watching the West Indies growing up and players like Curtly Ambrose and Brian Lara, although I supported the England team because of the likes of Robert Croft and Matthew Maynard.

I was going to have a hell of a sporting career at one point! But whatever sport I was playing at the time, I genuinely believed I was going to make it. I was visualising myself being there and winning trophies. When I transferred that to rugby, it was probably one of the most powerful things I did as a kid. I was never really passionate about farming but it was great fun learning to drive the tractors, stuff that kids who grew up on a normal street didn't get to do. I used to drive the Land Rover to the top of the drive to drop the rubbish off. I managed to stick it in the hedge once, causing about £800 worth of damage.

Rugby or Nothing

I sprinted back to the house in a panic but my dad was cool about it. To be honest, I deserved a hiding! My mother, Morfydd, was a teacher in the local school. She was extremely hard working and it can't have been easy bringing up three boys on a farm. There was a lot going on. I wouldn't say I used to get away with everything but she never really had a go at me until I got into some sticky situations during my rugby career. Come to think of it, I never really got myself into trouble with her until I started playing for Wales! I'm the youngest of three brothers by a good few years. Rob, my oldest brother, went away to university, so he wasn't around too much back in the day.

Mark, the middle sibling, took over the farm, so he was always about and wasn't shy when it came to ordering me around the place. Because I'm a lot younger than my brothers, we never really fought or had that sort of relationship. They looked after me and I always looked up to them, which is probably where I went wrong, actually!

Despite being the youngest, I'm taller than both of my brothers. Mark was quite slight and was a middleweight boxer. He had almost 70 professional fights but the vast majority of them were as a journeyman. He won the Welsh Amateur Championships and then turned professional out of a gym in Bristol and won his first few fights before his first loss. Then he met a guy who said: "Look, if you become a journeyman, you can get paid and look after yourself." The farm was Mark's passion and picking up a bit of cash from the boxing helped with that. He fought Nathan Cleverly at the Millennium Stadium back in 2006 but lost on points.

Rob was a good rugby player and had a brief spell with the Scarlets. Back when he was involved, if it kicked off, it really kicked off and Rob, despite also being a scrum-half, was always right in the middle of it. He was a tough cookie. They were talented sportsmen in their own rights. We always had boxing tapes on so I got interested in all that. When they used to get dressed up and go out on a Saturday night, I would always want to go with them but I was obviously far too young. They had a big influence on me growing up.

You might be surprised to learn that I wasn't a naughty kid in school by any stretch of the imagination. I was never in detention, never got told off. I might have put a football through the window once but that was about it. I enjoyed school, I got on with everyone. When I was in form two, I was going out with a girl in form five. Standard. At that age, mind, being in a relationship pretty much involves just doing laps of the schoolyard together. But school was good, I just struggled with it a bit. I was the youngest in my year and I don't think that helped me too much. English wasn't my strongest subject. My reading wasn't great and I would dread the moment when we had to take it in turns to read in front of the class. If I knew it was coming, I'd just skip on to my paragraph and practice reading it over and over to be ready when my time came. I didn't enjoy speaking in front of people and it's something I've had to learn throughout my adult life. I struggled with exams and that side of things wasn't easy. I was very young for my age as well and I was a late developer physically. I started my rugby journey with St Clears under-9s and ended up playing No.8 for the West Wales 'B' team at under-11s. I was captain of the school team but I was miles behind some of the boys in my year in terms of physical development. I hit puberty later than most and remember going away on a holiday to Magaluf with a group of my mates – boys and girls. Everyone would be telling stories about what they were getting up to, as you do, and I lied about losing my virginity to fit in. It soon picked up though and I started getting a few, err, caps. I played my youth rugby at Whitland RFC and that's when I really started to fill out and things progressed. I was a well behaved, happy-go-lucky kid and I had a wonderful childhood.

When I first got noticed by Llanelli, I was over the moon but I had no idea what the next decade and a half would have in store for me. The first thing to understand is that I straddled two eras as a player. I played youth rugby for Whitland RFC and was just a normal kid until Llanelli came knocking in my late teens, at the turn of the millennium. So I had that experience of playing with my mates, enjoying a beer in the bar afterwards and then chasing the women on a Saturday night.

Even when I arrived at Stradey Park, the game was still holding on to so many of its old school values and traditions. We played to win but we also knew how to have a good time. Those days moulded me. However, my career also overlapped into the ultra-professional era. Around the middle of it, there was a huge wave of boys coming through that had been in the academy systems since the age of about 16.

From the day they were picked up, they were being told to behave like professionals, given diets and weight programmes. They never had the same experiences I did as a youngster. Some may think that made them better players and it probably did, but I'd also argue that they missed out on a lot. The game was changing and slowly throughout my career, my species was dying out. By the time I retired, there weren't many players left that hadn't come through the academy system. I had a taste of both worlds and, when they collided, it resulted in me getting myself into bother. Nothing ever got in the way of me working hard and playing well for my club, country or the Lions. But when it was time to enjoy myself, I was going to take advantage of that. Some coaches and clubs didn't understand me in that sense and they didn't like it. But that's who I was. I take full responsibility for the poor choices I made off the field during my career and we'll go on to discuss some of those a little bit later. But I was a product of my environment.

The coaches wanted me to be on the edge, they liked me when I was volatile. All Warren Gatland and Rob Howley would do in training was just try and create pressure and stress in different ways. They used to push my buttons, that's for sure, and sometimes it got the best out of me. But when players explode, crack or break, they have to take an element of responsibility for that. What did they expect? Rugby players are only human beings. They used to light the fuse, stand back, and watch us explode.

I was recently doing my level three coaching qualification and we were given a task. The example was that we had a player who wasn't delivering, they were disruptive, in trouble all the time and having a bad influence on other players. My approach to that situation if I was the head coach would be to look at myself straight away.

You have to assess what you're doing as a coach and the environment that you've created if you have a player like that. I'd start asking myself if I'd created a supportive environment, are there people he can turn to if he's having issues? Does he feel comfortable approaching me? If we've created an environment where we're constantly shouting and the feedback is regularly negative, then of course somebody is going to lose their temper.

Steve Hansen, the former Wales coach, summed things up pretty well for me. He said that rugby players are essentially modern-day gladiators. Steve went on to guide the All Blacks to World Cup glory in 2015, so he knew a thing or two about rugby, and he was spot on there. We would go into the arena and show scant disregard for our own bodies and health.

During my playing days, we weren't always aware of the harm we were doing to ourselves and we know a lot more about things like concussion now. Looking back, it's incredible what I put my body through on a weekly basis. But you get an incredible adrenaline rush the moment you have some giant second row running down your channel and you have that split second when you realise that you've got to put your body on the line for the sake of your team.

It's the flight-or-fight response and I was always up for the fight. At times you feel almost invincible. I had many of those moments during my career. But you've got to be a certain type of person to be willing to do that week after week. If you want an individual to do those things on a rugby field, you can't expect them to be flawless. That sort of thing will have an impact on how you behave.

I'm aware of the way I was perceived during my career but there was so much going on in my head. I know I used to come across as this extremely confident, at times arrogant, guy on the field. And I was those things. I used to live up to this idea that I was a fighter, a warrior, a gladiator.

Someone who would scrap tooth and nail to win. It was mainly because the coaches drilled it into me but I also had supreme confidence in my own ability because my attitude was that if you didn't have that, you were putting yourself at a disadvantage. If you believe your opposite number is better than you, you've already lost.

When you're a kid you believe that you can take on the world but when we grow up, sometimes we lose that and we start listening to the negativity and the doubters. We should hold onto that belief we have as kids and I'm proud of the fact that I was able to do that for the majority of my career but there were some wobbles along the way.

I often get asked who my toughest opponent was and the answer is always the same; myself. At times in my career, I was too proud to say I was struggling, whether that was physically – like before the 2013 Lions Test series against Australia – or mentally. I used to get nervous and doubt myself before matches all the time. You would never have guessed it by looking at me on the field but I was very good at putting on a show.

Before my first big start for Wales against New Zealand in 2004, I remember looking at my boots in the changing room and they were old and a bit worn. I started beating myself up for not getting new boots. I was having negative thoughts about not being ready for this moment. I didn't think I was fit enough, didn't look good enough and I played poorly that day. From that moment onwards, I learned to suppress all those negative thoughts and feelings and get my head right before games.

That day, I made a commitment that if I ever got another opportunity, I'd just be confident, enjoy every moment and remember why I fell in love with the game. If I hadn't found a way to bury all that self-doubt, it would have been crippling.

I would always blame myself first when things went wrong. The buck stopped with me and I never sought to shift it onto other people. I was a scrum-half and I touched the ball more than any other player on the field. To me, that meant I had more influence over the game than anyone else. I would always blame myself if we lost, I'd beat myself up and I'd hate myself. I was horrible. I'd torment myself over the smallest of errors and sometimes over things that, looking back now, were never my fault. Then I'd handle it the wrong way by having a drink so that I could forget about it. Then people would think that I didn't care because they saw me going out and getting drunk and immediately everyone thinks that you're not bothered about the fact you've just lost a game. It was the complete opposite. But sometimes people can be too quick to judge.

As a professional athlete, people make very quick assumptions about you because they only see you for such a small amount of time. They think they know you because they've seen you run around a field for 80 minutes. When you break it down, it sounds quite silly. I couldn't handle losing. I knew what I could do, the value I could add to the attack, the physicality I can add to the defence. I always thought that if I played my best, then my team would win the game because I felt I could be that influential with and without the ball. That's a lot of pressure to put on yourself and when it went wrong, it consumed me. I couldn't let it go. It would fester and manifest into bigger problems and issues.

It all comes from not being able to forget about an incident that happened in a game, getting annoyed with it, fuelling it by adding alcohol. It's like pouring petrol on the fire instead of dealing with the issue. If you look at the times when I ended up on the front pages rather than the back pages, there was usually something else going on in my life and this was me trying to cope with it.

Another obstacle I had to overcome was that I was never a good communicator. I struggled to get my point across and say what was on my mind until I had a beer. Problem was, after a few pints I'd usually come across like a complete idiot and then people would just dismiss whatever point I was trying to make, even though I was always right, by the way. Then because people regularly dismissed my opinions, I became less inclined to give them. I was never big on speaking in team meetings and I got annoyed with players and coaches who just sounded off for the sake of it. Some people just spoke because they felt like they had to. It can get quite silly and I'd be sitting there thinking: 'Really? Do we really need to be told this? We're the best players in the country.' Some coaches make the mistake of thinking that because somebody pipes up in a team meeting regularly, then they must be a good communicator. That's not always the case.

At the Ospreys, for example, the coaches used to big up the overseas contingent we had for saying pointless stuff in team meetings. It's a doing sport, your actions define you. Anyone can talk a good game. I used to get really frustrated with people saying the obvious things in meetings. On the field is where I was most comfortable, under the bright lights and in front of 80,000 fans. That's where I did my talking. I had the confidence to do anything on that stage but behind closed doors I was poor at speaking in front of people. I started a business studies degree at UWIC – now known as Cardiff Met University – back in the early days and about six weeks in they wanted us to do presentations in front of the lecture group so I packed it in and decided it wasn't for me because I couldn't speak in front of everyone.

I probably found myself in the news a bit more than I'd have liked during my career, I can't deny that. But whatever criticism came my way never really weighed me down because I knew nobody would assess my performances as harshly as I did myself. That being said, you don't go looking for it, you try to avoid all the negative press but it always gets back to you in the end. Your mates tell you or your family mention it. Everyone has an opinion but I tried not to get too bothered by a bad rating in the newspaper, although it was always nice to get a nine out of 10!

Some players are very aware and switched on to what is going on around them. They're in tune with what's being said and written about them and all that sort of stuff. I was aware of all that to some degree but, ultimately, I was there to win games for Wales. That was it. Nothing else mattered. Anything that didn't help me do that was just white noise.

What did annoy me, though, is that when I did something really skilful, I felt like pundits were never willing to give me praise because I was pigeonholed as this big, physical scrum-half and nothing more. I've sent team-mates over for tries with an offload out the back door, put clever little kicks in behind to set up scores and hit booming 60-metre touch finders. But they never got mentioned on the TV coverage. They would get completely overlooked. That used to wind me up more than any criticism because I always felt that if it was someone else throwing those offloads, people would talk about it for weeks. I was supposed to be this big, aggressive player but I wasn't supposed to have silky skills.

People just didn't give me credit for that sort of thing. If Sonny Bill Williams had thrown some of the offloads I did to create tries like the one for Leigh Halfpenny in 2012, they'd have made YouTube clips of it and we'd all be going on about it to this day.

On the commentary of that game, Jonathan 'Jiffy' Davies doesn't mention it at all but praises Halfers for holding his run! I remember putting in this unbelievable kick against South Africa in the first Lions Test in 2009. The ball had gone over my head, so I had to track back. I've got absolutely no angle because I'm right-footed and tight to the right-hand touchline.

I sent this massive kick down field and into touch but Stuart Barnes on commentary doesn't even mention it. That sort of stuff used to wind me up because I felt I was unfairly characterised as one-dimensional.

So why did I make it? The answer is simple; because I only had one thing. I had one choice. One chance. It was rugby or nothing if I was ever going to make anything for myself. There was no plan B. If you have one focus and one goal, you're more likely to make it. There was nothing to fall back on. I didn't have a degree, my parents provided for me but they weren't going to just hand me money. I had to make it in rugby to be something. Winning was everything. I was desperate to win. Nothing ever got in the way of that. But I wasn't without my faults and I'm happy to admit that.

I'm proud of what I achieved on the field. Success means different things to different people. To some people it means having a family or running a business. Some boys may just have the goal of making it into a regional team, some boys want to get a Wales cap, others want to be named in a Lions squad. Everybody wants to achieve different things.

My version of success was winning Grand Slams and winning a Test series with the Lions. I wanted to be the one making the most tackles and making the most breaks. I used to actually write down goals ahead of a game like: 'Be 100 percent accurate with passing and kicking, be energetic, produce two marquee moments in the game.' I take a lot of pride in being able to do all those things. But when I look back over my career, I don't like the person that I was sometimes. Occasionally, I wonder what the hell I was doing on nights out and things like that. Without making excuses for my actions, I think the success I had on the rugby field brought that on a bit.

Nothing can prepare you for playing in front of millions of people, or having hundreds of fans come up to you on a night out after winning a Grand Slam. The pressure is on a different level. It's tough to deal with and I didn't always manage it in the right way. Deep down, I've always been a good guy but there are plenty of times when I woke up on a Sunday morning and hated myself for making poor decisions and putting myself in the compromising positions that I found myself in. But that's who I was and, in many ways, it made me the player I was.

Happily, I'm in a far better frame of mind nowadays. I have a beautiful family and I'm very content with life. I wouldn't change anything about my career because we don't have time for regrets but I'd never go back there. I'm happy the person that I used to be doesn't exist anymore.

3

Going Places

After grinding away with Whitland youth, in 2000 I was asked to go and sit on the bench for the Llanelli Scarlets' under-21 team towards the end of the season. Growing up down west, I'd supported them my entire life and to just wear the jersey at the age of 18 and play at Stradey Park was unbelievable. I finally felt like I was making progress because before that nobody had really paid attention to me and plenty of coaches had told me I wasn't good enough. Because I'm over six foot and playing scrum-half, everyone was telling me to change position but I wanted to play nine, and I broke down a lot of walls to make it happen.

I came off the bench a few times that year and I was then asked to come back for pre-season. We played Neath at the Gnoll and that was the game that kick-started my rugby career. It all started there. I had an absolute stormer, scoring two tries, including one effort from inside my own half. That was the moment the penny dropped for a few people who still doubted me and they realised that I was actually pretty good.

The following week I got called into the Wales Sevens squad and jetted off to Chile and Argentina to play on the circuit. I was right up for the Sevens because I was playing for Wales at the end of the day. It was a pretty cool experience at that age, flying away to all these places and representing your country. Sevens is the most amazing stepping stone for players. You can't hide on the Sevens field, there is just too much space and you will be found wanting if you're not up to it. One thing I remember from the Argentina leg is this incredible nightclub in Mar del Plata where all the women were absolutely stunning. One of them gave me her email address and we were messaging for months afterwards, despite the fact I was obviously never going to see her again. Very quickly from there I was asked to go up and train with the Llanelli senior team and suddenly I was sharing the dressing room with the likes of Scott Quinnell, Salesi Finau, Chris Wyatt, Leigh Davies – the list goes on. It was an unbelievable time in my life. Things are different now and, back in those days, not many youngsters got called up to the first-team environment. These days it seems like a load of players progress from the academy into the senior team at the regions every year but, back then, there might have been two or three of us moving up from the under-21s. Training was a whirlwind. We were doing full contact drills and suddenly I had the likes of Quinnell and Finau running down my channel! There was no hiding place for a skinny scrum-half who had barely turned 20.

It was a real baptism of fire. I knew I had to just go full tilt, otherwise it was a guarantee that I'd get hurt. Scott was coming to the end of his career so he spent a fair bit of time with the physios to get himself right for a Saturday. But he would only need one or two training sessions in the week and he was always immense on the weekend. He was one of the best ball-carriers I ever played with – nobody could tackle him!

Scott is a genuine legend, especially in that part of the world, and I was just desperate to prove myself to people like him. I remember scoring a good try away in Connacht and he was playing. It meant a lot to me because I wanted to prove to his generation that I was good enough to wear the jersey. He hammered me in training once, it was like being hit by a rhino. I was holding a pad and he knocked me back a number of steps before I eventually lost my balance and fell on my backside. It was like a cartoon sketch. It was so bad that the boys started laughing at me. But he's always been the same, Scott, a lovely guy who is so passionate about rugby.

He was great for the younger players in the squad, a very supportive figure. I didn't get to go out on the beers with him too often. By the time I arrived, he had a family and other things that needed his time. It was a bit of a shock to the system for me actually because, from my days with Whitland, I was so used to all the boys playing on a Saturday and being on the beers after the match. But now I was playing with guys who had other things going on.

In my first few games at senior level, there was one call and one call only; give it to Finau. I'd be shouting out to find out what the move was and every time it would come back: "Just hit Finau!" I was thinking to myself: 'Have we got another call or...?' To be fair, he was one of the hardest blokes I played with. He was 16 stone of Tongan muscle and when he got the ball he was like a runaway train. He was an absolute legend at Stradey, playing over 200 games for the club. He looked after me as well, it's great to have a guy like him on your side.

Towards the end of the season we played Swansea and their South African winger Shaun Payne basically double knee-dropped me in my face. The game went on, I scored two tries and I was really starting to make a name for myself. Finau comes up to me in the dressing room after the game and says: "Don't worry Mikey, I had him for you!" I didn't know what he was talking about.

A few days later, I was watching the tape back and as I'm getting up to run off after Payne's knee-drop, Finau comes out of nowhere and uppercuts him with this huge punch. If he did it these days he'd have been suspended for months. I'd have hated to play against Salesi but he was great to have on your side! He never really used to come out on the beers but he always had some advice for me.

I was trying to bring the physicality that I'd been dishing out in the age-grade stuff but obviously this was a different ball game. Salesi used to give me advice around putting on some muscle, although I never got as big as him! Around this time I was just trying to make a name for myself. I'd gone from being a big fish in a small pond with the under-21s to being at the bottom of the food chain in senior rugby, which was cool. It was an uncompromising environment to be in but I was never intimidated by it.

If I'd gone into my shell, I'd have been eaten alive. The only way you survive training sessions with some of the big bruising ball-carriers that we had was by throwing yourself into it with everything you had. In turn, you earned respect.

I'd only played a handful of games for the Scarlets when I was called up to go on Wales' summer tour of Australia and New Zealand in 2003. That was mayhem. We all met up in the car park at Cardiff West services on the M4. The boys were going on strike about pay and I'm stood in this service station thinking: 'What are we on strike for? We're playing for Wales!'

I was obviously young and naive and I certainly wasn't going to voice my opinion at that age. The older boys had their heads screwed on a bit more and what used to happen is the younger players would get shafted a little bit because we'd all play for Wales for free and the Welsh Rugby Union exploited that a bit back then. There was a genuine chance that boys were going to refuse to go on the tour and play.

They wanted to create a bit of chaos and they achieved that because we ended up missing our flight and had to spend the night in a hotel near the airport in London. Gareth Thomas stood up and said that youngsters had to speak up in the meeting. Can you imagine me standing up, with about five Scarlets games behind me, saying: "Ahh I'm not happy with the pay here boys, it's shit." I was playing for Llanelli under-21s a few months previously! I didn't make a peep in that meeting. Quiet as a mouse. No young player is going to go into that environment and start complaining about the match fee! I didn't realise this at the time but what those boys were really striking for was my generation.

Whenever Wales play rugby, it generates millions. Later on in my career, I learned that you have to look out for yourselves and make sure you're getting paid what you deserve. At the end of the day, serious injuries are a reality of a contact sport like rugby and your career can be over in the blink of an eye. Alfie was a great captain.

Later in my career we lost a game and the management said that none of the boys were allowed to drink that night. Gareth was having none of it, his response was: "No, we need to have a drink together, we need to bond now more than ever." He pretty much told the coaches that it was going to happen. As a youngster, I loved that. Gareth always had the boys' best interests at heart and protected the players as much as he could. Anyway, back to the services. Some sort of agreement was reached and we eventually made our way down but I didn't play in any of the matches.

I was loving life, going out during the week and sneaking back into the team hotel in the early hours of the morning, coming in through the fire exit and things like that. In the matchday programme for the Australia Test, they did a two-page spread on me under the headline: 'The next big thing.' I absolutely loved this. I was only a kid really so I grabbed about 10 copies. It was so cool to see that in the programme, in Australia of all places. I stayed on after the tour with Daf Jones in a place called Coogee Bay. Every night we went out, I made sure I took a copy of this spread with me and if I spotted a girl that I fancied, I'd just slide it across in front of her, just to let her know who the next big thing was. Terrible tactics. They were good times. I was just a kid being a kid.

Being involved in all the preparations for the 2003 World Cup was amazing but, honestly, I didn't feel like I deserved to be there. I didn't really want to be there because I knew that it wasn't my time. I wanted it to happen, of course I did, but I wanted it to happen when I felt like I was ready for it. I know Steve Hansen, who was head coach at the time, was looking at my development and stuff like that but I didn't see that at the time. I wasn't anywhere near mature enough for that opportunity. I was never really made aware of what his plans were for me until I was told that I hadn't been selected for the 2003 World Cup squad, which came as no great surprise to me but, fair play, Hansen called me into his office and sat me down. He explained why I hadn't been selected but told me that I was going to go on and have a great career. I thanked him and basically told him that I was just happy to be there. It was an amazing opportunity for a youngster. I was also a bit relieved to be honest because I feel like that would have been too much, too soon.

At the start of the 2003/04 season, I got a lot of game time at the Scarlets because Dwayne Peel was away with Wales. It was my first opportunity to have a run of games. I was third in line at this point. Guy Easterby was a senior player, Dwayne was a few years older than me so a lot had been invested in his development.

He had a big history with the club as well, his grandfather was the physio, he had a great relationship with head coach Gareth Jenkins. Gareth was polite with me and would always say hello but I remember being in the canteen one day and Dwayne walked past the table that the coaches were sitting on. Gareth was like: "Hiya Dwayne, how are your grandparents? How's your mum and dad? How's your dog? How's your cat? How's your fish?" This is nothing against Dwayne but that's just how it was. So regardless of how good I'd been for the under-21s, I was up against it from the start and even back then I could see that it was going to be tough for me to establish myself as first choice. But I had a good run of games to prove myself while Dwayne was away. Not long after I returned from the Wales camp, I started against Munster away from home and had an absolute shocker.

I was naive, thought I was the big dog having been away with Wales and that I could just go out and boss things. It was a bit of a reality check for myself because I still had much to learn. I was also my own harshest critic and I realised that wasn't the finished article. Despite my performance, we won the game and as the season went on I continued to develop. That year, Matthew J

Watkins joined from Newport. He was a little bit older than me and he really looked after me back then. He helped me get my first agent and was always fun to be around.

He'd take the mick out of me, calling me 'big nose'. Matthew was also an outstanding rugby player as well so, as a team-mate, he was the complete package. He sadly passed away in 2020 after a seven-year battle with cancer. It was heartbreaking when I heard the news. It was an absolute honour to play alongside him and call him my mate. In the year that Matthew joined, we made it to the Celtic League final.

Unfortunately for Dwayne, he got injured before the final against Ulster, so I started. That was a huge game, the biggest I'd played in up to that point in my career in front of a full house at Stradey Park. It was Stephen Jones' final game for the club before he departed to join Clermont – although he did return two years later. We won the game and it was an incredible occasion, one of the many special occasions that took place at the old ground. Personally, I'd just helped the side win the league in my first year in the senior team, so I was absolutely buzzing.

After we won the league, we went on an all-dayer, going through the pubs up towards Aberystwyth. The boys made me get up and sing 'Angels' by Robbie Williams in one pub which was an absolute nightmare. But I was soon in my element at the pool table. It was a lovely set-up, the owner had obviously splashed out on the table and had expensive cues, the full works. Anyway, after a few pints, I missed a black and in my frustration snapped the cue over my knee. Instant regret. All the boys found it hilarious but I immediately thought to myself: 'What have I done?' I was very apologetic to the owner and obviously gave him money to get a new one. Later in the day, we decided to get changed into our evening clothes outside another pub.

There's a picture somewhere of a few of us completely naked getting into our evening attire. This is all the sort of stuff that I'd never have been getting away with later in my career but it was different times. During that season, I was getting a sponsored car. These days, players get fancy Land Rovers and the like but back then I was getting a brand spanking new Nissan Almera every 10,000 miles. It was a smart car, I won't have a bad word said about it. Trouble was, my name was plastered all over it. To be honest, I was embarrassed by this because I hadn't really done anything yet and I still needed to earn my stripes.

When I turned up to Wales camps, I used to park at the far end of the car park at the Vale because I didn't want anyone to see it. Unfortunately, the car park at Stradey is not as big and I remember Ian Boobyer one day parked as close as he could to my car and slammed his door into mine as he got out before shouting: "Hiya Mike! How are you?" I couldn't believe it!

He used to terrorise me back in those early days, grabbing me, chucking me in bins and all that sort of nonsense. I tried not to snap because it usually gets worse if you react! I bounced him once in a training session and everyone stopped on the spot and went absolutely mental because they could all see he was giving me a hammering. I enjoyed that one. That year the boys planned a social event in Llanelli one Sunday at a place called Le Caprice. It was a big team bonding session and everyone had to go. I'd gone out on the Saturday night in Cardiff, wasn't feeling too fresh so didn't bother.

I just stayed in my house and chilled. Very quickly I get a phone call from captain Leigh Davies who, in a very sharp tone, asks: "Where are you?" In a very quiet, husky voice I explained that I wasn't feeling too good and made a lame excuse. Leigh wasn't having any of it: "If you don't come down here now, don't ever come training again." Suffice to say I got my arse down the M4. Turning up late, I had a pasting off the boys and a load of drinking fines. Then I had to go up on the balcony and sing a song, which is my worst nightmare. A bit like in training, though, you have to go flat out otherwise you'll be eaten alive. So I belted out You've Lost That Lovin' Feeling, gave it everything I had. The boys loved it, went back to their business and I was off the hook for my late arrival.

I hung around with people like Vernon Cooper and Chris Wyatt a lot and those boys knew how to have a good time. They used to have this clique called 'The Longs' and they were the instigators. Basically, it was all the tall players who used to hang out together. I impressed them with some off-field antics on a pre-season tour – the women were stunning – in Slovenia once and the following day I was called up to the back of the bus to become a 'Long'.

A few months later I was on a dance floor once in a Swansea nightclub and one of them got hold of me and they were like: "Mike, you're a Long, you don't dance, you just stand by the bar with us and drink." Wyatt was a hell of a boy. They used to call him 'The One Man Riot', which gives you a bit of an insight. I used to be part of a carpool with him. A group of us used to meet up just off junction 34 of the M4 and share lifts down to Llanelli for training. It was me, Chris, Iestyn Thomas and Dale Burn. It was carnage. Chris would always turn up with a McDonald's, he'd always have a fag in his hand. He was proper old school.

We were playing in a big European game away in France somewhere and the morning of the game he's sat at the table with me, eating a jam doughnut, drinking some coffee and having a fag. But then he goes out to play and absolutely kills it. Wyatt was an amazing player who had great hands. He was so freakishly gifted. He was also a legend, who never took things too seriously. I used to watch the likes of him on TV and looked up to them in many ways, so to be playing alongside them was unreal.

I was part of the Wales squad for the 2005 Six Nations when we won the nation's first Grand Slam since 1978. I sat on the bench for the final two matches but never got on the field. I never expected to get on against Ireland in the final and I wasn't bothered about it because it was a big game and Dwayne was playing well. But I thought Mike Ruddock could have thrown me on when the game was in the bag against Scotland the week before. In fact, it made no sense to leave Dwayne on the pitch and risk him getting an injury.

Anyway, I was told that if I played less than 15 minutes against Ireland, then I'd have to play for the Scarlets against the Cardiff Blues on the Sunday. Obviously, I didn't come on but I still went up and got a medal and did the lap of honour with the boys, waving to all the fans. I felt like a complete tool. I didn't want to be there. I was chuffed for the boys but, come on, I hadn't touched the ball. With this in mind, the bus took us to an after-match function and Cardiff was going absolutely mental. The scenes were just incredible. After the function, a handful of people were jumping on the bus to go back to the Vale and the majority of the squad were heading into town to celebrate. Knowing that I was playing the following day, I was getting ready to jump on the bus back to the Vale when Ruddock tapped me on the shoulder: "Mike, are you coming out with us?"

"Ahh I can't Mike, I've got a game tomorrow," I replied.

He flashed me a confused look before saying: "Mike, we've just won Wales' first Grand Slam in almost 30 years."

"Yeaaahhh, go on then," I said without needing too much convincing.

So out into Cardiff I went. It was hard not to get swept up in it all. Anyone who was out in Cardiff that day will remember it for the rest of their lives. It was unbelievable. Let's just say I had an enjoyable evening and didn't end up making it back to the Vale that night. So the following morning, my mate came to pick me up and took me back to the Vale so I could grab my kit. As I was loading up the boot, someone drove past and said: "Are you coming out?"

"Nah, I've got a game today but I think some of the boys are going out!" I replied.

They looked a little confused and then my mate had to explain that the person was asking if we were coming out of the parking space. Not my finest moment. My mate drove me down to Stradey and by the time I got there I was feeling a bit more like myself. By this point, I'd already signed for Cardiff, so it was a huge game for me, really. I wanted to show the Cardiff boys what they had signed and I was up against Ryan Powell, who would be my competition for the jersey the following season.

The previous night didn't have too much of an effect because I managed to put in a really good performance and get man of the match. Then it was straight back up to Cardiff to meet up with the boys. Happy days.

During my time in Llanelli there was this shady bloke who started hanging around the players. I don't know where he came from but he'd turn up to training every now and then in a Bentley or a Ferrari, which obviously caught the eye. Next thing I know he's appearing on nights out, and he was there when we had a golf day in Cardiff before going out for beers. It transpired that he was claiming to be an agent who looked after footballers and had organised some testimonials, so he was getting into the more senior boys about that sort of stuff. He was looking after some of the boys' insurances, which all passed me by a little bit. Then one day the boys started talking about these houses in Spain. The initial deposit was about £3,000 and then you had to put roughly another £10,000 down and then there was another payment.

But essentially he was saying we could buy cheap and make money on them. I overheard these conversations and thought I could afford it and didn't want to miss out if they were all about to make thousands. Me and my two brothers got involved in it, we only went to the first stage of £3,000 it turned out to be a big lie. He took the money and ran. It was a complete scam.

These guys are very clever because £3,000 was exactly the sort of money that a rugby player back then could part with quite easily. If the initial deposit had been £10,000, boys would never have gone for it. There were no houses, nothing. Some of the boys went a bit further than I did but it was absolutely brutal. Years later I managed to get my money back but it was a bit of a warning for me to be a bit more careful with my money.

I wasn't getting any proper advice at the time. Much later in my career, me and Dan Carter were at the Monaco Grand Prix in the Red Bull VIP area with Hollywood actors, American football players and all this jazz. It was an amazing set-up. I was busting for it, all the glitz and glamour, free day on the sauce. What's not to love? I walk up the steps into the VIP area and the first person I see is this guy who shafted us at Llanelli. And he's not hiding in the corner with his head down trying to avoid me, he's coming up to me and going: "Hey Mike! Let's have a drink!" I didn't say anything because I didn't want to cause a scene, I had a drink with him and then made an excuse to leave but the front on this guy was unbelievable.

When you're in a rugby environment, you're surrounded by good, honest people, for the most part. Bullshitters don't tend to last too long in the environment so, as a rugby player, I hadn't come across shady people like this bloke. You become quite a trusting person and you take things at face value but the outside world is full of people that talk absolute nonsense and will say anything. There's a real lesson here for any youngsters out there. I was lucky to get my money back.

Towards the end of my time in Llanelli, I got myself in a bit of bother. Myself and Barry Davies, a great full-back and an even better bloke, went out for a meal in Cardiff and ended up getting caught up in a bit of a night out. The following day, I turned up to training 40 minutes late, Barry was also late. When I got there, the fitness coach Wayne Proctor could smell the alcohol on me and he said: "You're in to see Stuart Gallagher." He was the chief executive back then. I went into Stuart's office and the way I tried to talk myself out of it is by saying that I hadn't gone out the weekend before and I'd just had a personal best in fitness testing.

So my excuse was basically that I was celebrating my PB. Barry was begging me to be quiet. We just had a bit of a slap on the wrist, there were no real dramas. To be fair to Stuart, he didn't kick off or anything like that. He was an old school operator, who just saw me as a young guy enjoying myself. He also knew that I was well aware of the fact that I'd messed up, so he was pretty relaxed about it.

Nowadays, if a youngster did that, there would probably be a huge fuss made but Stuart was level-headed about the whole thing. At the end of the day, when you're young, you have to be able to enjoy yourself. But at the same time, you can't be turning up late and things like that, so I knew I was in the wrong. Proctor absolutely hammered me then in a two-hour fitness session, so I paid my dues.

Mike Phillips

It wasn't an easy decision to leave Llanelli because it was my boyhood club. I'd supported them my entire life but I knew I had to move on. They'd put me in the centre a few times and it felt like they were trying to mould me into something. People in the Wales camp wanted this to happen as well but I had no interest in playing anywhere other than scrum-half. Even at this stage, I was still having to prove that scrum-half was my position. The Blues offered to make me their first choice scrum-half and I had the opportunity to go to the Ospreys as well. Some of the suits at the Scarlets were pleading with me not to join the Ospreys but I had to leave because I wasn't going to get the game time I wanted in Llanelli. I left there on great terms. I was living in Cardiff, so it was nice not to have the two-hour round trip to training every day. But they hadn't had a great season the previous year, finishing ninth out of 11, so there was a bit of work to do.

We had the Scarlets in the third game of the season, which was obviously going to be massive for me. There had been some talk that players leaving Llanelli to join Cardiff never did well and I wanted to shut the doubters up. I had a good block of pre-season behind me and was feeling good. Everything went my way that night, it was a lovely summer's evening, the conditions were perfect and it was a big atmosphere. I played out of my skin, scored a try and that was huge for me against my former team-mates because they were a good side. It was a bit of a leap forward for the Blues at the time as well.

Earlier in pre-season, Andy Powell had signed not long after me and after beating the Scarlets that night, we went out into Cardiff. Powelly was staying at my house but at some point during the night, I'd lost him. I was sitting in the Philharmonic bar with a few of the boys when some of them came rushing in to say it was kicking off outside. Glasses were being thrown and they needed help. So I went out and got caught up in the middle of this ruckus.

Before I know it, they're slapping the cuffs on me and throwing me in the back of a police van. I sat there, with my hands behind my back, for a little while, panicking about what the hell was going to happen next. Suddenly one of the coppers jumps in the back with me and says: "Mike, we were actually over your house earlier tonight." So I'm thinking: 'Great, they know who I am and they know where I live, they're just going to take me home.' But I was a bit concerned as to why they'd already been over my house that evening so I asked: "What went on boys?"

To which one of them replied: "We had a phone call from your neighbour and when we got there, Andy Powell was trying to break in."

"Ahh, he's a bit of a boy isn't he?" I laughed.

But it wasn't really a laughing matter because I then ended up spending a night in their lovely B&B. I remember waking up in the morning and a police officer said not to worry, that it wouldn't be much longer and asked if I wanted a newspaper to read. So he threw in a *Western Mail* and there was a massive picture of me scoring on the back page and there I was sitting in a police cell. That was a bit of a moment. It was all sorted but my main concern was my mother finding out.

A few days later it got into the *South Wales Echo*, which is only available in Cardiff, so I naively thought my mother down west wasn't going to find out. The following day it was in the national newspapers and she was ringing me up at six in the morning asking what I'd been up to. She was alright about it when I told her some blokes were throwing stuff at us but that was my first lesson, really. I was just trying to help my mates out but it spiralled out of control. From a young age, you're taught to look after your mates and stick together. But when you become a professional athlete, you get faced with a horrible decision. Do you help your mates and risk ending up in the headlines or do you not help your mates and protect your reputation? It's sad really because I viewed my actions in that situation as just being a good bloke. Someone was throwing glass at my mates, so I went to help. But then obviously I end up in the newspaper and people forget there are two sides to every story.

There was one rather memorable training session in around October in my first season. Nicky Robinson, who I knew well from our days with Wales under-21s, said to me: "Have you heard who we're signing?"

I hadn't.

"The biggest name in world rugby," He said.

"I'm already here mate," I replied.

"Alright, second biggest… we're signing Jonah Lomu," came Nicky's response.

"What? Jonah fucking Lomu?" I said. I couldn't believe it. You know when you hear news and it takes you about 30 seconds to get your head around it? This was that kind of moment.

It was just totally surreal. The word 'legend' gets thrown around a lot but he was rugby's first superstar. An absolute bonafide, cast iron legend. I'm not sure I left the greatest first impression on him, though.

When he turned up at the training ground in his car for the first time, he drove past at the exact moment that I was out the front of the training complex being sick, having enjoyed one too many pints two days earlier.

By the time he got out of his car, I'd gone back inside and I'm not even sure he ever found out it was me. His first game was against Calvisano away in the European Cup. I won man of the match that day and had to go for an interview with the broadcasters straight after the match. As I'm walking back to the dressing room, there are a few boys still around and Jonah's next to me. He spots the little trophy they've just given me for man of the match and says: "I'm going to get on Mikey's shoulder next week!" I'm just in awe and thinking to myself: 'What on earth am I hearing? Jonah Lomu is talking about needing to get on my shoulder!' It was just unreal.

When you play with people like that, you just want to show them how good you are. One day we were flying off somewhere after doing a captain's run, so it was a bit rushed after training. The pitch was muddy and I got out of the shower afterwards, started drying myself and just went: "Ahh bloody hell mun!"

Jonah looks over and says: "Mikey, what's the matter?"

"Ahh nothing mate, I just forgot to wash my boots in the shower," I replied.

"I'll take them in for you, give them here," he says.

I couldn't believe that Jonah Lomu was offering to clean my boots!

"Errr, nah mate, it's alright!" I said. I couldn't let him do that. The guy is rugby royalty. But that's the kind of bloke he was.

Look, it was unbelievable to have a player like that around, I still can't believe I was in the same team as him to this day. But he was coming to the end of his career at this point so he wasn't the Jonah that we all remember from the 1995 Rugby World Cup. In the years before he arrived he'd been ill and had to have a kidney transplant. He played 10 games for the region and unfortunately broke his ankle. That was incredibly sad because that season was his comeback after the illness. He still attracted a huge crowd wherever we went. Jonah probably brought in an extra 5,000 or so fans at every game that season. They all wanted to see him.

We were playing at home once and he was warming up under the main stand at the Arms Park, with his big headphones on, doing some fast feet and some stretching. I was sat down reading the programme, minding my own business. Dai Young, who was head coach at the time, caught my attention. He looked at Jonah and then looked at me with a face as if to say: 'How wild is this? Jonah Lomu is on our team!' It was just an incredible experience and I count myself incredibly lucky to have shared a dressing room with the game's biggest name.

Dai, who hadn't long retired, was brilliant with me. He man-managed me perfectly. They didn't go mad about the incident in Cardiff because they knew my side of the story. I remember turning up to training late once and Dai didn't give me a pasting over it, which was nice. But Dai had a wicked sense of humour.

We were playing away against Perpignan once and there was an incident with Wayne Evans, who I knew very well because we went to the same school growing up. He's a top bloke and was one of the other scrum-halves in the team. He boarded the bus to the captain's run without his boots and wearing flip-flops. I don't know what was going through his head, he must have just not realised where we were going. Dai is just hovering in the middle of the bus chatting to a few of the boys and Wayne is one of the last ones on the bus. Dai says: "Where are your boots, Wayne?"

"I didn't know we needed boots," Wayne replied.

"Wayne, we're going training mate," said Dai.

With that, Wayne scuttled off the bus in a bit of a flap and ran back into the hotel to get his boots. Dai lets out an exasperated sigh and says: "Boys, make sure you have a pint with Wayne after the game, it's going to be his last trip." Dai was so sharp like that. In one training session, the forwards were practicing receiving kick-offs. I was just standing around watching and one kick goes up, nobody claims it and it lands in the middle of them all. So Dai asks: "Lads, what happened there?"

A few of the boys start saying that it was the sun's fault because they couldn't see the ball.

To which Dai shouts over: "Ahh right, okay, don't worry, I'll go and move the sun for you now!" Before walking off, probably muttering a few expletives under his breath. He always had a one-liner.

There was a bit of a different vibe at the Blues compared to the Scarlets. First of all there was a bit of a divide because some of the squad were from the Valleys and they had a little clique and then there was the Cardiff boys, or the city slickers. There was never any animosity or anything like that, but they just had different personalities and enjoyed life in different ways. I enjoyed bouncing between the two and getting the best of both worlds. The Llanelli boys were far looser on nights out as well. I think that comes from the fact that most of them grew up in rural areas like myself and you could go on nights out without getting into too much bother in that part of the world. That being said, there was the odd occasion.

At Llanelli, we always used to go to Le Caprice after the game. It was a big venue and was basically the place we'd go before deciding whether to go to Swansea or Llanelli on a night out. It was a cool place and they'd always be replaying the full match by the time we got there. When I was a youngster, I always used to stand next to the big screen and make sure everyone in the bar knew that I was coming on and if I was about to do something good! It wasn't always good vibes though.

One night some guy in his Scarlets top started having a pop and giving me shit about a performance, so I had a go back and gave him a few words before my mate quickly reminded me that I was now a professional rugby player and it probably wasn't a good idea to be doing that. There was also a time when Arwel Thomas had to stand up for himself. He signed for us on a one-year deal but had just spent years making a name for himself at Swansea, who were our big rivals.

One day, someone came up to him in the car park outside Stradey and started giving him verbals. You just don't do that. Arwel stood up for himself and walked away. He was a hell of a boy and a brilliant rugby player. We played a few Sevens matches together earlier in my career and we managed to get a rare win against Fiji. I didn't really contribute a great deal but Arwel absolutely tore them up. With all that space on the field, he was a nightmare to defend. He was great on the beers and it was always a good night when he was around. But back to the point, it wasn't always plain sailing down west but in Cardiff players were far more aware that there were eyes on them when they were on nights out and things were far more likely to end up in newspapers.

Leaving the Cardiff Blues wasn't easy. I spoke to Dai personally and gave him my reasons but that was tough because I got on well with him. One of the worst things about leaving was that I knew he wasn't going to be coaching me. I loved playing for Dai. He was a great bloke and everyone respected him because of what he'd achieved. The problem was, I played

50 games in two seasons for that club, we finished fourth and second in the league, I played some great stuff. I was annoyed that they didn't offer me a new, longer contract after the first year. If they'd offered me a three-year deal after my first season, I'd have taken it for less money just to have the security. But they let it drag on right up until the end of my two-year deal.

I tried getting hold of the chairman, Peter Thomas, when it came to crunch time and he was on holiday. It left me feeling like they didn't give a damn but I had to look out for myself and make sure I still had a job the following season. It was around that time that the Ospreys came to the table with a big offer that, given the relative inactivity at the Blues, I couldn't turn down. But I didn't want to leave the Arms Park, I was the main man there. I loved living in the city and playing there. I was a bit cut up by the whole situation and my head was all over the place. I went for a meeting with Gareth Jenkins, who was Wales head coach by this point, and I broke down and got very emotional. I was asking: "This is all getting a bit too much for me. What do you think I should do? What is the best thing to do here?"

I'd been at the Scarlets and the Blues and now I was joining the Ospreys. I didn't want to be that guy who just jumped from club to club. I was worried about how I would be perceived, even though I had good reasons to move. Plus the Ospreys had put a really big offer in front of me that the Blues couldn't match because they had a policy that you could only earn so much money until you became a British & Irish Lion.

That's why they should have been more proactive and given me a longer contract after my first year because I'd have definitely signed it. Plus the Ospreys were building a hell of a squad and I wanted to be challenging in Europe, which we weren't able to do in Cardiff. Gareth gave me some good advice and said: "You have to look after yourself first and foremost. Don't be pressured into anything." He was very supportive. I also spoke to Blues legend Martyn Williams, who basically told me to just do what was right for me. It was never about the money for me but I valued myself and knew what I was worth. The Ospreys came in with about £190,000-a-year plus signing bonuses, which was probably one of the biggest deals in Wales at the time.

While I was in negotiations with the Ospreys, I never spoke to head coach Lyn Jones, although I knew he'd tried to sign me a few times in the past. It was all done between my agent and Ospreys director Mike Cuddy. I actually signed in the back of a car just off the M4. It was all a bit mental. But after everything was official, Lyn turns up to my flat in Cardiff one day totally unannounced with a big coffee machine under his arm and two cups in the other hand.

It was the first time I'd ever met him but by this point, I'd heard a few stories about his shenanigans. First thing he says to me as he comes through the front door is: "Right, where's your kitchen?" No pleasantries. So I showed him where it was. I had a nice big open-plan flat back then so I was just watching him plug this coffee machine in, then he turns to me and says: "How do you like your coffee?" And he starts whipping us up some coffees. This was pretty much all he'd said to me at this point. Then he clocked my snooker table. I'd splashed out £5,000 on a table that was almost full size, with the proper lights and scoreboard. All the trimmings. I remember one night after a game for the Blues – we'd taken a young side up to Leicester – I was telling the boys that I just forked out all that money for a snooker table and James Down, who was a young lad at the time went: "Five grand? bloody hell, I'm only on three grand-a-year!" Which gave everyone a laugh.

Anyway, Lyn was impressed by that and then he started trying to figure me out over a coffee. He was asking me loads of questions about rugby and life. I really liked Lyn and I only played under him for one year. I was gutted when he left because he was such an intelligent guy and he always thought outside the box. He used to come up with clever plays and we bent the rules under him. He was good fun as well, like a mad scientist. I didn't like the way he was pushed out of the door.

Around the time I joined the Ospreys, I had a big party at my house. Loads of people came over. Friends brought friends and there were plenty of people there that I didn't know. Obviously, it was a good time, there was plenty of beer drunk and I took myself to bed while the party was still going on downstairs. It's important to note at this point that I was alone when I fell asleep. The following morning, I'm a little bit hazy and the house is in a bit of a mess but that's the least of my worries. I get a knock on the door from a journalist who told me he was from the *News of the World*. He asked if I was Mike Phillips and if I was married or had a girlfriend. So I answered yes to the first question and no to the second. Next thing, he shoves a bunch of pictures printed out on pieces of paper in my face and says: "Do you have a comment for these pictures?"

I look at these pictures and they're of me, fast asleep in my own bed. Trouble is there are two girls there with me all of a sudden. They've put my jersey on – with Phillips and No.9 on the back – and they're posing next to me. They've posted the pictures on their Facebook pages and the newspaper has got hold of them. Now I've got a journalist in my face asking for a comment. I was sleeping in my own bloody bed on my own, what was I supposed to say. So I joked: "Well, I'm living the dream, aren't I?"

He replied: "Right, this is going to be in the *News of the World* next week."

It was ridiculous. Even in my own house, in my own bed, I still wasn't safe. It was all fun and I don't blame the girls, they were just having a laugh. But it was another headache for me to deal with. The newspaper article made me out to be a victim of social media but they still ran the pictures. A few days later my mother was onto me asking why I had two girls in my bed and telling me to settle down and find 'the one'. I said: "Well, I'm sorry mum but there were actually three."

"What do you mean three?" She asked.

Not being one to miss a chance to wind her up, I replied: "Well, who do you think took the picture?"

She had a laugh about it in the end.

It was at the Ospreys that me and Justin Marshall crossed paths. We'd played against each other twice while I was at the Blues. I got the better of him when he was at Leeds. He then definitely did a job on me when he was playing for the Ospreys and they beat us 27-10. I'd already signed for them by then and he made a comment about me signing to go and sit on the bench behind a 34-year-old. Fair enough, you've got to take it if you dish it out. I was giving him some verbals as well, telling him he was past it and things like that. They were dominating us up front a little bit and I was starting to get pretty frustrated with it because the platform wasn't great. He made a couple of breaks, which did my head in! He had a final dig at me towards the end of the game and I just pushed him and stormed off. I was more annoyed with my own team than anything Justin had done. I felt like we lacked aggression and physicality that day. If anything, it just confirmed to me that I was making the right decision by joining them. During my last team social with the Blues, they got a full New Zealand kit with No.9 and Marshall on the back of it. I had to wear that all night. Decent banter to be fair. I didn't go to the Ospreys with any animosity towards him. I was excited to work with him, thinking: 'Great, I'm going to have this legendary All Black that I can learn things from, he's going to tell me all the secrets.' But it wasn't like that at all. I don't think he gave me one piece of advice. I remember getting picked ahead of him for a game against Gloucester and he threw his toys out of the pram and didn't train. I had massive respect for everything that he achieved in the game but that surprised me a little bit. He was coming to the end of his career so he wasn't always the best trainer but, fair play, he could turn it on during matches when he wanted to. He was a competitor, an animal. We weren't exactly going out for pints with each other but we never really argued either. We just got on with it.

There were times when I got a little bit frustrated with the attitude at the Ospreys. Some of the coaches absolutely loved New Zealanders and didn't need a second invitation to big them up.

This is not a slight on the players in question, by the way. We had some phenomenal overseas talent in that side with the likes of Justin, Jerry Collins, Marty Holah, Filo Tiatia. Those boys came and added real value and that's what you want. But I felt like we talked them up and the expense of talking up the Welsh players in the side sometimes, which didn't sit well with me. We used to have the Marty Holah drill, the Ricky Januarie something or other. I don't know if it did anyone else's head in but it did my head in. Why were we doing this? Again, they were great blokes and this is nothing against them personally but we didn't we name drills after towns around the region or, heaven forbid, something Welsh? This might be going off on a tangent here but why do we always lose to New Zealand? It's this sort of stuff. We put them up on a pedestal.

That Ospreys squad was lively on a night out. There would usually be a few shenanigans on a night out. Sometimes there's a little wrestle or a scrap. Some Mondays we'd go in and boys couldn't look at each other after the weekend and then people start cracking jokes and moving past it by the Monday afternoon. Then we'd all start talking about how much fun we had and we'd all be looking forward to Saturday again. But almost everyone on that team was the same kind of bloke, more so than any team I've been on. We were all like-minded people. We loved busting our arses in training, playing hard and winning together, but then we all also enjoyed enjoying ourselves after matches as well.

During the final few rounds before we won the league in 2010, we ended up playing Ulster, Leinster and Munster all away from home in an 11-day period. The game against Ulster had to be rearranged twice and we ended up with this tough run of fixtures.

To really get some buy-in, we labelled it an old school tour amongst the players and made sure that we had some fun along the way. It wasn't an old school tour, really, and we wanted to get good results in these games because we had a shot at winning the league. But we made sure we got some team bonding in along the way. We smashed Ulster in a midweek match in the first leg of our mini-tour and things got a bit wild that night. Boys were wrestling with each other but were then best mates the following day. I think anyone who has played rugby can relate to that. It happens! The following morning, Sean Holley is ripping into us and talking about how disgraceful our behaviour was. He laid into me because I was questioning why we were naming calls after Kiwi players but because I'd had a few, I wasn't putting my point across very well. I had a little wrestle with Andrew Bishop, it was nothing nasty and he's a great bloke. It was just boys being boys.

That night, one individual also threw a glass and it was a bit rowdy. Anyway, in this meeting, Holley starts listing things off about why our behaviour was a disgrace.

"We've had boys saying derogatory things about each other," he said.

All the boys, slumped in their chairs, rolled their eyes but accepted where he was coming from.

"We've had boys wrestling."

Yeah, fair enough.

"We've had boys throwing glasses."

Out of order. We accept that. But then came the big finish.

"And someone has shit the bed."

Suddenly everyone perked up in their seats. Straight away, we're all thinking: 'WHAT? Who has done that?'

The first few things he raised were fair enough. It was just general rugby nonsense and nothing too hectic. Bit of arm wrestling, bit of pushing and shoving. The glass shouldn't have gone but these things happen. Nobody was expecting the final one. We calmed it down a bit after that. Before Holley was finished with his speech though, he turned and had a go at me: "Mike, you were a mess last night!" Everyone was a mess! So that annoyed me no end.

A few days later, we managed to sneak a bonus point against Leinster and then beat Munster to round off a successful little trip. I'm convinced those bonding trips work and we'll go on to discuss a few more in this book. We went on to beat the Dragons, then Glasgow in the semi-final before returning to the RDS and beating Leinster to win the whole thing.

In pre-season the following year, we went up to North Wales for a bit of training and then stocked the bus up with beer for the journey home. It was an awesome few hours on that journey, we sang loads of songs and just enjoyed each other's company. We got back to Swansea and all the boys were going out. Gav left his bag in Hooky's car and then they got split up during the night but Gav had to get something from his bag to go home. The bottom line is, he launched a brick through the car window, grabbed his bag and went home. Monday morning comes around and we're all chatting about how we had a great night, sharing stories and generally having a laugh, but James is looking a bit glum and says: "Boys, someone threw a brick through my car window!"

With a concerned look on his face, Henson says softly: "Oh James, that's terrible, absolutely shocking behaviour – bang out of order, that is!"

I'm not sure how long passed before Gav owned up.

That Christmas, I was saved by some frozen pipes at the Liberty Stadium. I spent Christmas Day with my girlfriend at the time, Aimee. We lived in Chippenham but we spent the day with her family near London. They were a good crack and the wine started flowing a bit. Nothing too hectic but just a good time. The following morning, her driver drove me back to Cardiff to pick up my car and then I took myself down to the stadium to play against the Scarlets on Boxing Day. I was arriving at the ground, regretting the wine with a bit of a dodgy stomach.

Some of the fans were trying to grab my attention so I gave the thumbs up and kept driving around to the players' car park. But then I noticed that the fans were particularly eager to get my attention so I stopped the car, rolled the window down and asked what was up. One of them told me the game was off. I was so relieved. I went into the changing room then and it was confirmed to us. Apparently some of the pipes in the stadium had frozen overnight and it was deemed unsafe for some reason. Anyway, we came back the next day, I was feeling fresh and we put 60 points on them. So it all turned out alright. It just went to show how mental my life was at that time though, commuting back from London to play games and stuff like that.

One of the best things to come out of my time with the Ospreys was the 'Fab Four'. It was something that Wales team manager Alan Phillips started calling me, Shane Williams, James Hook and Lee Byrne. Originally it was the 'Fab Five' and Gavin Henson was a part of it but he went off and did his own thing and we keep calling ourselves the Fab Four to try and stay relevant! Whenever we're out in public together, it's always the same. Youngsters will go up to Shane first and be a bit starstruck, then they'll go to Byrney and say: "Ahh Lee, I love watching you play." Then it'll be Hooky's turn and there will be a young fly-half saying he wants to play like James when he grows up. I'm usually on the end of the line thinking: 'Oh, I wonder what nice things they're going to say to me.' Usually, what I get is: "Mike, my nan thinks you're bloody gorgeous!" Happy days.

Gav was a bit of a lone wolf. I first came across him at Wales under-18s trials in Carmarthen. He was more developed than anyone, he had his hair and he had a presence about him. Even back then, he just looked like he had so much time on the ball, the way he was kicking and passing, it was just so much better than everyone else on the field.

I didn't get selected for that side and went back to play for Whitland youth. At the end of that season, I was playing for Pembrokeshire and we played against Wales under-18s in Narberth to give them a warm-up match for the world championships. For some reason, they picked me at fly-half for this game and Gav was my opposite number. All I remember is thinking to myself: 'If this guy doesn't play for. Wales, the rest of us haven't got a chance.' He was miles ahead of everyone. He went to the world championships and won player of the tournament and Wales didn't even get anywhere near the business end of the competition. Dan Carter was playing in that tournament and they still gave it to Gav. People say he should have achieved more in his career. I don't know if those kinds of comments are fair because there's a lot that goes on but I haven't come across many, if any, players with more talent than him. He was under a lot of pressure and scrutiny, some of it he brought on himself, just like I did. But when I signed for the Ospreys on a big deal, he used to say: "Pressure's on now then!" My mentality was that I was on that money because I deserved it. I was the man, in my own head. He was coming at it from a different perspective. He was such a special player but he needed good coaches and he didn't always get that.

Me and Byrney first crossed paths at the Scarlets. He was a bit of a late bloomer and he turned up one pre-season and just smashed the fitness. I always loved the pre-season testing because I prided myself on bossing the runs, particularly mid to long distance. He arrived and hammered me on them. He was an unbelievable trainer, so dedicated to what he did. He is a great guy and an outstanding player. Around 2008, without doubt, I think he was the best full-back in the world. He was brilliant in the air, was great at regathering his own kicks and could cut some brilliant angles from full-back.

Hooky was also an outstanding talent. I don't think coaches understood him. He was the kind of guy who you just had to let play. Just let him go. They tried to bombard him with information sometimes and it shackled his natural ability sometimes. He was at his best when coaches just told him to go out, play his own game and enjoy it. He was an instinctive player. Coaches got down on him a bit and if they'd just handled him better, then who knows what could have happened. Really early on in our careers, we were both sat on the bench against Australia in Cardiff.

The game kicked off and we were just having a bit of fun making silly comments like: "Look at us by here playing for Wales, mad init?" But he got sent on quite early after Stephen Jones picked up an injury. He absolutely smashed it and it was only his third cap. But I can guarantee you he wasn't worrying about moves, patterns and tactics. He was just playing what was in front of him and that's when he was dangerous. He kicked a penalty in the 71st minute to help us draw the game 29-29.

There's not a lot that hasn't been said about Shane's career. What can I add? His highlight reel is remarkable. He could finish like few others on the planet. He didn't just used to beat players, he'd embarrass them on occasions. People couldn't get anywhere near him and it was great to watch. A game could be passing him by and then all of a sudden he'd spring into life and produce the one bit of magic that won us the game.

All of them were just out of this world in their own ways but the best thing I can say about the Fab Four boys – and Gav – is that they are all genuinely good guys. We were having the time of our lives back then. Playing at the top of our game, helping Wales win things and just enjoying ourselves afterwards. I'm glad to call them good mates to this day.

My second away trip with Wales was to Argentina in 2004. I came off the bench in both matches, we lost the first Test but won the second one. Before flying home, we had our traditional Kangaroo Court, which is basically where a judge – one of the more senior boys – dishes out a load of drinking fines and everyone gets a little bit merry. We were doing this in the bar at our team hotel. It was the last game of the season and we were flying.

Next thing, the All Blacks arrive and they're staying in our hotel. I clocked them arriving – keep in mind I had three Wales caps at the time – and I was saying to the boys: "They're not all that, there's nothing special about them, it's all talk." Just stupid stuff like this. Jerry Collins came over – this was the first time I met him – and I started ripping into him a bit, telling him he wasn't that good and just having general banter. The following morning, at breakfast, Adam Jones comes over to me and says: "Mike, do you remember telling Jerry Collins that he was shit at rugby last night?" That didn't make the hangover any better. Then about 18 months later, New Zealand came to Cardiff for the autumn internationals. It was my first start in a really big game for me. Until then, I'd only started against Romania, the USA and Canada. I'd completely forgotten about the incident with Jerry but then a journalist says to me: "Mike, apparently Jerry Collins is looking forward to playing against you." I was a bit confused as to why but it was in my head a little bit then. Matchday comes around.

At the Millennium Stadium, the two changing rooms are probably about 80 metres apart and the entrance to the pitch is right in the middle. So when you leave the home dressing room, you walk down this corridor towards the away one but then turn left before you get there to enter the pitch. When we got to the stadium that day, I dropped my bag off in the dressing room and then went to go and have a look at the pitch. As I'm walking down the tunnel, who's coming towards me? Jerry. So I flick a switch. Straight away I can remember Adam's comment in that hotel in Argentina, the comment from the journalist in the build-up to the match.

I'm thinking: 'Alright then, here we go, I'm just going to stare at him all the way down. What's the worst that can happen?' I looked at him all the way down the tunnel. Then another thought popped into my head: 'If it kicks off, so be it. I'll probably get my head kicked in but I'll go flat out for 10 seconds.' So I stared at him all the way down and he's keeping his eyes on me. We're getting closer and then when he gets near me, he puts his head down and walks off. In my head, I thought it was a massive psychological victory: 'Get in! Here we go, I've done him.'

As it happened, I played shit and we lost 41-3. Lesson learned. But I've always been proud of my mentality in the early days. I might have been intimidated but I never showed it and I needed that to survive in the early days, especially at Llanelli! The thing with the All Blacks was that they were always talked up so much and I think we'd lost the game a lot of the time before we'd even taken the field. But I didn't know any of their players back then because I didn't grow up with Sky Sports like a lot of the boys. So I never used to watch Super Rugby or the Tri Nations and it was never ingrained in my head that these players were special. Later in my career, I became team-mates with Jerry at the Ospreys and I asked him whether he remembered the incident and if he'd taken offence. He said he thought I was being funny, which was a relief. He was an amazing guy. When we were team-mates he'd say: "If you get into any trouble, just come and see me."

He looked after all the boys. I was falling asleep in a nightclub one night and some girl took a picture of me. Jerry grabbed her camera straight away and just deleted the picture. He was an unbelievable drinker as well. My word, he could drink. I made the mistake of going in rounds with him once. At the time, I'd just moved from a flat in the middle of Cardiff to a house a bit further out. After trying to keep up with Jerry, I thought I still lived in my old flat and went back there at the end of the night instead of to my new house.

That was an interesting one. Jerry had his own way of doing things, he wouldn't turn up wearing the right kit but nobody ever said anything to him. I remember Scott Johnson came up to a few of us and told us to tell Jerry to basically sort himself out. I looked at him and said: "You fucking tell him, I'm not telling him!" Scott was great at trying to put me in my place and all the youngsters like he was a big dog but he wasn't going to tell Jerry Collins!

Welsh rugby frustrated the hell out of me sometimes with the way it was run and the attitude of promoting overseas talent ahead of our own. But I do have some great memories of my time with the regions. It was amazing to play regularly with some of my best mates and I was able to win a bit of silverware along the way. For better or worse, my time in Wales moulded me into the player that I was. But, in the end, the constant nonsense that I had to deal with – some of which I brought on myself – all got a bit too much and I had to get out of the bubble.

4

New Era

The year 2007 was a whirlwind for Welsh rugby. Of course, it is famous for the disappointing Rugby World Cup campaign and the scandalous way head coach Gareth Jenkins was sacked 24 hours after the tournament. It's also the year Warren Gatland arrived.

Prior to the 2007 Rugby World Cup, Gareth took us on a two-match tour to Australia. I started both matches, and they were big games for me because it was a chance to push my case to start at the World Cup. We pushed the Wallabies close in the first Test but ended up losing 29-23 and then got completely blown away 31-0 in the second encounter. To be honest, that felt like more of a social tour. There was a fair bit of drinking that went on and it felt like the purpose of the trip was as much to bring the group together as it was to prepare on the field for the World Cup. A few of us had been out one night and we had to be on the bus the following morning at 9:00am for training.

I was sharing a room with James Hook and we both woke up in our beds at 9:00am on the dot. We flew out of bed, got changed in a hell of a panic and I've never run down a flight of stairs so fast in all my life. We were a few minutes late and turned up, well, looking like we'd just rolled out of bed. James walks on the bus first and I follow him. As I'm walking past Gareth at the front, he says: "Apologise to everyone." So I literally put my hand up, said sorry and then plonked myself down.

That night we were at another function having a few beers again and Nigel Davies, Gareth's assistant, turned to me and basically told me to get stuffed, which I thought was a bit harsh. Gareth was actually alright about it, he just told me to make sure I set my alarm. The tour was a lot of fun, we did a lot of socialising, but we were there to play rugby at the end of the day. Gareth is a great bloke and I got on well with him but, looking back, he should have been Welsh coach a good few years earlier. By the time he was in the hot seat, the game had moved on beyond his methods. He was an absolutely outstanding motivator but I think he needed somebody underneath him who was a bit more in tune with the demands of the professional game. There was no edge about the environment.

There were a good few players around at that time who only needed half a chance to go out and hit the beers. I was one of them! It was the last generation of players before the real academy youngsters – the Sam Warburtons and Leigh Halfpennys of the world – came through. That's not a dig at those boys but the game still had an attachment to that old school mentality of enjoying yourself off the field as much as on it. When we got back from Australia, we went on these pre-tournament camps to France and stayed in the middle of nowhere.

It was my first taste of a World Cup but there just didn't feel like there was a buzz about it. Even during the tournament, when we were traveling around the country, it was just a bit flat. Four years later, in New Zealand, we were getting hakas every time we checked into a new hotel, the country was hooked on the tournament, fans were everywhere we went. The 2007 tournament fell way short in comparison on and off the field.

I'd trained well before the tournament and got myself into great shape but, a bit like during my time at the Scarlets, Dwayne was Gareth's preferred choice and I had to stomach that. He was named as captain for the first match of the tournament against Canada, which sent a clear message to me. The frustration was building up in me at this point. I thought I deserved a look-in but it was pretty clear to me that I wasn't going to get one under the regime. We came out of the blocks very slowly in the first game and were actually 12-9 down at half-time, but stayed calm and came back to win comfortably in the second period. I was thrown on with 10 minutes to go in the second game against Australia with the score 32-13 in their favour. I got the start against Japan and earned man of the match as we steamrolled them by 70 points. We were allowed out into Paris after that win over Japan, which was probably a bit of a loose call by the coaching staff but we took full advantage. To this day, it is still one of the best days out I've ever had. We had ex-SAS guys looking after us to make sure we stayed out of trouble.

First we hit the Longchamp races and enjoyed ourselves in the Royal Box with the champagne flowing. From there, we went to a lovely restaurant for lunch and then we went to see a cabaret show and we were all up on stage having our picture taken. As we were leaving each place to go to the next, we were zigzagging down the Champs-Élysées. We had policemen escorting us and they were literally stopping traffic because the Welsh boys were on the sauce. We ended up in some nightclub near a river. There were no major incidents but it was a big old day out.

This sort of thing was fairly common though. I know for a fact New Zealand went to Monaco the week before they were knocked out of the tournament by France. When we got back to the hotel, I remember Gareth was excited because we'd all been out to switch off and chill out. Now it was going to turn back to the rugby and we had seven days to prepare for Fiji.

The day of the game was a bit of a shambles from the start. We were staying about two hours away from the ground and there wasn't a toilet on the bus. Because it was a matchday, all the boys were fully hydrated and we were having to go to the toilet in some makeshift pot. It was disgusting. How can that be allowed to happen at that level? Things didn't get much better after the game kicked off. I was back on the bench and I remember watching from the stands thinking: 'What the hell are we doing?' We played it all wrong that day.

Against a side like Fiji, you have to be pragmatic and almost play boring rugby. But it was almost as if we were trying to turn it into a game of sevens, which suited them down to the ground. We were taking quick taps and lifting the tempo which was the exact opposite of what we needed to be doing. It was an open, expansive game and Fiji were loving it. Half-time comes and we're 25-10 down. Nigel Davies, who I didn't have a great relationship with, comes up to me and gives a little pep talk about how I need to be the one that makes the difference in the second half.

By then I was a bit disillusioned by it all. I felt like it was my time to take over the No.9 shirt at that tournament, which is only natural, and I was a bit fed up. So I was thinking in the back of my mind: 'Oh, now you want me?' Despite my frustrations, it was a chance for me to come on and win the game for Wales but we couldn't get it done. Michael Owen went right up in my estimations that day.

Some boys went missing in the last 10 minutes of that match, staying on the floor a little bit too long and not wanting the ball because they knew that the writing was on the wall. I think some of the boys had begun worrying about what the reaction was going to be back home after we got knocked out. But Michael was demanding the ball right until the final whistle and was really trying to seize the initiative. We obviously fell short, losing 38-34 in what was probably an outstanding game for the neutral.

You could hear a pin drop in the dressing room after the match. I think Alfie tried to break the silence but nobody really listened. The boys were in disbelief. We got back to the hotel relatively late that night and a number of us just hit the beers in the bar and went pretty much all the way through until the morning. There were a lot of sorrows to drown. I had about one hour's worth of kip and then wandered into a team meeting when we were told that Gareth had been sacked, a few hours before we were due to board the flight home.

The way that all went down was completely out of order. I may not have had the opportunities I thought I deserved under Gareth but I got on okay with him, he'd done a hell of a lot for Welsh rugby and they should never have treated him that way. He flew back to Wales with us and got on the bus that was taking us back to the Vale.

The resort has two entrances just off a country lane. The first one you come to will take you to the hotel reception and then about half a mile down the road is the golf club entrance. They knew that the press would be waiting outside the hotel reception so they stopped the bus on the country lane and let Gareth get off. I was sat on the left hand side of the coach, so as it turned right through the Vale's main gates, I watched him walking, alone, up this country lane towards the other entrance. It was so wrong and very sad, actually.

Later in the year, word began to filter through that a guy called Warren Gatland was taking over as head coach and he was officially appointed in November 2007. I don't mean this disrespectfully but I'd genuinely never heard of him. I had no idea what to expect but I was excited because it was a fresh start and I thought that might bring me some opportunities. There was a noticeable shift in atmosphere when Gatland arrived. I remember his first team meeting and all the boys were sitting up, nobody was pissing about.

Things were quite relaxed with the previous regime but a switch had well and truly been flicked when Gats arrived. He was very serious from the start, brought a lot of edge, a lot of detail but also the game plan was incredibly simple. It was easy to run as a scrum-half. Look, at times, I completely disagreed with it but it laid the foundation for us and gave us a structure after what had gone on at the 2007 World Cup. They had such a short time frame to get ready, they kept it simple and it worked.

I had a great relationship with him when he first came in. I felt like I could be myself around him and because he backed me, I felt like I had my feet under the table for the first time in a Wales environment. It was tough for me before then because I'd been pigeon-holed a little bit. Wales is such a small country and if someone has an opinion about you in Carmarthen, it'll soon travel to Newport and it's very difficult to change perceptions about you as a player. People thought that because I was tall, I was also slow and ponderous, which was nonsense. Having an outsider like Gats coming in was amazing. People tried to influence him but he was strong enough to stick to his guns and make his own judgements on players. I became his number one pretty quickly and I never really looked back after that. People say he was good for me – and I have to admit that he was – but I was good for him as well! I performed well during his early days and that gave me the confidence to have a laugh and a joke with him.

During a tour to New Zealand in 2010, I had him in a headlock telling him I should have been made captain during the second Test against the All Blacks. Ryan Jones was the captain then but he went off injured and Jonathan Thomas took over. I felt like I was a good candidate for it given that Gethin Jenkins wasn't playing and Sam Warburton wasn't around then. But he made Jonathan captain and we were having a few beers afterwards because it was the end of the season. We were sat next to each other having banter and it just ended up with me putting him in a headlock and airing my grievances. He then admitted that I had a point but he probably only agreed with me so I'd let him go. He used to think I was the most confident player he'd coached but I was just comfortable around him because of how our relationship started. He stopped a training session once and said: "Those of you who think you are world class, stand on this side, and those that think you're a good player, stand over there." I'd always go straight to the world class side without a moment's hesitation and then he'd say: "Well, I knew Phillsy would go over there…" Before having a bit of a go at the players that didn't back themselves quite as much. I was playing the game a bit as well, to get him onside.

My relationship with Rob Howley, the attack coach for the bulk of my Wales career, became quite difficult during the latter part of my career.

I felt like he was particularly hard on me because I played the same position as him. But at the start, he was really good to me. Before he came to the Wales setup, he coached me at the Cardiff Blues. During that time, Dwayne Peel was still the man with Wales but Rob, who is super intense, did this thing where he measured the speed of our passing, somehow, and he was adamant that mine was faster than Dwayne's.

So he did have my back in the early days. As the years went by, though, it became apparent that we were just two completely different characters with different approaches to life and that's probably why we didn't see eye-to-eye very often.

I felt like I had Shaun Edwards' respect from the get go. We really got on. I'd rate him as the best coach I ever worked with, not only because of his coaching skills but for the way he was around the players. He liked what I brought to the table and he is the kind of bloke that you'd run through brick walls for. You just never wanted to let him down. He's a proper, salt of the earth kind of guy who gave it to you straight and he's a bloody good coach as well. Before he came in, someone like Scott Johnson – who was an assistant to Mike Ruddock before becoming caretaker head coach for a few games in 2006 – wouldn't even acknowledge that I was in the room, let alone talk to me. We'd be in a team meeting and I remember him talking about what he wanted from the scrum-halves and only referred to Dwayne Peel and Gareth Cooper. I was just there thinking: 'I'm sat right here, mate.'

I wasn't really in the frame to start back then but it's a right kick in the teeth when you get treated like that. It just adds to that sense that you don't belong there. So when you've experienced all that kind of stuff, having someone like Shaun come in was a real boost. It was just his demeanour, the way he spoke to the players, the way he treated them. He had a lot of respect for the boys, I certainly appreciated that and it went both ways. Boys want to play for coaches like him. Shaun sometimes got players' names wrong but it wasn't intentional and everyone used to just let it slide because his heart was always in the right place.

There are a lot of fake people around but he was a straight shooter and you can't ask for any more than that. He would always make a point of staying in contact with me when I was out injured, just dropping me the odd text here or there. Nobody else did and that's why you'll struggle to find a player who'll say a bad word about him. He wanted nines to play a specific role and I was a big part of the system because he wanted to make the most of my size. I didn't hang in behind the defensive line like a lot of scrum-halves do, I was used in the front line.

He would then want me to get around to the short side and organise there, which was my chance to have a breather. I remember one of his first defensive sessions vividly. We were running a drill and the boys hadn't organised properly on the open side, so I filled in the gap. Next thing, Shaun is screaming at the top of his voice to stop the session. Everybody froze like statues. People talk about Shaun's temper and he can go off when he wants to. He was screaming at me calling me everything under the sun before telling me to get back to the short side. Fair enough. Five minutes later, the same thing happens again. There is a big gap on the open side and the ball is coming my way, so I fill in the hole. He stops the session again and goes even more nuts and I can't bite my tongue: "I'm just filling in the fucking gap!" I didn't know Shaun too well at this point so I wasn't sure what was about to happen next. But it was like someone flicked a switch and you could see his blood pressure go down almost instantly and he just said: "Okay, yeah, fair enough!" And that was it.

Not all coaches are willing to be challenged like that, which is another reason I got on well with him. Before the England game in the 2008 Six Nations, he gave a really passionate speech about a family member who had passed away. We were all just absorbed by his energy and his emotion in the dressing room before the game. Boys were absolutely bouncing off the walls. Trouble was, in those days we had to go out on the pitch before kick-off for a team photo and everyone cooled off a little bit, which is probably why we started the game so terribly that day.

I hate Twickenham. There's just something about the place that makes your blood run a little bit hotter as a Welshman. Whenever I played England, I always got myself fired up by thinking about the fact they've got all the money behind them, we're a smaller nation, they look down their noses at us. Underdog mentality. That's what fuelled my fire when I played against them.

When the games were at Twickenham, times it by 10. There's just a certain level of arrogance about the way the crowd carry themselves. Driving into the stadium you have fans tucking into their champagne picnics out the back of their Range Rovers. I just couldn't wait to get stuck into them. Later in my career, when I was at Sale in the north-west of England, some of the boys up there took issue with the Twickenham crowd, which kind of says it all. I started two competitive games there and won them both, which I'm particularly proud of but, of course, the most famous was in 2008 after the new regime came on board.

We were quite relaxed before the opener against England. Shaun's ex-wife is singer Heather Small from the band M People and, on the way up to London, Tom Shanklin was putting her music on over the speakers and we were all hiding behind the seats at the back of the bus because none of us knew how he was going to react. Myself, Lee Byrne and James Hook all managed to get a few sunbeds in as well just to get the tan on point before the match. Look good, feel good, play good, as Gavin Henson used to say.

On a more serious note, though, I was thinking about all the times I'd watched Wales play at Twickenham as a kid and get absolutely stuffed, we're talking cricket scores, and I just didn't want that to happen to me. We hadn't won there for 20 years – it was the first time I'd been there, mind – and at half-time the outlook was bleak. We were 16-6 down and I was thinking to myself that I was just going to become another statistic. It was a pretty horrible feeling and I didn't want that for myself. We managed to hang on in the first half and Huw Bennett made an amazing tackle just before the break to hold them out. I was expecting the coaches to come in ranting and raving but it was calm and constructive in the changing room.

It was largely positive but the coaches had a bit of a go at Alix Popham because he'd jumped out of the defensive line a few times. Howley was pretty upbeat and the message from Gats was: "Get into the right areas, get hold of the ball and play some rugby. Keep the ball on the field and let's back our fitness. Nobody has trained harder than us."

We actually realised we were decent players and then went out with a bit more belief and confidence in the second half. One thing led to another, Hooky kicked a few penalties and we were back in the game. Midway through the second half, I was looking at their pack thinking that not one of them intimidated me. They looked disinterested, they didn't look like they had as much fight in them as we did. Suddenly I had this confidence, I thought they didn't want to be there and I believed we were going to beat them. We struggle with that sometimes in Wales but when we actually believe in ourselves, it becomes quite powerful. Lee Byrne scored a try heading into the final 10 minutes and we were level.

After Byrney's try, I took the kick-off and booted this ball as far as I could but it went slightly infield, which is not great because it kind of opens the field up a little bit more for the counter-attack. Really, you want to kick it as close to the touchline as possible. As soon as I've hit this ball, I'm thinking: 'That's not good.'

So I'm sprinting as fast as I can to shut the space down. Iain Balshaw goes to stick an up-and-under in the air around his own 10 metre line and I charge it down. Then I completely miss the hack through and somehow it ends up in Gethin Jenkins' hands and I'm about five yards in front of the ball. It was chaos but I managed to get myself back onside, take the pass and stretch out to score the try that put us in front.

What a moment. It was like an out-of-body experience. Alun Wyn Jones rags me off the floor and when it all settled down the realisation sets in that we're 10 minutes away from claiming a famous win. The feeling at the final whistle was indescribable. I just wanted to prove to so many people, including myself, that I was good enough to be playing at that level and I felt I'd done that. But more importantly, we'd won at Twickenham, shaking off a losing record that stretched back two decades. We all knew it was huge. If you could bottle up those feelings and emotions, you'd be a millionaire. We used to sing Saturday Night At The Movies by The Drifters in the dressing room if we'd won, that was our song, and Shaun Edwards kicked us off. It was party time.

The beers were flowing on the bus back to Cardiff that night. We were on top of the world. Untouchable. As we

Young winner: Playing for West Wales B Under-11s. I played number 8 and scored the only try of the game. Wearing that kit was unbelievable

Three of a kind: Me and my brothers. Above left, with my arm around Mark, and Rob the other side. Above right, happy times growing up on the farm – Rob, Mark and me

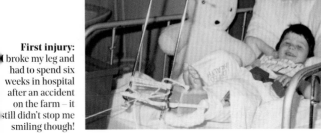

First injury: I broke my leg and had to spend six weeks in hospital after an accident on the farm – it still didn't stop me smiling though!

Class act: A school photo at Bancyfelin Primary. I'm third from the left, middle row. The school has produced an impressive number of outstanding rugby players

Big day: Lining up for Carmarthen and District Under-11s. A very proud occasion for me – captaining the team and getting to play at Cardiff Arms Park

Things I want.

1). I will for Wales more than 50 times. (Wales Firsts).

2). I will be famous.

3). I will be a great player for the whole of my playing career.

4). I will marry a netal snistst bird. who's really nice to me!

5) I will have lots + lot's of many.

6) I will have a nice house!

7) I will have a fantastic life, with a fantastic family.

✳.

((I will play for Wales U19 next year.)). ✳

Teenage dreams: A handwritten note from the early days – nothing wrong with ambition, is there?

Rising star: Winning man of the match for Whitland Youth versus Narbeth. I completely bossed the game

First of many: Wayne Hall presenting me with my Under-21s cap – the first Welsh cap of any kind I received

Enter the Dragon: My official Wales debut was against Romania in 2004 but my first senior appearance in a red shirt actually came the previous year in an uncapped game against the Barbarians

Meeting Mandela: I toured Argentina and South Africa with Wales in 2004, and shaking hands with Nelson Mandela before our Test match against the Springboks was a moment I'll never forget

cut above: Looking very stylish, I'm
ure you'll agree, with Gavin Henson and
al Luscombe. My form for the Scarlets
ight), meanwhile, helped earn me a
lace in the Northern Hemisphere team
at played a charity game (below) against
e Southern Hemisphere in 2005

Catching the eye: I played with Stephen Jones for both Scarlets and Wales, and he tempted me out of retirement at the end of my career, although I'm not too sure where his shiner here came from!

Big test: My first major start for Wales came against the All Blacks in 2005. Jerry Collins was looking forward to playing against me after I'd previously given him some stick!

At home: Long round trips to training were no longer an issue when I joined Cardiff Blues

Painful exit: We played into Fiji's hands at the 2007 Rugby World Cup. The defeat cost head coach Gareth Jenkins his job

Flying high: The Ospreys' offer was just too good to turn down

Celeb couple: With Amie Duffy. It was the longest, most serious relationship I'd been in at the time

Ups and downs: I had a great relationship with Warren Gatland (standing next to Neil Jenkins, who is on the far left of this photograph) when he first joined Wales but things became more strained between us towards the end of my international career

What a feeling: You can see how much it meant to me after we beat England at Twickenham in 2008 – Wales' first win there in 20 years

approached the outskirts of the Welsh capital, though, Gats announced that nobody was allowed into town that night, which was a bit disappointing to be honest because a few of us were right up for it. I'm convinced Ryan Jones, our captain, had a word with him!

Gav shouted down the bus: "I'd love to see you drop us after that one!" But everyone stuck to the rules and we all went to the bar at our team hotel instead. It was still a great night and everyone was enjoying each other's company. Eventually I end up sitting next to Gats and he leans into me and says: "Great game today but you could be world class one day." With a few beers in me and without a moment's thought, I replied: "I'm already world class, mate!" He loved that comment.

In the meeting on the Monday, my good mate Shane Williams gets up and starts apologising for his behaviour. I actually went to bed relatively early that night so I had no idea what had gone on. It turns out that when Warren tried to bring an end to the session, Shane wasn't ready to go and essentially offered Gats outside for a scrap. Not the greatest move in the world, as Shane himself admits. Anyway, he'd apologised privately to Gats and was now apologising to the team. Fair enough, we all do stupid shit. Case closed. After Shane is done, Gats stands up and says: "Boys, this is the first team I've ever coached in my life where the backs are the fighters, the drinkers and the shaggers!" I loved that. When he said that, I thought: 'This is the guy for me.' It completely killed any awkwardness and we were all able to move on and concentrate on winning a Grand Slam.

After every match, Shaun used to make a big fuss about the defensive play and for that game he chose my charge down. I made two or three charge downs in that match and he wanted to highlight those as well. Not all coaches are that detailed about things. My relationship with Shaun and Gats had gotten off to the perfect start. If I'd been a bit dodgy that day and made a few errors, I probably wouldn't have had the career that I did.

The Scotland game was a bit of a struggle although we ended up running out 30-15 victors in the end. I didn't particularly shine so they gave Dwayne the start against Italy. We never really got into our stride in that game and we were only leading 13-8 at half-time.

This is where the new management team were good for me. Before they came in, nobody really put pressure on the scrum-half to contribute defensively but suddenly the coaches wanted every player on the field to pitch in on both sides of the ball. If Dwayne wasn't making tackles in the past, nobody would say anything because he was very good with the ball. But the new regime wanted more defensively and I could do both. I came on just after half time against Italy and nailed almost everything I did and we ended up winning by 40 points.

That being said, I know better than anyone how much easier it is coming off the bench, especially against a team like Italy. That's a real bugbear of mine even now, when people say: "Player X came on and changed the game." My attitude to that is the game's been going on for 60 minutes and now everyone is knackered, of course they're going to have an impact. So I'm not trying to blow smoke up my arse here.

In the post-match review, Gatland played a clip of me making a break but I kept hold of the ball longer than I should have. So he was going through, saying it was a good break but I should have given it earlier etc. Then when he's finished his little speech, I've just piped up with: "Yeah, but it was a great break though, wasn't it?" All the boys chuckled and Gats had a little smile about it as well and I felt like I had him on side.

Previously, Dwayne and Scott Johnson were basically best mates, at least that's the way it felt to me. I remember them leaving one training session with the arms around each other. At times it felt like it was pointless me being there because I was never going to get a look in there. But what it did teach me is that you do have to build good relationships with the head coach and having that can work in your favour when it comes to selection. I built that relationship with Gats and got him on side very quickly. I was playing well, having some banter and it all worked in my favour. However, I did fear that I'd thrown it all away in the fourth match against Ireland.

In the build-up to the game, Shaun got me a little bit stressed because I felt like he wanted me in two places at once. Traditionally, a scrum-half is sweeping behind the first line of defence looking for the chip over the top but Shaun wanted me to be up in the front line so I could use my physicality. Obviously he didn't want me in two places at once but I had to be smart and read the game, read the fly-half's body language to try and predict what he was going to do. Shaun wanted me in the front line but I still had to cover those chips.

So I'd been trying to get to grips with this all week and then in the game, they had a lineout that came slightly in-field and I was just sat in behind the ruck when, really, I should have been organising the short side defence. I wasn't there and Shane Horgan made a break and to this day I have no idea how I managed to stop him scoring. I managed to get across and hold him up inches short of the line and then we won a turnover. Still, I remember thinking that Shaun was going to go mental on me for being out of position but instead he was cool with it because I managed to get back and make the tackle. He appreciated stuff like that. What he won't have appreciated, though, is what happened just before half-time. I can't tell you why I did it but I dropped a knee on Marcus Horan one minute before the break. Horan made a right meal of it but I can't deny that it was worthy of a yellow card and Wayne Barnes duly sent me on my way. We went in at half-time 6-3 down. I thought I was finished. We were going for the Triple Crown and the Grand Slam but I'd just jeopardised all that by doing something stupid.

I was genuinely thinking about David Beckham and the red card he received for kicking out at Diego Simeone at the 1998 World Cup. Beckham was vilified after that and I thought everyone was going to hate me. I'd let the country down, let my team-mates down – all these thoughts were going through my head. I was sat in the dressing room at half-time thinking there was no way I was going back on. They'd been savage earlier in the campaign with other players. Popham got dropped for a defensive error and Mark Jones lost his place for being injured during a phase and then getting up to run it off. Shaun's philosophy was that you can't be injured in defence.

Even if you've got one leg hanging off, get up on your other one and hop back into the line. So there I am in the belly of Croke Park and nobody is speaking to me at the break. Then Shaun came to calm me down and said: "Don't worry about what has just happened, don't try too hard when you go back on, just play your natural game."

That was nice and reassuring. I was just relieved they were even going to let me go back on as opposed to replacing me. I went on to play pretty well in the second half. Shane Williams scored and they came back with a few penalties but we managed to hold on and win. That was the first piece of silverware I won with Wales. We had a good night out after that game. We were allowed out until midnight and we ended up in one of the best nightclubs I've ever been in. I don't remember the specifics of the architecture but all the girls were stunning. I managed to make, err, friends with one of them but she wasn't allowed to accompany me back to the hotel.

It was a bit like they'd let us out for a few hours to run to the end of our lead and then pull us back. So we all went back to the hotel and watched Enzo Maccarinelli fight David Haye with a few more beers before Alan Phillips, team manager, called it a night. To be fair, I couldn't believe that they let us go out that night considering the Grand Slam was on the following week but, fair play, they let us go for a look. The France game was a bit cagey in the first half but we won pretty convincingly in the end. Shane broke Gareth Thomas' record for most tries by a Welshman and we came out on top 29-12. The one thing that strikes me from that day is just how confident we were. If you compare our mental state heading into that game to the way we felt going into the England game, we were like two different sets of players. The feeling was incredible. When you win a Grand Slam, you've arrived. Nobody can take that away from you and it just makes you hungry for more.

The feeling is like a drug. I'd also repaid Gatland's faith in me, which was huge going forward. It was the first campaign where I really felt like I was part of the team, contributing and adding real value.

That night, they sent us into Cardiff with five bodyguards to try and keep us away from trouble because we knew the city was going to be mayhem. It was a running joke that

I needed three on me! One of them had been working with Robbie Williams shortly before and he could not believe the reaction that the boys got. He'd never seen anything like it. It was absolute carnage, the boys felt like rockstars. I always used to get the same thing. There'd be a group of three girls and one of them would recognise me, one would just stand there and then the final one would be like: "Who is he? Who is he? I don't know who he is! Who are you?" I just used to stand there having absolutely no idea what to do. How do you react in a situation like that? But that night in Cardiff was on another scale, I'd never experienced that level of hysteria. I loved the attention and the adulation but I wasn't ready for the pitfalls, I didn't understand how you could get yourself into some real bother without really doing anything wrong. I learned the hard way later in my career! The following day we all met up down Mumbles to keep drinking. That day I remember feeling like I'd started to get the respect of the backroom staff as well. The physios, the medics, people like that. It felt like I was coming of age a little bit. I was having good chats with everyone, whereas previously that wouldn't have happened.

You can tell by someone's demeanour if they respect you or not, if they value your opinion or not. I was part of the squad in 2005 but I didn't touch the ball, whereas this time I felt like a real part of the squad. That was a great afternoon.

From that tournament onwards, me and Gats got on well. I knew I was his number one and that gave me a huge amount of confidence. I never once doubted my position in the squad and I loved it. When it came to the meetings where they'd announce the team after that, I'd just be sitting there thinking to myself: 'I wonder who's going to play second row this week,' or 'Tell you what, he might be getting a chance at centre.' Never once was

I concerned about my own selection and I felt that way for the next five or six years.

During that campaign, somebody was leaking the team to the media ahead of the official announcement and Gats wasn't too thrilled about it. He eventually found out who the guilty party was and wrote that person's number down on a white-board in the team room just to let everyone know that he knew who it was. I had no idea who it was and I wasn't really that bothered, although I know it wasn't one of the players.

These things usually get out because an agent might have a few players in the side and that gets leaked and then journalists piece it together from there. You don't have to be Sherlock Holmes to figure these things out to be honest. It was never something that bothered me. I didn't want to waste any energy on that sort of thing because I didn't really see it as a big deal. I think, as a player, if you're worrying about that sort of stuff then you've got your priorities wrong. Does it really matter if the opponents know the team a day early? I don't think so. But Gats was none too pleased. To this day I still don't know who it was.

After our all-day session on the Sunday, the Ospreys gave us the Monday off but we were back in on Tuesday because we had the semi-final of the EDF Energy Cup the Saturday after the Grand Slam. How about that for a bit of scheduling. We only had about two training sessions and a team run before that match and this is the genius of Lyn Jones. The majority of us had been in camp with Wales for the last seven weeks – the team that beat England had 13 Ospreys players in the starting 15 – so we played that day against Saracens using the Wales calls.

Lyn said it was a waste of time trying to get back into the Ospreys' plays, he told us to just go out and play like Wales. Same lineout calls, same patterns. Looking back, did I really need to be starting that day? I'm not sure. We had Justin Marshall on the bench, who could have probably done a job. Anyway, we won the game quite comfortably and Shane was out of this world. In the last 10 minutes, I carried the ball up and as I got tackled my knee twisted awkwardly. I'd just won the Grand Slam, we were winning this semi-final and I didn't want Justin to come on because, as we've discussed, he wasn't particularly great with me. So I refused to go down injured but they replaced me eventually. Stupid really, from me. I went to see the specialist after the game and told him that my knee wasn't great. This was the first real injury I'd suffered since I was about 15, so it was new territory for me.

He assessed things and told me that I'd done my anterior cruciate ligament and that I'd be out for six to nine months. Just like that. To say it came as a bit of a shock would be an understatement. I wasn't even in any real pain and I couldn't get my head around it. That was a massive blow and brought me crashing down to earth with a bump. I didn't deal with it very well. I wasn't the best patient. I was going out when I shouldn't have been and I wasn't focused on my rehab as much as I should have been.

Also, what you have to remember is that rugby players – and professional athletes in general – are creatures of habit and when that gets taken away from you, it's tough to deal with. I got left to my own devices. That's the time when you really need people talking to you, keeping in contact with you. You're away from the squad, you're isolated, your mind begins to wander. Personally, I got my confidence from playing rugby, I got a huge buzz from contributing to a team and when you win you feel like you're walking on water. To have that taken away really dented me a little bit.

It's almost like your armour gets stripped away and I felt a little bit worthless. To make matters worse, I never got injured so to go from that to being out for what ended up being nine months is incredibly difficult. It's not good but you have to learn from those times. To be honest, though, I wasn't ready to learn those lessons back then. It wasn't until I was far more experienced that I reflected on the things I could have done better. Looking back, I should have used that time more wisely, to do a course or add some other strings to my bow away from rugby. I could have been a bit more proactive perhaps but I didn't know where to start.

We didn't really have player development managers coming in and helping us out with that sort of thing like they have today. The game was way behind in that regard but it's pleasing to see things have improved on that front because injured players need support and something to engage their mind.

My recovery didn't really run too smoothly and I needed a second operation in the second half of 2008 to clear out some scar tissue and tidy things up in my knee. Obviously, I wasn't in a great place mentally and I soon found myself back in the newspapers. One evening, not long after the second op, I was out on Mill Lane in Cardiff with a few of my mates. I'm there just minding my business and next thing I know, I get whacked from behind. It was a decent clip and it sparked me clean out.

I ended up in the back of an ambulance and it got out in the press that I'd been hospitalised. A mate of mine was out that night with a different group of people and he actually found his way into the bed next to me after a totally unrelated incident, which gave us both a laugh. Of course, the perception then is that I'd gone out and made trouble for myself but, really, trouble had found me. The truth is that I'd had relations with a woman who I thought was single. Unbeknown to me, she was not. The guy who'd hit me was the boyfriend. He'd spotted me from across the street and wanted to have some sort of revenge. That was that. It was all a bit annoying and unnecessary. I never had any hard feelings towards the bloke, I have no idea who he is. I could have pressed charges and made a big fuss but what would that have achieved? I didn't want the distraction, I didn't want the bullshit. I just wanted to focus on the rugby. All I needed was to just get back on the rugby field. However, there were still a few more months before I would get there and I had to watch Wales' autumn campaign from the sidelines or, more accurately, in a bar with Gav. He was also injured and we decided to go out to watch the boys play Canada, the game when they wore those horrendous yellow jerseys. It was playing with a fire really because wherever we went, people were obviously noticing us.

As the day went on, things got a little bit boisterous and it caused a bit of a stir. The following day, I received notice that they wanted a meeting. What essentially happened was that random people were taking photos of us and we might have been a bit rude. Anyway, when I say they, I mean pretty much everyone! I was summoned to the training centre at the Vale. Gats, Howley, team manager Alan Phillips and Ospreys coach Sean Holley were all in there. I walked in quite cocky and I left the room feeling about two feet tall. They read out a list of complaints that they'd received about my behaviour over the previous few months. A lot of them were false but some of them could have just been overlooked, in my opinion. They weren't serious. This is where I started to get annoyed with Thumper because if somebody rang him up and said something, he'd immediately believe it instead of considering the players' side of things.

We were guilty before we'd even had the trial. I remember during my time at the Ospreys, I was injured and my foot was in plaster, and the club doctor rang me up and said: "Mike, I heard you were out on the weekend." The whole thing was nonsense and I told him exactly that. There were people out there talking shit and Wales can be very good for that sort of thing.

I wasn't whiter than white, not by any stretch of the imagination, but there is a lot of bullshit. It was things like having a word with a bouncer for him to try and let me jump the queue at a nightclub. Come on, how many people have tried that? I switched off about halfway through their list but some of them were to do with me being rude to people, but what everyone forgets is that I was only rude to people who had been rude to me in the first place. It was almost as if someone could call me whatever they wanted to but the moment I called them something back, suddenly I was the bad guy. It was nonsense.

The best complaint, which was totally false, involved Welsh boxing legend Joe Calzaghe. I was out one night and my ex-girlfriend and Joe happened to be in the same club as me. She was trying to wind me up by talking to him in front of me and all that sort of stuff. To be clear, Joe wasn't doing anything wrong and it wasn't him who filed the complaint, I've checked that with him. He just happened to be the one that got caught up in her nonsense. I've met Joe on a number of occasions down the years and he's a great guy who had a hell of a career.

Anyway, I left because she was doing my head in. At this meeting, one of the complaints was that I'd tried starting on Joe that night! Seriously, they thought I'd tried starting a fight with the guy who is the longest-reigning super-middleweight world champion in boxing history, the guy who never lost a fight in his entire career. Thumper went on reading the rest of his list and then said: "Do you have any comment to make?"

So I replied: "Look, I did not start on Joe Calzaghe. Are you mad? Why would I start on Joe Calzaghe?"

The meeting was a bit intense but I think they were trying to help. There wasn't really a warning fired but I got the message. They didn't have to say it but it was essentially them pointing out that if I carried on, I was eventually going to get myself in real trouble. I thought it was a bit ironic, mind, because these were the same people who wanted me to be a bit wild and aggressive when it suited them. It messed with my head a bit. When I came out of retirement to play for the Scarlets at the end of my career, I was chatting to Stephen Jones about some of the complaints they have to deal with about youngsters these days.

They had players turn up to training with marks on their face and the excuse was that they'd walked into a door on Saturday night. We were cracking up about some of the stories because every player has been there. I was thrown into the public eye very quickly and I had to learn very quickly, although to be honest it took me a while!

My main problem was I kept putting myself in stupid positions. Was it really a good idea for me and Gav to go out into the middle of Cardiff on a matchday? You're just putting yourself into a firing line. Don't get me wrong, it was always a great night out and you meet a lot of great people who are really nice, but it's also dangerous.

It was such a relief when I finally did get back out on the pitch in December that year. It was a nice little derby against the Dragons at Rodney Parade, just to ease me back in. I remember coming onto the field and getting booed from all corners of the ground. I was thinking: 'Pretty much the last time I played I helped win you lot a Grand Slam!' It's all good though. I loved the derbies and I was just excited to get back out there.

While I was out injured, I'd missed two Wales campaigns – a tour to South Africa and an autumn series – but I wasn't particularly concerned about my place in the squad. None of the scrum-halves really came in and grabbed the bull by the horns, plus I knew my value. I'd just played a key role in a Grand Slam and I just didn't see anyone as a threat. That being said, I was ready to make up for lost time because I knew there was a pretty big tour just around the corner.

5

Dragons and Lions

J ust fuck off, will you?"

Rob Howley's pushed my buttons one too many times and I've snapped. This is how one of our bust-ups started in 2009.

During the Six Nations that year, our game plan used to work the forwards hard. They used to have to get around the corner all the time, hit double rucks. They ran a fair distance and, for me, it wasn't really efficient. It was also the fact that sometimes I had to give it to a forward going around the corner to run into three defenders, just to get to a part of the field that they wanted us to be in before we launched the backs. This was in the back of my mind but I never really voiced my opinion on it. They were adamant that this was how they wanted to play so I stuck to it 95 percent of the time. Where me and Howley butted heads was that I felt someone else should be able to step in at scrum-half just to get the patterns going if we turned the ball over, rather than wait for me to get there from the other side of the field. Two games into the tournament, me and Rob had a falling out.

We did a play in training which meant the ball went straight to the other side of the field and I had to belt across to get to the breakdown. I thought it was better and quicker for Stephen Jones to play nine at that ruck, with me slotting in at 10. So I called across: "Steve, play nine!" Which he did and we swapped roles for the next phase. There were no errors, I dropped the forwards off and things went smoothly. It saved me running 30 yards and rugby's all about conserving energy.

After training we had this huddle and Howley said something about me not getting to that ruck in front of everyone. The red mist descended. I'm livid because I know I'm busting my balls running here, there and everywhere. We're walking off the pitch and he's looking at me with this cheeky smile. He goes to make a comment but before he gets the words out, I jump in: "Just fuck off, will you?"

I'm storming off the training field and he's trying to stop me. I tell him to piss off one last time before jumping in my car and going home. We had the weekend off and he's ringing me, I'm not answering, so he starts texting me telling me to answer my phone. I message him back telling him I'll speak to him on Monday. I obviously cool off a little bit over the weekend and Monday comes around but I'm still a bit annoyed.

He pulls me into a room and we had a bit of back and forth, nothing too shouty, just a difference of opinion. He said he was trying to get the best out of me and all this stuff. My response to that was that I was working my arse off and I told him to stop being so negative all the time. He then starts saying: "You're going to go on the Lions tour—" and I cut him off: "I know I'm going on the fucking Lions tour!" In the back of my mind, I was thinking: 'Who else are you going to pick?' That was just the confidence I had in my ability at the time. The coaches liked that about me though, they liked that edge and they used to put a lot of pressure on me.

They wanted me to contribute heavily in defence, they constantly used to say our aggression came from me and not many teams would put that responsibility on their scrum-half. They wanted me to offer stuff in attack, set the tempo, take on kicking responsibilities. It's a lot for one man's shoulders. Which is fine but that's why my emotions were always delicately balanced. They wanted to get a reaction out of me and this is an example of that. They were always winding me up.

I played with a lot of emotion and it was almost inevitable that it was going to spill over from time to time if they kept poking and prodding me. We'd just won seven games in a row and I was delivering for him. You should never swear at your coach the way I did but I felt like he didn't need to be having such a downer on me.

Me and Howley had plenty of run-ins down the years but when everything settled down, things were always alright. He thought he was right, I thought I was right, but we were all just trying to do our best for the team. If we ever had a bust-up back then we'd always follow it up with a bit of a joke. It didn't stay like that, mind you.

Despite my confidence, I knew I needed a big Six Nations. I was on top of the world after the Grand Slam the previous year but my knee injury had put me on the back foot a little bit. I was fairly confident of making the Lions squad and knew that a good Six Nations championship would cement my place on the tour to South Africa and convince the coaches that I was still the same guy after the injury.

Dragons and Lions

After the success of 2008, we were on for another Grand Slam in 2009 after dispatching Scotland and England. In the win over the old enemy, Stephen Jones kicked a load of penalties, Leigh Halfpenny scored a try and we saw them off 23-15. There was no game the following weekend so we had a few days off and some of us decided to go and have a few beers. It was me, Gavin Henson, Lee Byrne, Andy Powell and a few others.

There were about seven or eight of us in total. We'd been out for a few beers somewhere and then, in all our wisdom, we decided to go to the Queen's Vaults pub on Westgate Street. You can kick a ball from the front door of this pub and hit the Millennium Stadium. It is not the kind of place where the four of us were going to be able to remain anonymous. Gav got a bit lively and I actually had my head switched on for once. I was looking around the pub and I could see the regulars were getting agitated.

It felt like the kind of situation that might spiral out of control and end up with us on the front page of the newspaper. The boys left and went on to another bar and a performer was setting up. So I decided to get on the microphone and apologise to the regulars, explain that we've just had a good win but mainly just apologise. Powelly was stood next to me and we thought we'd done a good job of turning things around. We walked out of there thinking we'd got everyone back on our side, we were almost high-fiving going out of the pub!

Next thing I know, we bump into the boys and there are police cars turning up. Something had happened in the next bar and it was all kicking off. Nobody was arrested but it made it into the newspapers. The police officers had asked us to wait by them while they assessed the situation but Andy, who hadn't done anything, kicked off a little bit so they threw him in the back of the van to cool down. He was just frustrated because he hadn't actually done anything wrong. Next thing, the van starts rocking back and forth. It was like they caged King Kong!

They soon let him out, though, and nothing really came of it. The next morning, Powelly rings me and says Gats is pissed off. I'm there thinking: 'Christ, I was actually not in the wrong this time!' This was just a case of me being blamed because of the way they perceived me. If something went on and I was in the vicinity of it, then it must have been my fault. As it turned out, Gats never actually said anything to us because, at the end of the day, we'd just won our seventh game in a row and I'd started all of them. If we'd lost seven games in a row, it would have been a different story. It was in the week after this incident that I had my big falling out with Howley. In light of all that, it was a bit of a clean-off move from me to lose my cool with him, seeing as I'd just been in the newspapers for the wrong reasons. But it just went to show how strongly I felt about what he was asking me to do and the confidence I had at the time. There was also probably a bit of a frustration there because I didn't feel like I deserved the stick I got after that incident in the Queen's Vaults because I was trying to smooth things over!

On the pitch, though, things were going well for us but then we slipped up against France in Paris. We actually led the game 13-3 at one point but went on to lose 21-16, which was incredibly annoying. I dealt with the defeat the best way I knew how to at the time, by getting absolutely battered in the hotel bar. The following morning, still half drunk, I was a bit rude to team manager Alan Phillips. He told me I had to go and settle my bill at the hotel reception before I got on the team bus, to which I replied: "You pay it, that's your job." Not exactly my proudest moment. I was completely out of order and I was in an absolutely foul mood after losing. They gave all the players a packed lunch and I launched my banana down the bus in frustration. I was a complete dick and my behaviour here was a lot worse than the night of the McDonald's incident.

As the journey back to Cardiff continued, we started flirting with the idea of going out that night because it was a fallow week in the Six Nations, so we didn't have a game for a fortnight. Ryan Jones came up to me and said that it probably wasn't a good idea to go out again because the Lions was around the corner and all the rest of it. My attitude was that I was already on the plane, which was a really bad, shitty attitude to have and I'd never encourage similar behaviour from anyone these days. So I went out again that night. This time we went to Abergavenny because we thought nobody would know us there. For better or worse, those were the decisions that I was making at that time in my life.

We dispatched Italy without much hassle but it wasn't a great day for my good mate Powelly. He'd tell you himself, he had a poor first half, giving away penalties and knocking the ball on all the time. Half-time comes around and as we enter the dressing room, I hear him shout: "For fuck's sake boys!" Before punching the concrete pillar that was keeping the Stadio Flaminio upright. Then he stormed into the showers – he was frustrated with himself more than anything – but they were tiny and there was nowhere for him to go. He filled the entrance to the shower and he was breathing so ferociously that his shoulders rocked back every time he drew a breath. I was just trying my best to hide the fact that I was laughing my head off.

Anyway, we beat Italy and then had a chance to defend our title on the final weekend. We needed to beat Ireland by 13 points and they were trying to win their first Grand Slam in 61 years. So there was plenty riding on the match but we were our own worst enemies for a lot of the game. We gave away far too many penalties and we just couldn't win a lineout. On the occasions when referee Wayne Barnes actually gave us a penalty, we'd kick to touch and lose the ball. I remember telling Alun Wyn Jones that the next time we won a penalty, I was just going to tap and go because we were losing every ball too often.

He's a proud man and insisted that I give the forwards another chance because he'd figured it out. That's the way he is and he usually gets it right to be fair. I made a good break late in the game. It was scrappy ball off the top of the lineout and I didn't want to just ship it on. So I managed to power through a few of their forwards and it put us in position for Stephen Jones to kick the drop goal that put us one point ahead with six minutes remaining. That was one of my favourite breaks. I was just shrugging Irish defenders off me left, right and centre, the crowd was going absolutely mental.

You feel like you can do anything in those moments. The next bit still kills me to this day. We received the kick-off, carried outside the 22 and I thought rather than box kick, I'd throw it back to Stephen for him to clear and he put it out on the full, giving Ireland a perfect position. The only reason I threw it back was because it was a higher percentage play and I felt like there was less chance of him getting charged down than me. I thought he could bang it long, we'd get a good chase and I fancied us to defend around the halfway line but from good field position, Ronan O'Gara clipped over the drop goal that earned Ireland the Grand Slam. The fact I didn't take ownership of that moment still bugs me. My heart was racing because I'd just bounced about 10 of their players to put us in position to kick our own drop goal, so I tried to be calm and play smart. Sometimes you just get it wrong.

Even though we hadn't defended our championship, I was still confident that I'd be selected for the Lions tour that year. I was very confident in my own ability at this time and knew that I was playing well. During the Six Nations, I felt like I played better than my opposite number, who was ultimately my rival for a Lions spot.

We had Scotland first and I'm facing Mike Blair. I look down at the first scrum and see he's taping his boots up. I knew I could outperform him straight away. I was looking for any excuse to dislike my opponents. I was horrible on the field but that's just where my mindset took me. It probably made me horrible to play against. As far as I was concerned, he was trying to take that Lions No.9 jersey away from me.

Looking back I feel like a bit of a tool but my mindset at the time was: 'He's got shit boots, he's crap, he can't live with me.' I wasn't there to make friends at this stage. Even though we lost to Ireland, I felt like I played better than Tomas O'Leary too. You know where you are in the pecking order and you have to back yourself so I was confident of not only being selected for the tour but also being first choice. You should be backing yourself. I see videos going around these days of players getting excited when they're called up and I don't really understand it. It's a bit different if you're a teenager who gets called up out of nowhere and the Lions is a special thing. But if you're the calibre of player that is being selected for the squad, you should be confident enough in your own ability to expect that to happen. When I got the call-up in 2009, we were at the Ospreys training ground. I don't want to sound ungrateful or big-headed but I don't view that day as a big moment for me. I knew it was going to happen. I genuinely believe that you need to have that mindset if you're going to achieve great things. I felt like I belonged there.

Mike Phillips

I was incredibly excited to get going with the Lions that summer because I was feeling good about my game, I was confident and there was so much to be achieved. Team bonding on tours like that are more crucial than ever because you are trying to unite players from four different countries. We'd just spent a Six Nations trying to hurt each other and now we were team-mates. With that in mind, we had a few drinks in the bar the first night we met up at Pennyhill Park, which is usually where England train.

The following day we were all supposed to go sailing as a team bonding exercise and very quickly it became apparent that the trip wasn't going to take place. We were all getting on so well in the bar on the first night and suddenly it's 2:00am. It was a case of: 'Lads, why are we going sailing boats tomorrow? Let's just stay here for another few hours.' So we did and we had a ball. From that moment on, you start building bonds. Riki Flutey, who I didn't know at all, busts out a karaoke machine, which travelled with him all over South Africa, and got everyone going.

Typically, all the Welsh boys would need a beer or two in them before they said much but everyone just got along really well. Andy Powell was always in the middle of the fun but he actually kept his head down a little bit early on in the tour. Everyone obviously knew he was a bit out there but where he really made his mark was when Paul O'Connell made him chief announcer on the team bus.

On the way to the airport to catch our flight to South Africa, everyone had to go up on the mic and introduce themselves by saying something nobody knows about them. Half the team were trying to be funny and half the team were trying to be serious. Andy was the last person to get up on the mic and he said: "Hi everyone, I'm Andy Powell and I'll be your go-forward on this tour."

98

At this point, all the Welsh boys were cracking up laughing but you could see the players from other countries were still trying to figure him out. On the flight then, for some reason, he starts pretending to speak German but he's talking absolute nonsense. But he was making people laugh and if he's making people laugh, then he'll stick with the joke. He's got one of those faces that you just laugh at anyway, so he doesn't really need to say anything. I'm sure everyone has that one mate who tells the same jokes over and over again but you laugh at him every time because his delivery is spot on. That's Powelly.

He was important on that trip, just bringing an energy to the group and constantly lifting spirits around the place. People don't see that. On the tour, you have film crews following the team around and there were players doing their own video diaries. My approach to all that was to stay away from it because the whole focus for me was the Test series. The warm-up matches mean nothing, it's all about the Test series. That was my mindset.

My honest opinion is that you're only a true Lion if you play in a Test match. It's lovely to be selected for the Lions but you want to be a winning Lion as well. It's all about winning because there have been very few successful touring teams. When you play for the Lions, in your little spot in the dressing room there is a plaque with your name and number, then underneath it are the names of winning Lions. So there was Matt Dawson, Gareth Edwards and so on. I wanted to put my name alongside theirs, not get too caught up with all the baggage that comes with touring as a Lion. It wasn't about showing off on camera, that's not me. It was all about keeping my head down and making sure I bossed it on the field to help us win the Test series.

Not everyone had the same approach and it does take time to warm to certain players from other countries. Someone like Flutey was a bit of an extrovert, he was quite out there. When he whipped out his karaoke machine on the first night, which was a great bit of team bonding, my initial thought was: 'Who's this guy trying to show off?' But once I got to know him, though, I thought: 'This guy's really cool actually.' He was really funny and great for the squad.

In rugby you have these perceptions of people because you're looking for any little excuse you can find to get angry about them, you want them to give you a reason to smash them. Whenever I'd look at the opposition, straight away I'd think 'He's a dick, don't like him' and I've never met the guy. But because he's trying to take food off your table in many ways, you want to hammer him. So you don't look for the good in other players, you look for the bad in them.

Rugby's a really weird sport in that way. So I'd just spent the last few years trying to smash players from England, Ireland and Scotland and now they were my team-mates. I don't know how I'm perceived in Ireland but I did have some great tussles with them down the years. Since I've retired I've heard the likes of Conor Murray say he'd walk into the room and see 'MP' on my kitbag and think 'oh shit' and Rob Kearney worried about how he was going to put up with me on the tour to South Africa.

Players from that part of the world seemed to have a perception about me but I quite liked that because you're not going on the rugby field to be liked. It is quite nice when they say "actually Mike was a legend" rather than the opposite. There was that interesting period at the start of the tour when you're figuring some people out. When you're away from the field it's totally different because you get to know people and you open up a little bit and form those bonds. What I found was, at the end of the day, most rugby players are generally all the same. We're all cut from the same cloth.

Of all the rivalries I had with Irish players down the years, the biggest one was with Ronan O'Gara and we weren't even opposite numbers. I really respected Rog and I used to go at him because I knew how important he was to the teams that he played for. I faced him in my early days at Llanelli, when Munster came to Stradey Park, and I just decided to have a go at him relentlessly, calling him shit and everything else under the sun. I was obviously young at the time and a lot of it was probably to do with me being nervous and trying to get myself up for the game. It was a huge opportunity for me. Back then, youngsters didn't start as regularly as they do now and Munster had all their big guns out. I was onto him all the time in that game and it got to the point where Robin McBryde, our hooker, turned around and went: "Mike, I've had enough of it, it's got to stop!" So I did. Paul O'Connell laughs about that to this day. I've always had the attitude that whatever happens on the field, stays on the field, and I'm pretty good at just forgetting about stuff when I leave the pitch.

What I don't realise is that sometimes I can hurt people's feelings and they remember it more than I do. In the warm-up ahead of the 2009 match against Ireland, I was going through my kicking drills and my ball bounced into their half. I went to get it and had to run past Rog. We were probably about five metres apart. He's just absolutely ripped into me, calling me all sorts: "Get back in your own half you Welsh…" It took me back a bit and by the time I'd picked my ball up, the red mist had descended.

As I ran back past him, I fired a load of verbals at him, calling him useless, shit and all the rest of it. He probably hated me ever since I had a go at him at Stradey! This was before kick-off! We went into the dressing room then after the warm-up and I was telling Stephen Jones and the rest of the backs what had happened and Steve was pissing himself. Every time me and Rog faced each other, we were at each other. We were just two passionate blokes who loved winning.

Anyway, when I arrived for the first day of camp, I flung the door to my room open and who should be lying on one of the beds? My new room-mate Rog. I thought he'd absolutely hate me after the way we'd been at each other's throats but we both just burst out laughing as soon as we clocked what was happening.

Before we knew it, we were getting on like a house on fire. We'd sit next to each other on the team bus, have really good banter. Whenever Stephen Jones would get on the bus, Rog would be in my ear: "Here he comes, the King has arrived." My girlfriend at the time had packed a load of things for me to open when I got to South Africa. There were a few pictures of us in there and I put them on my bedside table. Rog was absolutely pissing himself saying things like: "Mike, we're going away for about eight weeks, not eight months!" That was a bit of ammunition for him but I thought it was a lovely gesture! He was great fun, very quick-witted. He would often sing the lyrics to You're A Superstar by Love Inc. whenever I was around, which gave everyone a laugh.

He got quite frustrated with how much game time he was getting on tour but I was completely blown away by his skills in training. He was such an accurate kicker of the ball and his distribution was brilliant. He was a great communicator and an absolute animal on the field. He was very passionate, very proud and just a superb bloke.

I was on the bench against the Royal XV – a composite team of provincial players – in Rustenburg. We were out in the sticks and staying in these chalets. I remember speaking to a member of staff in reception asking if there were any snakes about and stuff like that. He was talking to me about black mambas, saying there could be one in your room and you'd never know it. Tidy. I was sharing a room with Lee Mears at the time and we basically spent our entire time there watching the TV series Californication and searching the room for black mamba snakes. There were only 12,000 fans at the game.

Really, this is a team that we should have been beating quite comfortably. But it was the first game of the tour, we were still getting familiar with each other and we were struggling to find our groove for the first 60 minutes. We were 18-3 down at one point and it would have been the first time the Lions had lost their opening game on tour since 1971. That was not a piece of history that I wanted to be a part of so there was a bit of pressure on when I came off the bench in the 66th minute. Some late tries from Lee Byrne, Alun Wyn Jones and Rog got us out of jail and then the tour was rolling. I picked up a dead leg in that game. If I'd picked up a similar injury playing for the Ospreys, I'd have fobbed the physios off and played through it. But because it was the Lions, I had a bit more of a professional head on my shoulders. I didn't have a beer that night because I wanted to make sure my leg had every chance of recovering.

I realised just how big this was. It was the first time I'd ever done that really! I was very focused on making the Test team. I started the next game against the Golden Lions and was then reseted for the match against the Free State Cheetahs. I came back to face the Sharks in Durban, which was a big game for me. I played out of my skin that night, was named man of the match, set up a try and scored a good one. That game cemented my position as a Test starter, which was my main aim.

I expected to start the Test, it wasn't cocky, it was just confidence and I think you need that. So when I played well that night it was a big moment because it confirmed my spot as first choice scrum-half. My man of the match medal actually got stolen from my hotel room after that game, which was a bit of a shitter.

Don't get me wrong, I love rugby as much as the next person but some of my old team-mates really love rugby. They live and breathe it all day, every day. One such team-mate was Adam Jones, he is absolutely mad for it. Two days before the first Test, I'm sat at the same table as him having my breakfast. He's chatting to someone else and for some reason he's picking a world XV. I'm listening in but I'm not really that arsed until I overhear him say: "Right then, second rows... Matfield and Bakkies, got to be innit?"

At this point I nearly choked on my cornflakes. I had a bit of a go at him: "Bomb (Adam's nickname), that's your problem! You respect them too much, you shouldn't care how big they are, you're as good as them!" He told me to calm down but he knew where I was coming from and he has since admitted that I was right – to be fair, I usually was – and he even said so in his book. We all knew they were good rugby players but we were playing them on Saturday and we didn't need to be bigging them up two days out from a Test match.

By the time the first Test came around, we were fairly comfortable with where we were as a squad. We'd put in some good performances in the warm-up match but now it was time for the big games. The first Test was immensely frustrating. We started very slowly, we were making mistakes, giving away penalties and dropping the ball over the line. We actually played the more entertaining rugby, made more breaks and I think we were the better team but we'd basically handed them a 26-7 lead.

During the game, I let a real chance go begging. I made a good break and got dragged down just as I'm approaching the line. As I go to stretch out, Bakkies Botha comes from nowhere and knocks the ball out of my hands with the try line at my mercy. I was absolutely gutted, obviously, and it was at a crucial time in the match. It would have been a good try as well because I beat about five of them and it would have got us back in the match. So I'm pissed off and I get up to see him smiling at me with all his mates. So I'm thinking: 'Ahh bloody hell, I'm going to have to say something to him here.' So I came out with something like: "Well done mate, you're all on steroids anyway so fuck off." At this point, I was expecting at least a push and for something to kick off but he just looks at me and says: "Oh, you have sexy blue eyes." Fair play to him, I didn't have a comeback for that. I was completely taken aback. Even as the ball was being put into the next scrum, I was still totally confused, thinking to myself: 'What on earth is he on about?'

Tom Croft scored a try to get us back in it and I remember being stood on the field in the last 10 minutes thinking that the Springboks were completely knackered. They were gone. I hate this kind of mentality but if there were another five minutes on the clock we'd have won the match. I did eventually score with a few minutes remaining and I was really pleased with how I finished the game and I was absolutely loving it.

I lifted the tempo, ripped the ball off Pierre Spies and then took his headguard off before throwing it away. Then I ran through their pack telling them all to fuck off as I went. After I scored my try, I dropped my shoulder into Victor Matfield. To be fair, I was just being an absolute dick. This is probably why nobody likes me in rugby! Unfortunately, though, we couldn't get the job done. That first Test is so important to win because you're in the driving seat and you have two chances to win the series but we hadn't managed it. We were sat in the changing room after the match annoyed that we'd started so poorly. It was a real opportunity for us to lay down a marker and we ended up losing 26-21.

On a personal level, this was a massive opportunity, going up against the world champions but more specifically Fourie du Preez, their scrum-half, who was the best No.9 in the world at the time. I respected him and I wanted to test myself against the best. If I could get the better of him, then I would be No.1 in the world. That's how I looked at the personal duel. He's since called me his toughest opponent, which I took as a compliment.

Straight after the final whistle, their hooker Bismarck du Plessis gets right in my face, and I mean as close as you can get, and screams at me. He didn't really say anything, I think he was trying to roar like a lion, which was weird behaviour whichever way you look at it. But he was definitely trying to make a statement. So that pissed me off and then it comes to the point where we're supposed to shake hands and clap them off the field. Number one, I'm annoyed that we lost and number two, du Plessis has just given it large in my face. I'm close to exploding here. Their captain, John Smit, tries to shake my hand and, basically, I tell him to go and fuck himself. I don't want to shake anyone's hand after what's just happened on the final whistle. Du Plessis had been disrespectful so I wasn't in a rush to show them any respect. This is where context is important. Most people just see me telling Smit where to go but they didn't see what had happened a few moments earlier. I shouldn't have let Smit have it but I was wound up. That said, I think if people knew what had happened to me, they would have understood my reaction a little more. Maybe I should have been big enough to shake his hand but there's a reason why I reacted the way I did. I know Smit wasn't thrilled about the incident but he hadn't seen his team-mate antagonise me and it got under my skin.

Having lost the first game against the 'Boks, we headed to Pretoria needing a win to keep the series alive. Defeat would mean them winning the series. Ahead of the match, our defence coach Shaun Edwards got into us about their bully mentality. During the game, I remember Matfield pushing O'Driscoll, trying to intimidate him. I wasn't having any of that so I went over and pushed Matfield. I had no intention of hitting anyone but it was just about letting them know that we weren't going to be messed with. It all kicked off after I pushed him and I just walked away but I was just trying to spark a bit of fire in the boys. South Africa are immensely aggressive.

It was a mindset thing. I didn't care what Matfield's reputation was when we were on the field, I wasn't going to let him impose himself on us.

Anyway, in a team meeting before the second Test, Shaun Edwards pulled some poor bloke up to the front and actually demonstrated what we were able to do if it all kicked off. They would try and dominate you physically and there were little things going on off the ball all the time. So Shaun gripped this player by the scruff and was ragging him backwards, all the while saying: "This is what you can do. Don't throw a punch but this is what to do!"

I was feeling pretty good heading into the match. I'd played well in the warm-up games and the first Test and I was just looking to keep the good form going. The messages from the coaches were to basically stick to the same game plan and just execute it better. We also had to get parity up front but, unfortunately, there wasn't a lot I could do about that. Mentally, I was in a great place. I never usually spoke in team huddles but before that game I said: "Boys, everything we do, we do it with confidence. Every decision we make today is the correct one and we have to have a bit of arrogance about us." I felt like we had to have that mindset if we were going to beat them.

I remember turning up to that game on the bus and to say it was a hostile atmosphere would be doing it a disservice. Normally, when you turn up at an away game in the Six Nations, opposition supporters are fairly respectful and you might get some quiet applause or whatever as the bus drives into the stadium. There was none of that in Pretoria. There were beer cans being launched at the bus, it was pretty hostile. I thought it was a bit much but it got me right up for the match.

Most people will remember the eye gouge that took place in that match. In the first minute, cameras picked up Schalk Burger ramming his fingers into Luke Fitzgerald's eyes. When I saw the replays, I thought: 'Happy days, that's a red card'. To my surprise, the referee pulled out a yellow. He bottled it. Pure and simple. It was a hostile environment, Burger's 50th Test match, early in the game. The French ref just got it horribly wrong. Burger was banned for eight weeks after the match but that was of no use to us at the time. If he had got the card he deserved, the Test series probably looks a lot different but there is little we can do about it now. The margins are so small at the very top. I look back at the two real highlights – this tour and the 2011 Rugby World Cup – and both occasions were heavily influenced by refereeing decisions.

If Burger had got the red card he deserved that day, it could have changed the course of history. That being said, there were other reasons why we lost that day. The second Test in general was a brutal affair. If it was played in this day and age they'd have finished the game with 10 men on the pitch. Adam Jones ended up with a dislocated shoulder after being cleared out of a ruck by Botha, who later received a two-week ban for the incident. Gethin Jenkins fractured his cheekbone and then there was the huge hit from O'Driscoll on Danie Rossouw.

I don't think Brian would have carried on after that collision in this day and age but they were different times. We got off to a great start in the second Test and went 10-0 up inside the first 10 minutes. But then JP Pietersen scored a try which got them back into the game and I blame myself for it. I wonder whether I could have been in a better position to make a tackle as he cut through at the back of the lineout. I didn't make the critical error that let him through but I sometimes think about whether I should have been in a better position to stop him. I still ask myself that question now.

The way the Test series was decided was unfortunate. I really felt for Rog because he carried the can for it all when, in reality, we should have killed the game off in the first 30 minutes. That Jacques Fourie try kills me to this day. I was defending in the wide channel and Rog and Luke Fitzgerald were outside me.

We were operating a blitz defence so I flew out of the line to try and stop the ball getting wide. If Rog and Luke had been flatter, we'd have killed the move there. But given how the men outside me were positioned, I should have drifted off and we could have smothered them into touch. Rog then got bumped off and I tried to get back and make the cover tackle but I was too late. Stephen Jones kicked a late penalty to get us back on level terms and we all know what happened next. Rog gave away a penalty just inside the South Africa half for tackling a man in the air and up stepped Morne Steyn. I was stood to the left of the posts, just praying for the ball to bounce back into my arms off the sticks or anything. Watching the kick sail over, you just feel so hopeless because there's nothing you can do to stop it. As soon as it went over, meaning South Africa won the game and the Test series, I just felt this flood of regret: 'I wish I could have run that little bit harder, that little bit faster.' You just want one more chance to put it right but you can't because the referee has blown his whistle and you've lost the series. It's an agonising feeling.

Fair play to Steyn, I think the ball is still going! It cleared the crossbar by some distance. They all started celebrating. It hurts to this day. Don't get me wrong, I don't wake up screaming in the middle of the night, it doesn't haunt my dreams. But every time I see highlights from that tour – and they played a lot of them during the Covid-19 lockdown – it all comes flooding back. So in many ways, that defeat will live with me forever. If we'd been blown away then it would be easier to take but I think we were the better side, we just couldn't get the job done and you can't take anything away from South Africa. It was a very sombre dressing room. I just sat there with my head down for a little while in my own world. Head coach Ian McGeechan may have said a few words but they didn't register with me in all honesty. I was still trying to process it all. Rog had a bandage around his head and was probably a bit concussed. The boys were battered and bruised, a lot of them had blood coming from somewhere. A few of them would go to the hospital. We were proud of the effort that we'd put in but there was nothing anyone could say at that point.

I think players just need time to get their heads around that kind of disappointment on their own. If the coaches were honest with themselves, I think they made some poor calls. Hindsight is great but Adam Jones should have started that Test series, there's no doubting that. This is not a dig at Phil Vickery because he's a quality player who achieved a hell of a lot in his career. He's a World Cup winner and he was great off the field, a lovely, down to earth kind of guy. But he's a bit taller than Adam and I think Adam was able to get under South Africa loose-head Tendai Mtawarira a bit more.

Adam is also one of the best players I ever played with. If he's not in my team, I'm worried. If anybody else is missing, there was always someone else that could come in, but Adam was worth his weight in gold. I just knew how good he was. I felt like we could have used a bit more size in the pack to try and contain them up front. We got dominated there for much of the series. Also, Shane Williams might have been a little out of form at the time but he was World Player of the Year the previous season and he didn't start until the final Test, when he scored two tries.

We could have used his stardust earlier on in the series. The man very rarely let an opportunity pass him by. He was clinical and that's what we needed. Rog was the scapegoat for it all, which you never like to see. I respect him for trying to take responsibility and control of the situation. Some players go missing in the big moments – I've seen players stay on the floor a little bit longer than they need to. Rog didn't want to hide and you want to play with players who are not afraid to make mistakes.

We were in a hell of a state after the second Test. We went out, I was in a bit of a mess emotionally that night and I went on to drink too much. Everyone did the same thing to be honest. When I look back, I'm not really sure what I could have done about Fourie's try but at the time I blamed myself – I always did – and I couldn't deal with it properly so I just drank. The next day they had booked us on a safari so we jump on the bus and head out, all feeling worse for wear. Straight away, someone starts handing out some bottles of beer. The first one is a bit ropey but they start going down. Next thing I know, I've sunk five or six and suddenly what happened the day before is forgotten about and the world is still turning. So then a few of the boys – predominantly Welsh, I have to say – start getting into Paul O'Connell's ear: "Why are we going on a safari? Let's turn this bus around and get back on the beer!"

To be fair, Paulie delivered. There were always two buses travelling around with us and the call was made that the front bus was going to carry on to the safari and the back bus was going back to the hotel for beers. So we pulled over and all got on the right bus. As the beers went down, things got more and more boisterous.

It was James Hook's birthday and they'd got this amazing cake for him in the shape of a Lions jersey and it was sitting there on the bus, near the toilet. As I walked past it, I decided it would be a good idea to shout: "Matfield!" – referring to the South Africa captain – before head-butting Hooky's cake. Next thing, the cake is being flung all around the bus. O'Connell's getting into me: "Jaysus Phillsy! Will you calm down?" The next day there were still bits of cake stuck to the ceiling of the bus. But it was all a bit of fun.

Geech's speech before the last Test sticks with me. It was all about having to win the final match to set things up for the squad that followed us in four years time, it was about leaving the jersey in a better place. The Lions tour in 2005, when they got hammered by the All Blacks, from what I've heard, was a bit of a shambles. So 2009 was about putting the respect back into the jersey and I think we achieved that. We had a duty in that last Test to leave the jersey in a good place. That really resonated with me. The series was gone but it was still important to win that game and the boys did a job in the end. We clicked quite nicely that day. Shane and Ugo Monye scored their tries and we won 28-9 and it meant the tour ended on a good note. We ended up drinking until the early hours of the morning. It got to about 5am and it was me, Hooky and Shane Williams. We made the call that we were going to get changed and go straight through. No sleep, just beer. So I went back to my room to have a shower and put some different clothes on. Obviously, I passed out on my bed as I was totally knackered. The boys were having none of it, though. Somehow the sneaky buggers got a key for my room, came flying in and started jumping all over me.

We play wrestled for a little bit and then we all clattered into the wall. The bed was broken, the bedside table was flipped, for some reason I started drop-kicking the wardrobe and the door came flying off. Put simply, it was like a bomb had gone off. Straight away I realised I had to go down to reception and sort this out before anybody realised. So down I went and said: "There's been a mix up in the room and I think the wardrobe door is broken." I made my excuses, gave them £500 and that was that. Thankfully nobody found out about it because that could have been another issue.

Back to the room I went, got ready and off the three of us went for some more beer. The following day when the rest of the team got up, we gathered in the team room for a social and there were 15 bottles of champagne, which left us all wondering what the hell was going on. They were sent by actor Daniel Craig, who wanted to thank us for our efforts on the tour. Not many people can say James Bond bought them a drink, so that was cool.

Geech was there and I remember watching the video from the 1997 Lions tour and in the Kangaroo Court – a setting in which basically everyone gets punished with drinking fines, whether they were actually legitimate offences or not – he had to drink this massive whiskey, it must have been more than a quad-shot. In homage to that, I poured him a massive whiskey and made him down it. Having grown up with that DVD, it was so surreal to be coached by him. He's Mr Lions and one of these guys that you just don't want to let down. I could see that he respected me and it was amazing to have that, it gave me a lot of confidence to have the backing of a rugby icon like him. For those that don't know, Geech was head coach on four Lions tours and coached the midweek team in 2005. He's an emotional guy and after giving us a team talk in the meeting before we got on the bus for the final Test, he completely broke down in tears.

It was his last-ever team talk as a Lions head coach and he knew it was his final tour. It wasn't until I watched the behind-the-scenes documentary of that '09 tour that I realised this. He'd managed to hold it together until the last player left the room. The Lions is so special and these opportunities don't come around very often. It's hard to explain to people on the outside just how emotional it is to be a part of something like that.

And on that tour in particular we had a really close group, there were no egos, we'd been dealt some tough calls, an eye gouge, they were the best team in the world and it was an amazing Test series, we just didn't get the result. I think what happened with Geech was all that emotion just came pouring out. After that final Test, there were 10 of us still going at about 4:00am and I was sat next to Shaun.

All of a sudden, he starts teaching me how to box on the inside, so here we are sat by the table, head to head, play fighting with him jabbing me with punches on the inside. He's showing me how to slip punches and jabbing me in the ribs and he even threw some to the face. The boys were totally confused by what was happening. I absolutely love Shaun, he's a great coach and an even better bloke. He was the kind of guy that you never wanted to let down. Throughout the tour, larger-than-life strength and conditioning coach Paul 'Bobby' Stridgeon ran something called the 'Bobby Cup'.

It was an award that he dished out if we won back-to-back games on tour and it was given to the person who had contributed the most, whether it was on the field, off the field or for just generally being an all-round legend. He used to do these hilarious presentations. It was a great way of pulling the team together and good entertainment for the boys. The last one he did on that tour was to award a Bobby Cup for the tour as a whole and I won it.

The boys had won a huge trophy for beating the Southern Kings and Paul had put a new plaque on it and presented it to me! I was quite proud of winning that. For me, that award was for contributing significantly both on and off the field, which I think says a lot about you. Jamie Roberts still winds me up about the fact he won the official Man of the Series and he didn't even play in the third Test!

He knows I deserved it but I wasn't studying to be a doctor and didn't have a fancy education! Back to the man behind the Bobby Cup though, Stridgeon is a hell of a character. He's just a little bundle of energy and he's 100mph all the day. When he went back to his room at night he must have just crashed as soon as the door shut but he was vitally important for the team. We were coming back from training one day and the boys were loving the music on the bus, dancing and singing along.

So we arrive at the front of the hotel and Bobby shouts: "Take it around the block!" And got the driver to pull back out of the hotel and drive in a loop so we could finish the song. He was always up for a good time and you need people like that. He was also really good at his job as an S&C coach as well.

The frustrating thing for me is that my stock went up after the tour but we'd lost the series. It was a difficult one for me to process because, on a personal level, things had gone well. I'd played some of the best rugby of my career until that point but I wasn't able to put my name on that plaque alongside Edwards, Dawson and those boys. The praise was nice but it meant little really. My name wasn't in the history books as a winning Lion and that cut me. It was all that mattered, regardless of how well I thought I'd done personally.

When you achieve something as significant as representing the Lions, playing well and winning a Test match, you are literally on cloud nine. You feel like you can take on the world. I came back from South Africa feeling like I'd achieved something, got respect and I was on top of the world. I need to take responsibility for feeling this way and I was naive but I just thought doors were going to open after the tour and people would be rolling out the red carpet for me wherever I went.

In reality, after the tour, nobody else really gives a shit! Which is fair enough and it was a terrible attitude to have anyway. But with this in mind, I was in Cardiff and I was trying to get served at the bar but I felt like the barman was just ignoring me, serving everybody else but me. So I ended up letting him know what I thought of him and we had words, which obviously agitated me and put me in a bit of a shit mood.

A little while later I was in the back of the taxi on my way home to Penarth from the city centre and I was just dozing off a little bit but I noticed the driver taking a peculiar route to my house. I know the quickest way from the centre of Cardiff to my house and I felt like the driver was trying to take the mick, racking up the meter. So I got a little bit stern with him, as I'm sure a lot of people would in that situation, and said: "Look mate, I can see what you're doing, just take me home." He took me home, I paid him what I felt was an overpriced cab fare and nothing really came of it. After that I went to Las Vegas with a few of the boys from the Lions tour and, in the car on the way back from the airport, I just had this gut instinct that something wasn't right. Shortly after the trip, there were two policemen at my door asking me to go down to the station and answer some questions. The taxi driver had filed a complaint. I answered all their questions and was free to leave.

Mike Cuddy, the boss at the Ospreys, came down to the station with me to help smooth things over. The story ended up in the *South Wales Echo* so it was just another load of nonsense that I had to deal with, another stick that could be used to beat me with.

You didn't think I was going to gloss over that trip to Vegas, did you? That was a serious case of just letting the hair down after a hectic few months. There was a good crew of us on the trip from Ireland and Wales and we'd started planning it halfway through the tour, which just goes to prove that when you hear people talking about the bonds you form on Lions trips, they're not just talking nonsense. It's genuine. The cast list looked a little something like this; Alun Wyn Jones, Lee Byrne, Andy Powell, Gordon D'Arcy, Tommy Bowe, Jamie

Heaslip – Ugo Monye was supposed to come but I'm not sure he was up for drinking with the Welsh! I don't really want to go back to Las Vegas after that one to be honest! It's just not for me. I'd always rather go to a bar than a nightclub so it wasn't really my scene.

I'll chalk it up as one of those things you do when you're young and spending a shitload of money. We were out one night and I bought the table for us in a club and decided to buy the booze as well, thinking I was the big dog. When I was half-cut at about 4:00am I decided it would be a good idea to splash something like £8,000 on a diamond watch. Nonsense really. Byrney upped and left after two days. Poor tourist behaviour from him! It all got a bit too much for him! Bowe was on fire, D'Arcy was still clinging to his professional side. He loved the beers like the rest of us but he was eating seeds for breakfast. I just switched off entirely and relaxed. I hit the first two days hard, we all did. But then it caught up with me and I passed out on a sun lounger by the pool. I then booked myself a new room away from the boys to sleep for pretty much 24 hours solid. The boys had no idea where I'd gone and were a bit concerned but I was absolutely exhausted! That was a fun trip.

I look back on that 2009 tour as my favourite. Yes we lost but the games, the occasions, were incredible. They were physical, confrontational matches. Neither side took a backwards step and I was right in the middle of it all, loving it. We might have won in 2013 – more on that later – but I enjoyed the 2009 tour. It was my favourite by far.

I had some time to relax and reflect after the tour. It had been a whirlwind couple of months and it was nice to just switch off from rugby a little bit. I was having a chat with the agency that were looking after me at the time, just shooting the breeze and talking about anything and everything really. I mentioned that Welsh singer Aimee Duffy had caught my eye and someone there knew someone and they got a message to her asking if she wanted to go on a date with me.

We arranged to go for dinner at a restaurant in London, I stayed there until the early hours of the morning before getting a taxi back to Cardiff and things went from there. We'd starting seeing each other in September and Christmas obviously appeared on the horizon pretty quickly. Things were going really well between us and she starts saying things like: "I think I've gone a bit too crazy on your Christmas present!" But I didn't really think much of it to be honest. Suddenly, she'd start dropping massive hints about wanting a dog on a daily basis. She kept asking: "Where's the puppy? Where are you hiding the puppy?" In my mind, I was thinking: 'Well hang on just a second, a dog isn't just for Christmas!' And all that stuff. There was no puppy. I'd only known her a few months! I was living in Penarth Marina and one day she told me she was down West Wales visiting her family. I was driving out of the Marina and I passed the boat shop. I looked out of the window and noticed this speedboat, then I clocked the people standing next to it and then I put two and two together: 'Shit! She's buying me a bloody speedboat for Christmas!' There she was with her sister and a driver buying me a boat. Gavin Henson also knew I was getting it. I don't know how but he did.

A few weeks previously, he pulled up outside my flat in this massive yacht. I was chilling out one day and all I could hear was someone hammering this horn, so I looked out and there's Gav on the deck, shouting at me. That's when he told me that Aimee was going to buy me something extravagant but he didn't mention what it was.

After I saw her in the boatyard, I had absolutely no idea what to get her. So now I'm thinking: 'Shit! I've got to get this puppy now.' I left it late, as usual, so started frantically searching on Google and found somewhere that I could buy her a dog, so I was up the Valleys on Christmas Eve buying a beagle. So I managed to pull that off. I woke up on Christmas morning and she managed to put this speedboat outside my house with a big bow on it. It got me a few looks that morning. I didn't know my neighbours at the time but I've got to know them since and they've said they looked out the window and thought: 'Flipping hell, Mike's got a bloody speedboat!' It was a bit wild to be honest.

That dog got me in a bit of bother once. My brothers and their partners came up to visit us in London one weekend and we rented a boat to go up the Thames and have a few drinks. Then we went out for food before going back to the house and having a few more drinks. We were having a great time. But back at the house the dog started barking a bit and a neighbour came around to complain.

He was regularly drunk and had come around a few times before but he always did it when I wasn't there. This time, I was the one to open the door to him. As I did, the dog ran out of the house and into the middle of the road, so I totally ignored him and ran after the dog. I grabbed the dog before anything disastrous could happen and here comes the neighbour, charging towards me angrily. He grabs the dog's neck and shouts: "Shut that dog up!" I feel like I'm under threat at this point and he's got his hand around my dog's throat, so I gave him the Mike Phillips palm to the chest and it knocked him to the floor.

He got back up and came at me again, this time swinging punches, so I gave him another one in self defence before walking away from the situation. As I'm heading back to the house, I notice two people walking past and I immediately start worrying about them going to the press.

So I spoke to them and invited them into the house, had a couple of drinks with them and they were cool. They saw him grab the dog and said I didn't do anything wrong. We eventually get around to chatting about what they do for a living and then they tell us that they were both journalists! You couldn't make this stuff up. I was a bit worried about whether or not they were going to print what they'd seen but nothing ever came of it.

I'd had a few girlfriends before but Duffy was the longest, most serious relationship I'd been in at that time. We were together for two years and we had a great time together. She was fantastic. I'd never met a girl with her own stuff going on, she had a very successful career of her own and was making her own money, she had her own life. She also used to send me really nice messages after games that made me feel good about myself. They were quite deep sometimes but I needed that sort of stuff. Journalists, fans and even family members sometimes can be quite critical of your performance so it was nice to have a constant source of positivity. We got on really well but things eventually fizzled out and I decided to bring it to a halt because of a few things that were going on.

I just felt like the relationship was no longer working and I'd started to give up quite a bit to be with her. I wasn't going out with my mates at all. When we won the league with the Ospreys in 2010, I went straight back to London to be with her instead of celebrating with the boys. It got to the point where the coaches at the Ospreys pulled me aside and asked: "Who's this new Mike? We want the old Mike back." They wanted the more aggressive Mike back, the wilder Mike who played – and lived – a bit more on the edge. I thought that was a bit much.

When I was fired up and getting into everything, I was being told to calm down and here the coaches were having a go at me for being too chilled out. Talk about mixed signals! It just got to the point where I couldn't see myself being with her for the rest of my life so I decided to end it. Plus there was all the commuting between Cardiff and London. It all started to get on top of me a little bit. Things ended pretty amicably and we went our separate ways.

6

World Cup Woes

The training camps ahead of the 2011 Rugby World Cup were hell.

Everyone remembers the camps we went on to Spala, a tiny Polish village that isn't really near anything at all. This was Gats playing one of his games. He was constantly trying to test players and break players or, perhaps more accurately, see which players survive. All our comforts were taken away, the rooms were very basic, the food was pretty average. It was cold, grey and pretty fucking miserable.

To put it mildly, we were a long way from our state-of-the-art training base at the Vale Resort, a four-star hotel on the outskirts of Cardiff. The accommodation was simple. A relatively small wooden bed, a bedside table and somewhere to hang your clothes. There was absolutely nothing to watch on TV so we were relying on a database of movies on our laptops to stave off the boredom. One of the main reasons for going was because of the cryotherapy chambers they had there. They are essentially these boxes where the temperature plunges down to around -160 degrees celsius. You can get individual ones or

123

ones where a few of you stand in there for a couple of minutes. The cold therapy is supposed to aid recovery and allow us to train harder and more frequently. We were cramming two intense days of training into one and were able to back it up the following day.

We'd be up at sunrise for breakfast, then a typical day could be a running session first thing followed by some cryotherapy and food, then it was a rugby-specific training session followed by another trip to the human fridge and a weights session in the evening. The chambers weren't very commonly used in rugby at the time but I think we made them fashionable and now most teams are using them.

They would say to us: "Right, we've got these ice chambers now so you can train harder." Whether it was scientifically proven or not, it flicked a switch psychologically and got into our heads. The other reason for going there, in my view, was for Gats to see which boys would crack. It was a horrible place and the training was horrendous but there was a great focus around the team. We barely had any injuries in Poland. It was tough but everyone was in a great space mentally and hellbent on winning the World Cup. It really did galvanise the squad. After all the shit I'd been through with the McDonald's incident, I knew I had to knuckle down and I had a fresh outlook. I had a bit of a chip on my shoulder because I wanted to prove to everyone that, whatever had gone on away from the field, when it came to training and playing I was fully committed to being the best.

Whatever had gone on away from rugby, it was not going to affect what happened on the pitch. I felt like I'd lost a bit of respect in the eyes of the public and I needed to earn that back. I do have one regret about those trips to Poland though. On a rare day off they ran a trip to Auschwitz, a concentration camp run by the Nazis in the Second World War. Before leaving Wales, my father had told me I had to go to understand what people had gone through and all the horrendous things that happened there. But I was absolutely exhausted. I just slept for virtually the entire day because I needed the recovery and I didn't go. I never admitted that to my old man but I watched documentaries on it just so I could have a conversation about it if he ever asked! I wish I'd gone but at the time my body was in bits and I was so focussed on getting as fit as I could. I was desperate to top the fitness charts but I remember Lee Byrne being up there as the one to catch when it came to the running tests.

That internal competition was great and everyone was really digging deep. Coaches would be shouting: "Nobody is working harder than us." And we were determined to be the fittest team at the tournament. I was probably in the shape of my life after those training camps. Everybody struggled with the time in Poland in their own way but nobody really moaned. We had a good vibe in the camp. There were some young, fresh faces in the side like Jonathan Davies, George North, Taulupe Faletau. They brought some energy to the group and pushed the older boys. It was a great dynamic. There was one rather surprising premature departure though.

About four days into the first camp Gavin Henson disappeared to go and do some filming for his latest TV show 'The Bachelor' with Gatland's blessing. At the time it was a bit of a laugh and Gav was showing us the pictures of all the women that were going to be on his show but, looking back, it was absolutely mental that they just let him go. I love Gav and he's one of the most gifted players I've ever come across but I didn't hear of the All Blacks letting one of their players leave camp to film a dating show. It was madness. It didn't bother me personally because I was too focussed on being the fittest in the squad but it should never have happened really. During the trip Gav caught an elbow in the face and it gave him a black eye.

We were sharing the facility with other athletes and he walked into the canteen one day wearing sunglasses and I said: "Gav, what are you doing? We're inside!" And he just casually explained: "Ahhh, I've got a black eye, got to look after my image, haven't I?" That was Gav and he was very much his own man but immensely talented. He dislocated a bone in his wrist in one of the warm-up games against England and missed the entire tournament. I think we missed him in New Zealand. He just had that something extra, that little bit of talent and flair that can unlock defences and blow games wide open. He was also an outstanding goal-kicker and that would have been of use to us along the way. Gav was a man for the big occasion, just look at what he did against England in 2005.

I've just got this nagging feeling that if he was playing in the 2011 semi-final, he'd have done something, produced a bit of magic that would have got us over the line. It's just a hunch but he had that spark.

By the time we got to New Zealand, we were in really good shape. We were confident that we weren't going to be outworked because of all the training we'd done and Gatland had successfully convinced us that we were the fittest team at the competition. More importantly, every player in the squad knew that the bloke standing next to them had been through really dark places. So we knew we were physically prepared but we were about to find out if we could become the best team in the world.

South Africa first up was always going to be our toughest test of the group stages and I think we turned a few heads with how we performed but ultimately we lost the game 17-16. They went into the game knowing they were going to beat us and I don't think we went in and believed, to a man, that we were capable of beating them. Those are the margins at the top level. Talking about margins, though, James Hook clipped over a penalty, which made all the difference in the end, but it wasn't awarded because the officials thought it went directly over the top of the post. I thought it went over, but then I would say that. Losing that game, however, actually worked in our favour because we had an easier run in the knockout stages then.

Next we had Samoa, who absolutely battered us physically but we got through it 17-0. They should have had red cards and yellow cards all over the shop for some of their antics, especially when you consider what was going to happen to Sam Warburton later in the tournament.

I felt like they got away with a fair bit because there is a perception of teams like Samoa that this is just the way they play, hitting high and not wrapping the arms in contact. It's bullshit really and I think it's disrespectful towards them because there is more to them than that. Don't get me wrong, Samoa got shafted in that World Cup because they only had three days of recovery between facing Namibia and playing against us and that's not on. Some of their players had been pretty vocal about their schedule and that's fair enough, I'd support them in that, but I think it worked in their favour in our game and the referee let a lot of things slide. I think he probably looked at it and thought: 'Actually, Samoa are being shafted here,' and subconsciously just aired on their side a little bit when it came to 50/50 calls.

Off the field, things couldn't have really gone any better for us because we became everyone's second favourite team in New Zealand. As long as we weren't playing against the All Blacks, the locals were on our side. I think they took to us because we were the underdogs, we'd performed well and given South Africa a shock and we were playing some really entertaining rugby. It helped that things were going horribly for England off the field.

They were getting themselves in all sorts of trouble and it was being splashed all over the newspapers. All the attention was on them and it took the heat off us a little bit. We were certainly going out and enjoying ourselves after wins and I know Ireland were doing exactly the same but we managed to avoid doing anything too stupid, which I was particularly proud of. That being said, I did almost drop myself in it.

After the win over Samoa we had eight days off before facing Namibia and I knew there was a decent chance I wouldn't be starting that game, so we went out in Waikato for a few drinks. It was a good atmosphere, we were mixing with a few fans and the tournament was generally going well for all of us so it was happy days. Then someone in a daffodil hat comes up to me and says: "Mike! You're killing our backline. Stop taking a bloody step before you pass the ball!" Now, I tend not to take things like this to heart but it annoyed me a little bit because it's just a lazy analysis of my game. It's the go-to criticism of a scrum-half that people just spout off whether it's true or not and I took offence to it. Why did this person have to say it? We were having a good time! Long story short, I poured some of my beer over their daffodil.

I thought the worst that would come of it would be that they just ended up with a soggy daffodil but they got pretty wet and were obviously not best pleased. In the back of my mind I'm thinking: 'Ahhh Mike, what have you done?' The next morning, I wake up and I'm pretty paranoid because of the incident. If the person has complained to the Welsh Rugby

Union, I'm going to go down to breakfast and have a dressing down from Alan Phillips or, worse, they've gone to the newspapers. I was rooming with prop Paul James. He went down to breakfast before me, came back to the room and said: "Mike, you're on the front page mate."

My stomach dropped and I just went: "WHAT?" And with that he throws a newspaper onto my bed and the headline is: "Mike Phillips voted sexiest man at Rugby World Cup." Now that's a bit more like it! I never did get in trouble for that incident but it was a dick move on my part. I owe that person an apology. The newsagents loved me that day, though, because I bought them all out of newspapers!

I was, in fact, rested for the Namibia game but the boys did an emphatic job. That was a special match though because Ken Owens made his international debut. I was thrilled for Ken, who is one of the good guys. I remember him coming up to me when he was a youngster in Carmarthen, in a Wetherspoons of all places, to shake my hand. He was a confident young man, a very personable guy and he gets on with everyone. He's a really likeable guy and he does so much for those around him. It was great to see him make his debut.

In the last game before the knockout stages we absolutely battered Fiji 66-0. They were a shadow of the side that they can be and we put them to the sword that day. There was a bit of revenge about it after 2007 but we were an entirely different beast at this tournament with new players and a new set-up. We ran in nine tries and it was a real statement performance, coming off the back of the thumping we dished out to Namibia. The game was done and dusted early doors so I was brought off in the 55th minute, which was 10 minutes before Jamie Roberts was replaced.

The coaches were obviously keen to wrap me up in cotton wool for the next game whereas they didn't seem to mind risking Jamie for an extra few minutes! Anyway, he sits down next to me and tries starting a bit of banter: "I can't believe you haven't scored in this game." He'd crossed for two and I obviously hadn't. I didn't bite at the time but I remember thinking: 'Alright dickhead.' I'd matured a bit by now and I genuinely wasn't bothered about whether or not I was scoring, I was just as happy creating for other players and doing my bit for the team. Whereas in my early days I was guilty of making it too much about myself. That's probably why I played the best rugby of my career at that tournament. All that being said, Jamie's comment did fester and it lit a bit of a fire under me. I went on to score tries in the quarter-final and the semi-final, games that mattered. Not a 66-0 thrashing of Fiji!

Finishing second in our group set us up to face Ireland in the quarter-final and I always loved facing Ireland. I almost didn't make the quarter-final, mind. On our day off, myself, Andy Powell, Rhys Priestland and my agent at the time all decided to go and play a round of golf.

On one of the holes, me and my agent were driving our buggy along this grass verge, not exactly a cliff but a bit of a drop. Powelly decides it would be hilarious to try and ram our buggy off this verge by crashing his into it. I'm all for a laugh and a joke but we had a World Cup quarter-final in two days' time. Hell of a boy.

The Irish side we faced in the quarter-final was iconic. They'd beaten everyone in their group, including Australia, and were absolutely stacked with quality across the board. Paul O'Connell, a young Sean O'Brien, Conor Murray, Ronan O'Gara, Johnny Sexton, Brian O'Driscoll, Tommy Bowe, Rob Kearney... I could name the whole team. They had quality everywhere but we made them look pedestrian from start to finish. We just had more about us, looked more dangerous with ball in hand and just caused them problems whenever we wanted to.

Everyone in a red shirt played well that day, we made barely any handling errors and dominated. One moment stands out in this game and it's tough to describe, but with about 20 minutes to go I was putting the ball into a scrum and I just felt totally calm, everything about me felt perfect. My aggression level and my emotional level was exactly where it had to be. It was like I was gliding across the turf. I just felt at peace, completely in the zone, like the game was coming easy to me. It was bizarre but you spend your entire career trying to prepare for matches the right way and find the right balance emotionally but that's the only time I ever felt that way in my entire career. It was zen-like. Total perfection.

Shortly before that I'd scored my try down the short side, handing off Gordon D'Arcy and diving in just before my good mate Tommy Bowe can get to me. I enjoy bringing that one up whenever I see him. There are two great pictures of me scoring with Tommy just struggling to get to me. I love it and he can't stand it! I do enjoy posting them on social media from time to time. He's been searching the internet for years trying to find a picture of him skinning me but they simply do not exist! From that moment on everything just fell into place and I felt like I was on top of the world.

I was awarded man of the match and was just riding this wave of confidence and adulation. On a personal level, the tournament was going exactly as I'd hoped it would. In general, we just had a bit more footballing ability than Ireland, more stardust. Yes, we could slam it up the middle through Jamie but then you had the likes of Jonathan Davies, George North and Leigh Halfpenny all having really good tournaments. Taulupe Faletau had come into the side and was bossing it at the tournament. He was a young kid who had great hands, footwork and just a general all-round game. We hadn't had that kind of player at No.8 before.

The celebrations were not too hectic after the quarter-final because everyone had their head screwed on by this point I think. We went out for food and then chilled out in the hotel bar for a bit but there were no shenanigans. I personally looked at the tournament and realised that things were shaping up for us. We had France in the semi-final and we knew we were capable of beating them. Also, with the way that the draw had worked out for us, it was on my mind that we could get to the World Cup final without having to face a southern hemisphere team in the knockout stages. It was a huge opportunity and nobody wanted to mess it up.

We had a sports psychologist, Andy McCann, with us during that World Cup and he was a huge help to me personally. There is still a stigma attached to this sort of thing in rugby but all of the most successful people in the world, whether that's sport or business, have mental skills coaches. Rugby players are funny creatures. They blame themselves for defeats, they don't open up and talk about their feelings or emotions and some players can really struggle with the huge pressure that they are put under. At least that's the way I was, anyway. I saw Andy before every game at that tournament and we got into a nice routine. He would literally get me to say things like "I'm in the best place I could be in the world" and simple stuff like that. He made a little highlight reel for me before games.

To be fair, after that Ireland match, he might as well have just given me the full 80 minutes to watch! I saw Ryan Jones watching his once and thought: 'Hmmm, won't be too much on there!' At one point I thought I was going to miss the kick-off in the semi-final because I was sitting on the bus waiting for my highlights video to end! Andy was a big help. A sports psychologist is a really important figure in an environment like that and we didn't always have one. The way I look at it, these days, everyone is on a fairly even playing field when it comes to physical attributes, they're all big, fit guys. Having someone there to work on the players' mental skills is probably going to be the difference between winning and losing some games nowadays and it's good to see that stigma being lifted little by little. I think that's the next step for professional rugby teams. We've seen the advancements in nutrition and physical preparation since the game went pro. Now I think we'll see teams looking to nail their mental preparation more and more as a means to take themselves to the next level. They will keep looking for ways to eradicate the doubts and the anxiety that can creep in sometimes.

The semi-final will stick with me for the rest of my life. The warm-up was slick, conditions were perfect, the ball was dry and I was feeling unbelievably confident. Untouchable, almost. Then in the final minutes before kick-off, the heavens opened and it absolutely lashed it down. It was a disaster for us because we were young, fit and we wanted to move France around. Whether it was true or not, it was drilled into our heads that they were big, lazy, unfit and unprofessional.

We wanted that quick ball but the moisture just slows everything down by a split second and it was the last thing we wanted. That downpour just before kick-off was the first in a series of events that evening that just made it feel like the world had turned against us. One thing everyone overlooks in this game is that Adam Jones went off injured after 10 minutes. That was a huge blow for us and I think it was more significant than the red card because France were renowned for their scrummaging at that time. Paul James, usually a loose-head, had to pack down at tight-head for 70 minutes and gave it everything. He was my captain at age-grade level and was a great player in his own right. He was a cracking scrummager as well and he did an outstanding job that night playing out of position but Adam, for me, is one of the best players to have ever played the game and any side would feel his absence. Then we all know what happened next. French winger Vincent Clerc hits a line at the back of a lineout and Sam Warburton has read it like a book and absolutely nails him. If you watch it back, Clerc actually sees Warby lining him up and slows down. He pretty much surrenders the collision. For me, it's just not a red card. I remember seeing the card go up. It was like being in a car crash. It all just happened in slow motion but Alain Rolland, the referee, made his mind up so quickly. He just got it horribly wrong in my opinion. But that red card didn't cost us a place in the World Cup final. We still blew it because France were terrible that night. If anything, they stopped playing altogether and we missed three kicks at goal.

We didn't change our tactics at half-time because we felt we were right in the contest. Gats said: "Stick to the game plan. Everyone has to work 20 percent harder. We're fitter than them and we'll get our opportunities." To be fair, Gats had put us in that position before. We were winning a game against Scotland once and he took a player off in the second half to leave us with 14 men. He could be quite innovative like that sometimes. I changed my boots at half-time because, let's face it, we hadn't had much luck in the first half and I wanted something to change our fortunes.

World Cup Woes

It worked to a certain degree because I went over for a try with just over 20 minutes remaining. That was an incredible feeling. When I was a young kid growing up on the farm in west Wales, I used to dream of that moment and visualise scoring for Wales at a World Cup, side-stepping cow pats.

There I was diving over in the semi-final and I genuinely thought I'd given us a great chance of going through to the final but it wasn't to be. In the last play of the match, I threw myself into a ruck to try and win the ball back but their scrum-half Dimitri Yachvili got his hands on it and booted it into the stands. He then walks towards me and I think he's being confrontational about my attempted counter-ruck, so I pushed him. The centre Maxime Mermoz, who I'd just hit in the ruck, then got in my face but, fair play, Yachvili ragged him out of the way and just put his hand out and then I shook it as if nothing had happened.

Thankfully I saw sense and did the right thing. The dressing room was quiet. You'd hear the odd person shuffling around or the clatter of a pair of studs hitting the floor but nobody really moved. I just sat there in my little spot staring at the floor, trying to understand it. Gats spoke but, a bit like after the second Test on the 2009 Lions tour, I don't think anyone listened. I certainly didn't. What can you say in that situation? Nothing, is the answer. Words are empty, hollow.

All that's left is regret, doubt and anger. Could I have done more? I've certainly asked myself that question many times over the years since. Neil Jenkins, who was our kicking coach, broke the silence. He stood up and tried to take responsibility for the defeat because we'd missed four kicks at goal and lost by one point. It was never his fault but he felt like it was. That's what you get in a professional environment – honest people who are prepared to take ownership of disappointment.

He got very emotional and broke down because he just cares so much. I never blamed any one individual for losing games and I certainly don't lay the blame for that one at anyone's door. Everybody in that dressing room did everything they could to get us to a World Cup final but we just didn't produce the goods as a group. It was there for us and we couldn't get the job done. I eventually went over and had a word with Warby. It wasn't his fault we lost the game and I just wanted to tell him that. It was clear that the next few days, weeks and months were going to be tough for him. He was going to beat himself up over it and I worried about what the reaction of the public and the media was going to be.

He was still a young guy and I felt for him. I needn't have worried too much because it went the other way for him and he was very well supported by the public through the whole thing. I often think things might be a little bit different if I was the one who'd smashed Clerc! It wouldn't have been worth me setting foot in Wales ever again had I been the one to get sent off but they were clapping Sam all the way down the street on the way to his disciplinary hearing, literally! In all seriousness, Warby is the kind of guy who will have been his own harshest critic. I'm glad there wasn't really a pile-on in the media or anything like that because it can get ugly, fast. I played with Sam for many years but I wouldn't say we ever got really close.

We celebrated the wins and handled the defeats in different ways. He took on a hell of a lot for such a young guy at that World Cup. He was learning on the job in terms of the captaincy. Obviously, there was a huge amount of mutual respect there and we got on, but we were just from two different generations. Jeez, there were certainly times in my career when I wished I had Warby's head on my shoulders. He was a great player, a stronger ball carrier than people gave him credit for and he was clearly exceptional over the ball.

After we were knocked out we went on an all-dayer. We had plenty of reasons to drown our sorrows. Nothing was planned but we had Sunday and Monday off, so we had a bit of an opportunity to hit the beers. We all went off in little groups, which I regret a bit, we should have done it together as one big group and basically hugged it out but we didn't come together until later in the afternoon.

Anyway, myself, James Hook, Lee Byrne, Shane Williams and Aled Brew ended up in this quirky part of Auckland and found a funky bar that was playing old school music and just started hitting the cocktails, mainly because I don't think we could handle any more beer after the night before.

Again, we were just having a great time, but the bar bill was racking up into three figures so we played credit card roulette. Shane lost and then when it was time to pay the next bar tab he got stung again, much to the delight of the rest of us. When we were out in that bar my mum called. So I wandered out into the alleyway by the bar, leaned up against a wall and spoke to her for a bit. I got pretty emotional on the phone and started crying. I hadn't really spoken to my mother since the McDonald's incident, we'd never really addressed it. But I knew how much I'd let her down and how furious she was about the whole thing. I knew how embarrassed she was about it all. I was also conscious of the fact that my name had been dragged through the dirt and there was huge pressure on me to produce the goods in the tournament – and I'd done that.

I also wanted to make my parents proud of me and felt I'd achieved that as well, while also putting some respect back on my name in the eyes of the public. I'd righted a lot of wrongs.

It was a real cocktail of emotions. All of those things mixed up with a stomach full of alcohol led to me having a bit of a moment in that alleyway and it was just good to speak to her after everything that had happened.

It was a tough week after the semi-final defeat. Let's be fair, nobody really wants to end up in a third-place play-off match, but I just looked at it as another chance to put the jersey on. Whenever you pull on that shirt, it's an honour and I got myself right for the game mentally and physically as the week went on. It got around to the point where I was just throwing some banter around to try and lift spirits in camp a bit, which led to me and Alun Wyn Jones having a bit of verbal jousting. Just silly banter, which spilled over onto the training pitch.

He was on the bench for the Australia game and I was starting. When we were heading out onto the training field, the coaches called the starting XV over to one part of the field and I said: "Hey Al, subs over there mate." And pointed towards where the replacements were warming up. The banter was no longer friendly. He turned and glared at me. That one didn't go down too well and he didn't speak to me for two days afterwards. That was just his intensity though, it would have cut him deep but it's why he is the most capped rugby player of all time. He's got no 'off' switch and when he's on the training field, it's all business.

The third-place match is the game that nobody wants to play in and few people will remember what actually happened in it but I was playing well so I was excited to get back out there and strut my stuff again. I put in a naughty little grubber kick which set up a try for Shane Williams and generally went about my business pretty well again. We lost by three points in the end but it obviously didn't hurt like the defeat to France did. Nowhere near.

When we were on the bus heading to the airport, Alan Phillips was going around asking players what they thought about the prospect of having an open-top bus parade in Cardiff to celebrate our achievements. I was sitting next to Alun Wyn on the bus when Thumper approached us to see what we thought about it and you can imagine what Al's reaction was. I was the same. I thought it was a ridiculous idea.

Look, that World Cup was a huge step forward for us as a rugby nation and for a young group like that, especially after what had happened in 2007. Gatland and all the players involved in that campaign deserve credit. But at the end of the day we came fourth and lost three games. We hadn't won the World Cup and if we're looking at the cold, hard facts we didn't really have much worth celebrating. We'd beaten Fiji, Samoa, Namibia and a very good Ireland side. Yes we'd played some decent stuff but ultimately we didn't have the balls to close out the semi-final and we should have. Me and Al both shot it down as a stupid idea and thankfully the parade never happened. The likes of New Zealand and South Africa would have been laughing at us. If you celebrate coming fourth, you're only ever going to come fourth. I had no interest in that.

Immediately after the tournament, I was on cloud nine really and was concentrating on the positives. It was the end of a long season, months of real hard training going all the way back to Spala were over and I was moving to France. Life was good and I was revelling in it. So when it came to the flight home, I wanted to carry on enjoying myself. We were in business class and we wanted to get stuck into the bar.

We got a laptop out and put some music on, did a bit of singing, had a laugh and team manager Alan Phillips was telling me to keep a lid on it because there were other people around. I fobbed him off and told him we'd keep it calm before going back about my business of getting drunk with my mates. Little did I know that someone then dropped a sleeping tablet in my drink and eventually it kicked in as we were getting closer to the UK. So I retire to my seat and go out like a light.

Shortly afterwards, I woke myself up just in time to be sick all over myself. As you can imagine, this was panic stations. I'm desperately trying to find a way of sorting this mess out and the smell… oh my God the smell was horrendous. I wiped it all up and started hurriedly rummaging through the wash bag they give you on these flights. I found some cleaning foam and rubbed that into my skin to try and get rid of the stench. I was sat next to a young Rhys Priestland, who was absolutely cracking up, but that was not a proud moment for me.

Much like the Lions tour two years previous, it's always been a really difficult tournament to assess. It's also one of my biggest failures because we couldn't beat France to make it to a World Cup final. It was a huge opportunity and I don't think there's been a better chance for Wales to win a World Cup since. That's why it hurts. But it's all very conflicting because on a personal level, I had a great tournament. I played well, answered all my critics, proved to everyone that I was a top player at the top of my game. A lot of newspapers and pundits were picking me as the best scrum-half in the tournament and that felt good. After all the nonsense before hand, playing well meant a huge deal to me.

7

C'est La Vie

I'd always wanted to play abroad. Having spent a lot of time in Wales and enjoyed plenty of success, I was ready to broaden my horizons even if my French adventure did come around a bit quicker than I would have liked.

I had a good relationship with Mike Cuddy, who was the Ospreys' managing director during my time at the region. I can only talk about my experience of him and he was fantastic with the players. He helped me out when that taxi driver filed his complaint in 2009, coming down to the police station with me to help smooth things over.

In early 2011, I met him at the Celtic Manor Resort, just off the M4 in Newport, to discuss renegotiating my contract. Calling them negotiations, though, is probably overstating it slightly. He literally wrote down some figures on a napkin. It was like something you see in the movies. It was a very good offer but there were a number of things that started to make the situation unattractive. I was still with Aimee at the time, dealing with that monster six-hour round trip to get to training three days a week.

Cuddy had offered me a four-year deal on good money which, for reasons that I still don't understand, I signed. I instantly regretted the decision. I should never have penned a four-year contract, it should have been a two-year deal. I didn't want to be tied down for that long because I could sense the feeling of wanting to experience something new was growing. I should never have signed that contract. It was a real mistake on my part.

I was ringing Cuddy asking if they could knock the length of the deal down a bit because I couldn't see it working over four years, especially with how things were off the field with all the commuting. I felt a bit suffocated in Wales at the time too. I became a little bit rude to Cuddy towards the end and I'm not very proud of the way I handled things at the time.

A few weeks later, Andrew Hore – one of the other suits at the Ospreys – came and found me in the canteen at the training ground and said: "You can go now, whenever you want."

That was a bit of a bombshell and not exactly what you expect to hear in the canteen of all places. Not to mention that it wasn't what I was asking for. I never wanted to get out of the contract, I just wanted to knock it down by a year or two – which a lot of the boys did, by the way – and suddenly I was out.

I didn't think he had to do it that way, in the middle of the canteen with people around. That being said, he probably didn't think I was being particularly professional when I was calling Cuddy up at 11pm trying to renegotiate my contract. I wasn't Hore's biggest fan. He got rid of Lyn Jones, who was head coach at the region for five years, one of Welsh rugby's great characters and a very talented guy, he always thought outside the box. I liked Lyn and I didn't enjoy the way Hore got rid of him. Whatever I thought of Hore, though, it was clear

C'est La Vie

I wasn't going to be there for much longer. The boys went on an end-of-season trip to Dubai that year but I didn't bother going. It was a rubbish situation. I had to look for another club and I was up against it. I was told I was leaving in March but teams have usually done the majority of their recruitment way before Christmas. By this point in the season, everyone's books are pretty full and they'll have settled on their squads for the following year. The timing couldn't have been any worse. This is when the McDonald's incident occurred. I felt like I was in no man's land. The Ospreys had pretty much turned their back on me, I was Wales' number one scrum-half and there I was searching for a club.

Luckily, Bayonne weren't done and they came knocking. Aimee and I travelled out there to have a look at the place before completing the deal. The club were making some big signings, trying to build something and it seemed like a good project to get involved in. All Blacks Joe Rokocoko and Neemia Tialata were on board. Aussie lock Mark Chisholm, who earned over 50 caps for the Wallabies, was also arriving. I was on the back foot and offers weren't flooding in because teams had already spent their budgets but there was a lot to like about Bayonne. They put together a very enticing three-year contract, which was worth in excess of €300,000. It wasn't a lot more than the Ospreys had offered but the rate of tax was more appealing in France! Nobody is going to sniff at that but it has never been about the money for me, it was about being happy. I'd had enough of the bullshit in Wales. Shortly after our recce, me and Aimee broke up and then the summer of 2011 happened. I needed a new beginning and a new experience.

You get an allowance from the club to spend on your accommodation over there and I went over mine by €700 per month – which I had to pay – to have a brand spanking new flat on the beach near Biarritz, overlooking the sea. I'd just bossed things at the World Cup, I was riding my Vespa to training, the sun shined more often than not, I was single – life was good. I was in a new country, with a new culture and it was an exciting time. One of the main motivations behind the move was to get myself out of the spotlight. I thought I could go to France, as some bloke who'd grown up on a farm in west Wales, and nobody would know who I was. I thought I could enjoy some sort of peace and quiet I guess. France is a big old country so I thought I could get a bit of escapism, become a little bit anonymous even. The plan was to get back to why I started playing in the first place. Just turn up, train hard, play hard and then enjoy yourself. What I didn't appreciate is that, in the south of France, the rugby players are the superstars and I'd just become one of the highest-paid players at the club. I'd been playing the rugby of my life at the World Cup and I was voted into the team of the tournament. So I was under a lot of pressure to deliver the goods.

But this was one of my favourite things about France. As a foreigner, when you turn up, you simply have to perform. You have no right to just arrive, pick up the cash and go through the motions, they just won't have it. You have to be winning games on your own.

The reverse happens in Wales and it did my head in. Players would come over – usually from the Southern Hemisphere – and we'd put them on this pedestal, whether they played well or not.

In France, it was a case of: 'You're the foreigner, you have to win us games.' It was a totally different mindset. If we lost a game, it was my fault because I was the outsider but if we lost at the Ospreys, it was never the overseas players' fault. I despised that about Welsh rugby. Why do we elevate overseas players who are usually just coming over to earn a bit of money? It should be about us. Even though it piled the pressure on me and it bit me on the arse a few times, I absolutely loved that attitude in France. I'm going over there, I'm earning good money and I should be winning them games. I got it and I totally bought into it. That was my attitude towards the whole experience, I threw myself into it 100 percent. I learned French, immersed myself in the culture, and always tried to sit with the local boys during downtime. I tried to make the most of it.

I couldn't wait to get into the training ground with some of the players I've just mentioned. Joe was one of the best players I'd ever played against. The guy was untouchable, he was on a different level. Unfortunately he was injured in his first year and, really, he shouldn't have been playing. But he is a nice guy and he felt like he owed it to the club to play. What a top bloke he is. Chisholm was a bit older, a family guy with five kids. Like we all did, Mark wanted to add value to the team, share his experiences and make things better at the club. Tialata, who played 43 times for the All Blacks, was also coming on board. Another one I haven't mentioned is Sione Lauaki, a big No.8 of Tongan heritage. He was a great character. He was also an incredible player who played 17 times for the All Blacks. I remember on our first night out together, we were both a bit pissed and I said to him: "I know you think you're the big dog… but I'm the big dog." He's a lot bigger than me but I didn't care. I decided he was having it, so he had it! It was just a bit of childish banter. Nothing serious, just two blokes being idiots. As soon as he laughed at that, I knew I had him and I was going to continue with it. Straight away I knew that he was my kind of guy and we'd get on. The next day, I walked into training and I could hear someone going 'Woof! Woof!' quietly under their breath. It was a bit unnerving actually. I turn around and it's Lauaki taking the piss out of me and we both start cracking up laughing. The way we clicked so quickly just went to show the importance of going out and having a good beer, there's no substitute for it in terms of building that team spirit. Tragically, Sione passed away in 2017. He was an amazingly talented rugby player and a lovely guy. I've got nothing but fond memories of him.

The club had spent a bit of cash and put together a very handy squad but the organisation itself was not ready to be great. Yes the players were outstanding but the foundations were not in place for the club to be successful. The infrastructure needed work. In my first year at the club, they sacked three head coaches. The whole culture was around throwing money at problems and hoping for a quick fix. The facilities were not where they needed to be if the club wanted to reach the heights they did. In many ways, it took me back to my days playing for Whitland and part of me really liked the set-up because everything was so old school. The stadium was old, the kit men had been there for decades. On that note, in every club I've ever been at, the kit men are always the heart and soul of the place. They're the backbone of any team I've been involved with. The gym was like something from the 1970s. It was dusty and the equipment wasn't as modern as the stuff we were using with Wales. There was so much potential in the place but, as far as I could see, it wasn't as professional as it could have been.

Matchdays were also a bit different. If we were kicking off in the evening, we'd meet up at 11 in the morning, have lunch together – they'd give you this massive steak before the game, which was the last thing we should have been eating – and then basically we'd do nothing for hours. We'd just be counting down the minutes until we could finally leave for the stadium. It used to sap a lot of energy out of me before kick-off. When I was playing in Wales it was great because you spent the morning of the match at home. I used to watch Braveheart, Rocky IV and Gladiator to get myself going and smash the pillow in my house 10 times. I'd get myself up for the game in familiar surroundings. In France, we'd have to go to a hotel and it felt a bit like playing an away game at home. Actual away trips were not easy either. I remember we flew to Clermont and got to our hotel six hours before kick-off but we were told that we shouldn't sleep and should stand around talking about the game. I could just sense that the boys were a bit flat and this was a few hours before we ran out at the Stade Marcel-Michelin, one of the hardest places to go and win in Europe. I was arriving off the back of a World Cup campaign with Wales, where things were ultra professional. We were looking at the science, taking our nutrition seriously and using cryotherapy chambers to recover for. Things were a little different at Bayonne.

We had a coach called Jean-Pierre Élissalde, who was a good player in his day but was a bit unique in his approach. I was on the bench for a game away at Toulouse once and we'd taken play down right to their line, so a good 60 metres away from the dugout. He gets up next to me and starts screaming and shouting at the top of his voice. I remember looking at him thinking: 'Mate, nobody can hear you. What are you doing?' It was all bullshit and bravado. They used to call it 'cinema' – it was all for show. A team-mate once told me that I had to wave my arms around more and create more of a fuss at the back of rucks because it would win us a few more penalties. I just couldn't take it seriously sometimes. Then there were the video analysis sessions. They were usually taken by a guy called

Christophe Deylaud, were completely different to what I was used to and went on a lot longer. It wasn't always easy to stay focused in them.

The fans were the best part of the club. They were probably the greatest fans I've played in front of at club level. They generated an incredible atmosphere. There were around 16,000 in the Stade Jean Dauger, our home ground, for every game. After you finished the warm-up and went back into the sheds to get your jersey on, the fans would start singing this song called Hymne de la Peña Baiona, which lasted a full three minutes. It was incredible, genuinely spine-tingling at times. Any player would love to play in front of fans like that. And they all knew who you were as well. If you played shit on a Saturday and they saw you on a street on the Monday, they wouldn't think twice before telling you that you'd played shit. In my early days in Bayonne, the locals were incredibly welcoming, stopping me in the supermarket or the coffee shop to say hello. They all made exactly the same point, though, and made sure that I was paying attention. It didn't matter what happened that season, they would say, as long as we beat Biarritz. The Basque Derby – that was the big one. I can still remember them coming up to me now: "Just win one game, one game. Beat Biarritz!" That was their main goal. Now I'd just come from a World Cup semi-final and my goals were massive, I wanted more Lions tours and World Cups. So, me being me, I used to tell them that we wanted to win every game, never mind just one.

But straight away it was made clear to me that this was a huge derby. Biarritz and Bayonne are five miles apart. The atmosphere in those games was absolutely electric, it was immense. The first time I played in that derby was an experience I'll never forget for so many reasons. It's a huge deal. You stay in a hotel the night before the match, the president of the club comes in to give you a huge talk about what it means to play for the team. I'd played in Wales games with less pre-match fuss. Kick-off was at 5pm but you'd wake up for breakfast and then there'd be endless meetings. I remember one such gathering and I was sat with the forwards. I couldn't believe what was to come next. Amongst themselves, they decide that at the first scrum they're going to let one go and make sure it all kicks off. By that, of course, they mean that someone is going to send a punch through on one of the unsuspecting Biarritz props. I stood there thinking: 'Yeah, I like where you're going with it. I like the fire. But shouldn't we, you know, be disciplined in the first 10 minutes?' We were playing away from home so we were already up against the ref. I didn't say any of this but in my head I was just thinking: 'Oh fucking hell, this is nuts.' Bizarrely, the game was played on a Tuesday night but it was a great occasion, the atmosphere didn't disappoint. I made a couple of breaks early on and it was brilliant. I went through on another one of my breaks and got brought down just short of the line, the ball was recycled and Sione sent our loosehead, Aretz Iguiniz, over in the corner. Perfect start. But as I'm getting up off the deck, all hell is breaking loose back towards the halfway line. It wasn't quite how the forwards had drawn it up in their pre-match meeting but our openside, Jean-Jo Marmouyet, was unloading punches on Biarritz No.8 Imanol Harinordoquy. Players ran in – I had no interest in getting involved – and there's the usual pushing and shoving. Suddenly I see an older bloke, in jeans and a jacket, wearing glasses, right in the thick of the scuffle. Turns out it was Harinordoquy's old man, who'd seen punches raining down on his son and decided to jump the barriers to get involved. He's now on the field fighting with our players. I'd seen a lot in my time but never this. You hear stories of it happening at amateur level but not at a professional rugby match! When things calmed down, Jean-Jo got off with a warning but, more importantly, the try was disallowed because of the scuffle and our perfect start was wiped out. I was gutted because I'd made the break that had initiated the try in my first derby for the club. Anyway, the game went on, I played well and it got to the final minute. We're winning by a point. We had the ball just inside our own half and I made the decision to keep the ball and run down the clock rather than kick it to them. I wish I'd kicked it. We knocked the ball on and then gave a penalty away at the scrum. Up stepped their fly-half, Julien Peyrelongue, to win it 21-19 for them with the last kick of the game. I was devastated, absolutely devastated. It was one of my first games for the club and we came that close to winning the derby. It would have been huge for the fans and the players would have been local legends for life. It was pretty heartbreaking.

After the final whistle, I'm not in a particularly good mood and I have to hold my hands up and say that I was a bit out of order with what happened next, but my blood was running hot and shit happens. I'm there with my head down, looking pretty glum, and their English winger Iain Balshaw – an ex-Lion – comes up to me, goes to shake my hand and with his English accent says: "Unlucky mate." To which I responded: "Go fuck yourself, mate."

Taken aback by what I'd said, he turned on his heels and went to look for someone else to console. It wasn't my finest moment but I wasn't always good at managing my emotions at times like that. I was wrong and I should never have reacted like I did. I was a terrible loser but my attitude was how can you be a good loser? I couldn't deal with that. By and large I had a

C'est La Vie

handle on it and I would be respectful after games but it used to do my head in when I saw players being overly friendly with opposition after a loss. I didn't like that at all.

That being said, give me an hour to get my head around the defeat and I'll be your best mate sinking a few pints in the bar. I'm old school like that. I met Balshaw a few months later and he was the coolest guy in the world. There were no issues there at all. Christian Gaijan, the coach who'd signed me a few months earlier, was sacked after the match. That sort of thing was fairly common in French rugby. Yes we'd lost the local derby but we'd lost by two points and given a pretty good account of ourselves. It was hardly a sackable offence in my view but that's the way it worked.

Three days after the last game in my first season, they pull us in for a meeting, which in itself is nuts because everything's over. The first thing all the players want to do is go on holiday and relax after busting their balls all season. The last thing they want is to get dragged in to talk about rugby. Anyway, in we go for this leadership meeting, where we all get split into groups and asked to come up with things that we can improve on for next season. However, I think much of our feedback fell on deaf ears. During this meeting, I was asked to go to the house of club president Alain Afflelou. He's one of the wealthiest men in France and owned an incredible property near Biarritz, it was like a palace. You go through the main gates and there was a huge villa with a number of châteaus dotted around the complex. It was a surreal experience arriving at his house and I had no idea what he wanted with me.

There and then, he offers me a contract extension. I wasn't sure about it, to be honest. We'd finished seventh in the league, which was a success for the club and explains why he was so

151

excited, but that wasn't my idea of success, especially given we'd just won another Grand Slam with Wales. That said, I loved the lifestyle and it was a nice balance. At the time, I was bouncing between the ultra-intense environment for a few weeks of the season with Wales and then back to the more chilled out vibe of south-west France. There's a common misconception in Wales that playing in France puts you at a disadvantage during international campaigns because of all the travel. That might be true if you're a new face trying to break into the squad and settle in but it suited me perfectly. I was one season into a three-year deal, so I didn't sign that contract.

We started my second season at the club terribly. We weren't really that competitive and found ourselves around the bottom of the league. We lost nine out of our first 14 league games, which included a 59-0 thrashing against Toulon and then a 48-3 hammering by Clermont. We recovered pretty well that year to get back to eighth in the league but it was in the third and final year of my contract that the shit really hit the fan. Again, things hadn't started particularly well. We'd lost six games and won three. The defeats included another hammering from Clermont and one from Toulouse. Once again we were near the bottom of the league. Then Europe came around to give us a welcome break from the league and we thrashed Grenoble 37-6 on a Thursday night in October on our own patch. It hadn't been a great year to that point so a win like that really lifted the mood. We weren't supposed to be back in full training until the Monday so pretty much every single player went out on the beers that night to celebrate a rare win. I vividly remember all the boys cramming into a bar. The following day, though, we had to go in for video analysis and recovery. Deylaud starts going through the game and it gets to the point around the 60-minute mark where I come on as a replacement. So just to perk things up a little bit I give it large. I used to call myself the 'vedette', which loosely translates to 'superstar', just to have a bit of a crack with the lads. I started shouting: "Here he is, the vedette!" And it got a bit of a laugh. I cracked another joke and it got a few laughs again but nothing really came of it and the session ended. Next we did a bit of recovery and then the club organised a barbecue on-site at the training ground. We hadn't had a team bonding session all season and I'm not saying this is the reason we were struggling but I think it was a contributing factor. Suddenly, someone starts handing cans out in the changing room but I didn't see any harm in it, especially considering we had the next few days off and we were about to have a good session. In fact, I thought it was exactly what we needed. Yes we were professionals but there is a lot to be said for having a few cold ones with your team-mates. It just brings everyone that little bit closer together and that's true no matter what level you play at. So the barbecue kicks off and the beers are flowing. In all honesty, we didn't need much topping up from the night before. After a few hours I decide to stand up and give a speech in French. I dug a few of the players out with some gags here and there, just generally taking the piss and it was well received. Then I poured my heart out, talking about how much I loved the place and the people. I was trying to connect the boys and bring everyone together. You have to do that as a team. If you become a family and if you have that culture, you go the extra mile for each other. In no way was I trying to degrade anyone, put any of the boys down or be negative. I was just trying to make the boys laugh and I achieved that. It was an attempt to lift the spirits. It was a good crack and everyone had a great time. But things were about to take a dark twist.

In the days that followed, the club alleged that I had turned up to the video analysis session drunk on October 11 and they suspended me. Two other players – Stephen Brett and Dwayne Haare – were also facing the same allegations as myself. I wasn't able to play in the next game against Wasps and I didn't attend the game against Montpellier. That annoyed me because I wanted to be there for my team-mates. They won the match and one of the boys put me on loudspeaker in the changing rooms after the game, they were loving it, all shouting and screaming, saying they'd won the game for me. I got on great with all the players at the club. It was a sad situation. I thought it was all going to be resolved but it wasn't to be. Ten days after the incident I had my disciplinary meeting but it didn't go in my favour.

The year before, I was being offered a new contract and now I was being sacked. In France, a certain amount of time has to pass after your hearing before a club can officially tell you that you're gone. In that window, it leaked out to the local press, which was unfortunate. My contract was terminated less than three weeks after the alleged incident. The other two players were fined. Talk about a rollercoaster. My good mate, and team-mate, Scott Spedding came around to the flat. He couldn't believe what was happening and was helping me try and make sense of it. A lot of the boys signed a petition to try and support me but it didn't work out. I had Jamie Robinson, the old Cardiff Blues centre, ringing me up to give me some support as well. He had problems of his own when he left Toulon, so was on hand to offer some advice. I was really disappointed with how it all finished in Bayonne, especially after the McDonald's incident.

That said, I want to take an element of responsibility for how things went during my time there. I should have had a better attitude towards the club. I should have gone in there and looked to change things with regards to the culture and coaching but I couldn't really influence things the way I wanted to off the field. I tried but I didn't really manage to change anything, so I just accepted that and went about my business. In many ways, I admired the confidence they had in the way they wanted to do things. But, it doesn't matter who you are, I think it always helps to learn from other people who have had different experiences. That's when you start getting better coaches, better players and better organisations. After I left the club, they went through a rough patch and slipped out of the league and I felt for the fans. It must have been awful for them because you could see how much they loved the club. But it just wasn't being run the way I would have done it. The style of man management wasn't what I had experienced before and the coaching wasn't what I was used to. I'd have loved things to turn out differently there because the place had so much potential to be great. It was a real shame. I didn't have time to dwell on it though because the autumn internationals were around the corner. I did some training on my own and Warren Gatland was great with me in all fairness, telling me to just get my head down and work hard. When the internationals came around, I didn't have a club next to my name in the match day programme, it just said 'unattached', which I thought was pretty cool. Not for the first time in my career, though, I found myself without a club at a really awkward period in the season. Not many clubs are looking to bring players on board halfway through the year and, after the international break, I was technically unemployed. I was negotiating a settlement with Bayonne – which rumbled on a bit – but I wanted to keep playing, no way did I want to be sat on the sidelines. The autumn games were a big chance to showcase my talents and remind people how good I was. The reality was, not many clubs were looking and I wasn't far off ringing Whitland to see if they needed numbers! At this point, the WRU were preparing to step in and offer me some sort of contract to get me through the season. At the time I was one of the best players in the country and it was in their interests to look after me. They weren't always great when it didn't suit them, mind! Luckily for me, one of the biggest clubs in Europe were interested and I signed for Racing Metro, as they were known at the time. They'd had an injury and needed cover. I signed a two-and-a-half year deal on similar money to what Bayonne had paid me. Ronan O'Gara, who I'd become close with on the 2009 Lions tour, was on their coaching staff and probably pulled a few strings. I had to ship all my stuff from Bayonne to Paris, including a Ralph Lauren sofa which traveled everywhere with me and now currently resides at my parents' house. Organising all that was a nightmare but I never got a chance to say goodbye to the boys or the fans, which upset me.

I picked out a place in Le Plessis-Robinson but had to stay in a hotel for a couple of weeks to find my feet. Soon after arriving I met with Laurent Labit, who was head coach at the time, and he presented me with a playbook that was about two inches thick. It was professional from the very start. I did my initiation – smashed a Welsh hymn called Calon Lan, standard – and then I just wanted to get stuck in. Paris was an unbelievable place to live. There was just so much history and so many things to do. You could be sipping coffee in the shadow of the Eiffel Tower one minute and sampling some unbelievable food in a fantastic restaurant the next. I was going to watch PSG play football, the tennis at Roland Garros, and fashion shows. And I loved the fact I was joining a quality side, who were driven and challenging for silverware.

My apartment in Paris wasn't the best, it wasn't a patch on what I'd been living in during my stay on the Biarritz coastline. It was a small, two-bed place with a tiny garden that was in the shade more often than it was in the sun. I wasn't too bothered about my accommodation there. I just took what the club were offering this time, I didn't top it up myself. My flat was about 500 yards from the training ground, there were few distractions, it was exactly what I needed and was the perfect place to just get my head down. During my time at Bayonne, I mentioned that I would often get recognised on the street. If you went out for a quiet drink someone would see you, people would talk shit and it would get back to the club and cause you grief. But I found that level of anonymity that I was looking for in Paris. Not even the likes of Dan Carter, who I played with in my final year at Racing, would get bothered. Even superstars in other sports like football could walk around without getting pestered too much because Parisians are very much into themselves, really. I'd heard stories of French players passing out on the Champs-Élysées and nobody batting an eyelid. It was a totally different place altogether. It was nice to be able to go out and enjoy yourself without worrying about who was watching you. There's a street in Paris called Rue Princesse, which is pretty much the only place in the city where you'll find rugby bars. There were a handful of spots there that would be frequented by rugby players and fans. I went down there once or twice but I hated it. I wanted to avoid it at all costs. I enjoyed mixing with fans every now and again but I'd been stung in Cardiff on so many occasions and even Bayonne a few times. When I was young, I didn't mind going out and being spotted, I wanted the attention. But it's funny how things change the older you get and I just didn't want to be recognised in Paris. Also, I was in Paris for God's sake, so I had almost unlimited options and so many other things to see and experience.

Things were extremely professional at Racing. The training facility was world class and the entire mindset was just different to what I had experienced in Bayonne. You'd walk into the training complex and have to change your footwear on arrival. It was all to do with flicking that mental switch when you turn up to work and getting into the right mindset. It's the kind of thing you see at some of the biggest corporations in the world. The weights room was unbelievable, kitted out with shiny, well-maintained equipment and then there were recovery facilities. They even built their own cryotherapy chambers just before I left. There was no hiding place at Racing either. Every form of training, whether it was out on the training field or fitness in the gym, was monitored and analysed very closely. All the players would be wearing heart monitors and there was a big screen on the wall displaying real-time heart rates for everyone, so you could see who was working the hardest and so could everyone else. The canteen was top notch, there were sofas and sitting areas for everyone to chill out in between sessions with all the coaches' offices nearby. Every player had their picture on the wall which made you feel a bit special. There were no excuses for the players if we lost a game because we had all the tools to prepare ourselves for matches. It was a different mentality to the south as well. In Bayonne, they really forced their culture on you and were deeply patriotic. Which is completely fine. But in Paris they let you explore it at your own pace and the French players wanted to learn English. They saw the value in that. It was far more relaxed in that sense. I don't have many bad things to say about my time at

Racing at all but the stadium they had when I was there – the Stade Yves-du-Manoir – was a shocker. One thing that stands out is that the toilets were absolutely horrendous. There was a lot of history in the ground and I didn't fully appreciate that straight away. The Olympics was held there in the early 1900s, the football World Cup final was held there and the French rugby team used to play home games there until the early 70s, so some Welsh legends strutted their stuff there. It was steeped in history but you could see it, if you know what I mean. It wasn't in great nick and there was a running track between the spectators and the pitch, which always impacts on the atmosphere. Now Racing play at their stunning indoor stadium, La Défense Arena, which cost over €300 million to build. But back then the stadium was a bit of a disappointment, it didn't really fit with how modern and professional the club was in pretty much every other department, and their new home is much more fitting. We did play the odd game at the Stade de France, which is a pretty impressive stadium. I played my best game for Racing there against Toulouse when we won 25-5 in the January of my first season at the club. I scored a try in the first half and we pretty much dominated from start to finish. I know Gats was particularly impressed with that performance because we spoke about it not long after when the Six Nations came around. One thing I didn't like is that he thought my legs had gone on the 2013 Lions tour. That pissed me off because it wasn't the case. I was carrying an injury on that trip but he never came to ask me about it, he just assumed I was getting old and I was past it. I'd heard him say it about other players before but he was wrong about me on that occasion. During the match against Toulouse, our Irish fly-half Johnny Sexton made a break from inside our half. He was getting caught so grubbered it towards the try line. I sprinted a full 65 metres to get on the end of that grubber kick, out-sprinting the cover defence to score. That game proved to Gats that I still had it.

The one thing that Bayonne had that Racing didn't have was the fans. If you combined Racing's professionalism with Bayonne's fans, you'd have an unbelievable club. The coaches were just as bonkers at Racing but there was more structure to the sessions and the coaching was better.

We had two head coaches there – Labit and Laurent Travers. Both former players but both had a mental streak in them. My first game for the club was against Harlequins in the Heineken Cup. One thing I didn't realise about Labit at the time is that he's got a twitch. After the pre-match meeting, I'm sitting there pumped up ready to go for my club debut.

He's looking in my direction and he's twitched. I think he's nodding at me as if to say 'are you ready to go?' So I just nod back to him to let him know that I'm bouncing. Right up for it. I'm not going to let him down. I look around and a few of the boys noticed what had happened and were absolutely pissing themselves.

I soon realised what had happened. Labit wasn't gesturing towards me or trying to interact with me at all, he was probably wondering why I was nodding at him! Travers was a former hooker who played for Brive around the time they got involved in that infamous punch-up with Pontypridd, which everyone calls the Battle of Brive. I've seen him described as 'a full-blown old style French nutter' in a newspaper report. They weren't far off. He was totally bonkers. In my final year at the club, we had a play-off match against Toulouse in order to make it into the semi-finals of the Top 14. The game was played on our patch but, in typical French rugby fashion, they stuck us in a hotel for hours before kick-off to sap the life out of us.

We eventually get on the bus and head to Colombes, where the ground is, and the journey out there is on a single lane road. We're driving along when suddenly the Toulouse bus pulls out in front of us. So now we're following their coach into our stadium. Travers was having absolutely none of it. He gets into the driver's ear and barks words to the effect of 'we're getting there before they do' with the odd expletive thrown in for good measure.

Bear in mind we're on the backstreets of Paris now, there's no overtaking on these roads because there's simply no room. The poor bus driver probably tried to explain this to Travers but he kept putting the pressure on and suddenly I felt the bus speed up. Now we're in a full-blown street race with Toulouse's bus. It was complete madness but Travers was adamant that we were getting to the ground first. Eventually we pull up alongside the Toulouse bus but we're traveling approximately one mile per hour faster than them so it was the slowest overtake you've ever seen.

We're all sat there with our headphones on, trying to get in the zone. I look across to see the Toulouse players looking back at us as if to say 'what the fuck are you boys doing?' And all we could do was just shrug and point towards Travers. We pulled in just in front of them and got to the ground first. We won the game 21-16 with Carter nailing six penalties out of six and Johan Goosen, an incredibly talented South African who could also be a nut job sometimes, adding another.

To this day, Travers is probably convinced we won the game because we won the drag race to the stadium. Both coaches were good guys but they were both mad. I've never seen a coach go as mental as Travers before a game, eyes popping out of his head, screaming at the players. I used to think he was going to blow up before matches.

They weren't the only ones with hot tempers, though. Club president Jacky Lorenzetti was not afraid to storm into the dressing room and let us have it if we lost. We came off second best against Lyon at home once. Jacky comes down to the dressing room and he's not happy. He's throwing stuff, the ice bucket goes. Losing home games was unacceptable and he let us know about it. But I don't have a bad word to say about him. He was one of the best owners in France.

I've got a lot of time for him and he hated losing as much as the rest of us. He is an unbelievably rich and successful man and you don't achieve what he has done without having that ruthless streak. But the boys loved him and he looked after us. He had my back after the way I was treated in Bayonne and I'll always be grateful to him for that.

In an interview with the BBC after I signed, he said: "In Bayonne, they said he liked to drink. He's won 80 caps for Wales, five for the Lions and won two Grand Slams. If that's what happens when you drink, then I will put all my players in a barrel of alcohol from morning until night." It was a bit of fun but I appreciated his comments. It proved to me that he backed me and that's all I ever really wanted. He had a crazy streak mind.

One pre-season he comes to give us a speech and starts talking about how he wants us to be fierce and aggressive in the upcoming season. Then he says he has a present for us, so we all get up and leave the meeting room, following him down the stairs, into another building and onto the artificial turf training pitch. The boys are looking around at each other wondering what the hell is going on and suddenly he unveils these two tigers in cages and uses them to illustrate what he's just said in his speech. Basically, he wanted us to be like tigers. That was an incredibly bizarre experience. Can you imagine one of the Welsh regions trying to pull that stunt? It would never happen but I don't think it would work. The boys would have either thought it was a joke or that their owner had lost the plot. But in France, those sort of flamboyant gestures were normal and players responded to it. I was just stood there hoping the tigers didn't find a way out of that cage, otherwise we'd have all been on the menu.

When I first got to Bayonne, I wanted to make a real effort to buy into their culture and become one of the lads. It was all about learning the language, I was always told that would be a big thing with the locals so I always made the effort and the youngsters at the club were brilliant with me. Charles Ollivon, who's now captain of France, was there at the time as a kid coming through the ranks.

At Racing, it was a bit harder to keep developing your French because there was so much English-speaking going on. Johnny Sexton, Casey Laulala, Bernard Le Roux, Juandre Kruger were there, as were the Welsh boys Jamie Roberts and Dan Lydiate, so there was a lot of English spoken. We had a good handful of my fellow Welsh internationals in the side for the bulk of my time at the club. Jamie and Dan were already in Paris when I signed and Luke Charteris followed a season later.

It was nice to have some familiar faces around. I felt bad sometimes because it's easy to slip into your own group but I was having extra French lessons to keep that coming along. It was Jamie's first time in France and being in French classes with him was always an exciting part of the week. Jamie, now a qualified doctor, is clearly a very intelligent bloke (I hope he doesn't read this) and has done his fair share of travelling.

He thought he was going to stroll into the French lessons and pick it up within a few weeks but he struggled a fair bit and it used to stress him out big time. "I'm not learning anything, I can't get it." He used to moan. Bear in mind this is a bloke who has done a lot of studying in his time.

I used to take the piss a lot in those sessions and I loved it. He got there in the end, though. He's a great character to have around the place. We always used to give Jamie shit for different things because he thinks he's chocolate. After he left to join Harlequins, I was giving a TV interview to Sky Sports and they asked what my favourite day at Racing had been so far, my reply was: "Jamie Roberts' last." It's all a bit of fun, though. Jamie's a good guy and he gives as good as he gets! We went to watch the Manic Street Preachers play in Paris once and, of course, Jamie knew them and we met up after the gig. That was awesome.

They're a great bunch and know more about rugby than me! Luke probably had the biggest impact out of all the Welsh boys there, though. He was amazing at Racing, they loved him and they didn't want him to go when he eventually left in 2016 to join Bath. His French was brilliant and, for some reason, before an away game I decided to give a quick team talk in the huddle before the match.

It's always a bit daunting to do that, let alone in French. After I'd given the talk, I turned to Luke straight away and asked how I did. He said: "Yeah it was great Mike! Not a lot of French in there but plenty of 'fuck this and fuck that' so well done!" Luke never got the credit he deserved as a player, nowhere near. Because he was so tall, there was a misconception that he was clumsy and slow. Similar stuff to what I faced in my career because I was tall for my position. But the reality is that Luke would often be the top tackler in teams, he regularly made over 20 and in 2015 he set a Six Nations record with 31 tackles against Ireland. He's a machine and he was invaluable at set-pieces.

In some ways, I have Jamie to thank for helping me meet my wife. He brought in this tradition called 'The Paris Dining Club'. Once a week, all the foreign players would meet up and it would be one player's responsibility to pick a different restaurant every week. We'd all go, enjoy the food and have a few beers, nothing too hectic. It was a great way of mixing it up, seeing the city and all it had to offer.

On one such night in my final season, we met at the bar Dan Carter had at his house, had a couple of beers and then went out to this lovely restaurant. It was me, Dan, Casey Laulala and Yannick Nyanga, who is French but everyone was welcome really. Halfway through the night, Dan returns to the table and some shots appear. He says to me: "Mike, those girls over there have just bought you some shots, you'd better go and say thank you." So I'm feeling pretty good about myself at this point. I stroll over to this table where three women are enjoying their evening, sit down and begin thanking them for the shots. They're looking at me, probably thinking 'who the fuck is this guy and what is up to?' I never found out who actually bought the shots that night but it certainly wasn't one of the three women. I reckon it was Carter. I was the only single one out and the boys were having a bit of banter. Anyway, the woman I sat down next to is now my wife. I chased her around that evening but she wasn't interested. It turned out she was mates with Yannick so he put me in touch, we went on a couple of dates and the rest is history.

As I've alluded to, ahead of my last season at the club, some good-looking Kiwi bloke named Dan Carter signed. He's achieved a thing or two, you may have heard of him. In all seriousness, it was amazing to play with Dan, who most people would regard as the best rugby player of his generation. Six weeks after the 2015 Rugby World Cup final, during which he scored 17 points and was awarded man of the match, he was making his Racing debut alongside me against Northampton in the Champions Cup.

He arrived in the week before the match and a few of the boys were in awe during his first training session. He was just jogging around, passing the ball and was very calm. He had a lovely demeanour about him and was top notch with everyone around the facility. He always looked as if he was in second gear. I don't mean that in a bad way, it was just because he made things look effortless. He was that cool.

After his first session Juan Imhoff, our Argentine winger, was jogging around next to him, taking the piss, making out as if he wasn't even trying. Then a few of us had a kicking competition, a crossbar challenge. Dan came dead last and then the running joke was that we'd signed Gary Carter, Dan's imaginary brother. For that game against Northampton, I called all the plays on the field because Dan hadn't had the chance to familiarise himself with the calls. I was almost like a captain.

It was great because he'd just won the World Cup and now he's following my orders. Plus we won the game by 30 points. Afterwards he was getting mobbed by fans on the way to a function and I yelled over: "There were more for my debut, Dan. Don't worry, it gets easier after a few weeks!" Then I got questions in the press asking me what it was like to play with him and, not being one to turn down the opportunity for some banter, my response was: "You're better off asking him what it was like to play with me." But in all honesty, it was a pleasure to play with him. I didn't realise how good he was until I played with him. His arrival was brilliant for me. Before he signed, Maxime Machenaud, my rival for the No.9 jersey, was starting a lot because he was the goal-kicker. But Dan was one of the best goal-kickers in the world, so I played far more regularly after he came to town.

He was brilliant off the field as well. He might have been one of the biggest names in the sport but he was still one of the boys. He would always come out for a pint and he could let his hair down with the rest of us. We went to watch PSG together but I never tagged along to the Louis Vuitton functions that he was invited to! It was at the Monaco Grand Prix when I realised just how famous he was. We had a great weekend there but he was turning heads among some very famous people. He was off doing little bits and bobs to keep his sponsors happy.

The year before, Jamie had talked us into a party at the Grand Prix with Albert II, Prince of Monaco. The big man had his uses sometimes, I'll give him that. I had a couple of good trips down there. But one of the best trips I had with Dan was to Hong Kong and, in all truth, I don't remember much of it! Racing were sent there in the middle of the season – a bit mad really – to play a game against the Highlanders, who were the Super Rugby champions at the time. It was all for the sponsors and the exhibition game probably generated a few euros. But, again, Jacky sorted the boys out. He got us into the nicest restaurants around but then the nights ended up in all sorts of bars. We were flat out on the beers for three or four days. Barely any training. Carnage. I was sharing with Dan on that trip and we were both well oiled and having banter with each other in the room one night. I was telling him I'm the greatest of all time and all this nonsense, posting my highlights on Twitter with silly captions. Dan's a very humble guy but I managed to talk him into doing the same. Luckily we came to our senses and deleted the Tweets before anyone had really noticed. That trip was chaos, we were probably drunk as much as we were sober. The motto became 'back it up'. I got on really well with former All Black Chris Masoe.

I think he took a shine to me after hearing stories from Jerry Collins about our time together at the Ospreys. He enjoyed the fact we looked after Jerry so he looked after me a lot in Paris. Chris, who was as partial to a beer as the rest of us, coined the phrase 'back it up'. The meaning being that we could go and have a drink but when it came to what limited training we did, we had to perform and 'back it up'. We had a little captain's run the day before the game and I remember Travers pleading with the players not to drink that night. I was looking at him thinking: 'Are you mental? I can't touch another drop.'

In that last session before the match, though, it was amazing because all the boys switched on and we were on fire. Barely a single ball went down. In the week leading up to the match there were a load of corporate events. I did a Q&A with Dan, who was his usual humble self and I had to bring the humour to proceedings.

Then Jamie Joseph, who was the coach of the Highlanders at the time, gave a very serious interview about the game while we were all on the beers. We went on to win 45-38, somehow. People probably underestimate how important it is, even at a professional level, to have team bonding trips like that. We went on to win the league that year and I believe that week in Hong Kong was an important part of our season.

One of the biggest characters at the club was Italian legend Martin Castrogiovanni. The bearded prop, who played over

100 times for his country, was very much his own man, a real larger than life character and in my final year at the club he proved it.

We were heading to Nottingham to face Leicester at a neutral venue in the Champions Cup semi-final. We were all sat on the bus ready to leave the training ground and start our journey to England when Castro hopped on and said one of his family members was ill and that he had to go and be with them. He wasn't coming with us. We all thought it was fair enough and wished him all the best, thinking nothing of it. He stays in Paris and we head to the East Midlands.

We win the game and secure our place in the final. Happy days. In the meantime, Castro hasn't gone to visit a sick relative at all. During his time in Paris, he became friendly with the footballer Zlatan Ibrahimovic and a few Argentina players, who were all playing for PSG at the time. They'd invited Castro to Las Vegas on a private jet, which was the real reason why he couldn't play in this European semi-final.

He'd have probably got away with it but Ibrahimovic was photographed by a pool and who was stood next to him? Castro and his unmistakable beard. Top off, having a whale of time. It didn't take long for the story to catch fire and the picture was everywhere, in all the newspapers. At first, a few of the boys were wondering what the hell he was playing at, ditching us to head off to Vegas like that. But we'd won the match and I saw it as a bit of fun. I can understand why the club were furious, mind. All hell broke loose in that respect and they sacked him. At the age of 34, that was the end of his career and he was never seen on a rugby field again.

The week after the match, Lorenzetti came in to give us a talking to and, to break the tension a little bit, our captain

Dimitri Szarzewski said: "Jacky, if we win the league or the European Cup, you have to pay to send us all to Vegas." All the boys were in stitches but we were only able to make a joke out of it because we'd squeezed past Leicester by three points a few days before.

The laughing didn't last forever. I was getting a little annoyed towards the end of my time there because Machenaud was playing more than me. We went on a run in the Champions Cup and I was an unused sub in the quarter-final against Toulon and then I came on for four minutes in the semi-final against Leicester, the game Castro went AWOL for. We made it to the final against Saracens, which was played in Lyon, but so much annoyed me about that day.

It was a bit of a low point for me. I was nowhere near match fit because I hadn't played much rugby at all in the weeks before. Machenaud got injured after 22 minutes so on I went. I didn't have any sort of form and wasn't feeling particularly great. I did okay that day but the team struggled generally. All week we planned to throw the ball about, loop passes over their midfield and throw cross kicks in to try and nullify their strength, which we all knew was their blitz defence. But it absolutely lashed down, I'd never seen rain like it. It suited their game plan down to the ground. They implemented a really detailed kicking game and then just applied pressure with their incredible defence.

If it was a dry ball, I think we'd have had a great chance but when the rain came, they were always going to be favourites. A few weeks after that I signed for Sale because nothing came down from the club in terms of a new deal. They thought my heart wasn't in it after it was confirmed I was leaving – they can be a bit like that in France – and I didn't really feature much from then on in. I wasn't selected to play in the Top 14 final that year and I was gutted. It was against Toulon at the Nou Camp, Barcelona's stadium. There were 99,000 people in attendance and I was left out of the side. I was a bit pissed off with it all because I was ready to give my all until my last match but there were no hard feelings. It never got frosty between me and Machenaud even though he was getting picked ahead of me. If anything, I just wanted him to go on and become a regular in the French team.

He used to put a lot of pressure on himself. I remember him making a mistake in a game and beating himself up about it so I passed on some advice, tried to get him to relax. Only he can tell you whether he listened or not but I never felt any animosity towards him. He was a passionate, hard-working guy and I respected that. We had an open-top bus parade after winning the league and I was able to enjoy that because I'd contributed throughout the season. We had a few days on the beers after-wards, those were great times. Jacky was booking up venues for us in the night and we all got absolutely trollied. The day we arrived back home, the Wales football team were playing against Northern Ireland in a last-16 match at Euro 2016.

The game was taking place at Parc de Princes in Paris and I'd managed to get some tickets. I'd barely slept the night before and I was nodding off at the game, which wasn't the best in all honesty. Half-time comes around and I say to my missus: "We've got to go because I'm in all sorts of trouble." So we left at the break with the score 0-0. Wales ended up going through to the quarter-finals after an own goal from Gareth McAuley in the second half but we were long gone by then.

And so my time in France came to an end. Things got

tough at times, particularly at Bayonne, but so much good came out of that part of my life. My French adventure ended with me winning the league, I'd found the woman that would become my wife and we've now got two little boys together. I've got nothing but fond memories of my time in Paris and it was actually nice to leave a club on good terms! But I still had more left in the tank.

Boys on tour: On a wing and a prayer in 2009 with my fellow British and Irish Lions

Feels good:
Celebrating a try in the
first Test against South
Africa in Durban in
June 2009

World in my han[...]
Ireland legends
Ronan O'Gara and
Paul O'Connell
look on as we head
to victory in the
quarter-finals of t[...]
Rugby World Cup
in 2011

Crossing the line again: A try at the Millennium Stadium against Ireland in March 2011

Cheers: Pictured here is the greatest of all time – and Dan Carter!

2013 and all that: In action on the way to a Six Nations title and a laugh in training with 'Bomb'

Wizards of Aus:
Enjoying the moment
after a famous 2-1
Lions series win over
Australia in 2013

The real McCaw: Getting to grips with New Zealand legend Richie McCaw in November 2014

Home and abroad: Wearing the sky blue of Racing 92 (above left) and (above) back on British soil with Sale Sharks

Au revoir: Time to say goodbye but I'll never forget my French adventure

Happy days: Plenty of good memories from my Instagram: With Niall Horan (top left), Puff Daddy (top right), being inducted into the Hall of Fame by Gareth Edwards (left) and 'the name's Phillips...' with James Bond aka Daniel Craig (above)

New horizon: It's no longer just about me – my only goal is to be the best husband and father I can be. That's all that matters

Looking ahead: I'm happy and the future looks bright. There is plenty more to play for

8

Winning Again

The 2012 Six Nations was huge for us as a squad. I wasn't as excited about our Rugby World Cup campaign as some people. We'd made the semi-final but I didn't view that as something to be celebrated. That being said, I did accept that we'd taken a step forward as a team, the fans were right behind us and the mood was good. Welsh rugby usually follows that kind of high with a bit of a low, we've always struggled to build on what have been deemed successful campaigns. Warren Gatland and the coaches deserve credit for what happened in 2012 and 2013.

There was huge pressure on us heading into the 2012 Six Nations because we had to back up what we'd done in New Zealand, which was basically outperform people's expectations. There was no point going out and doing that at a World Cup and then flopping in the Six Nations.

We had Ireland up first in 2012 out in Dublin and it was a huge game to kick things off. We'd stuffed them in the World Cup quarter-final and now we were heading to their backyard and they had all their big guns playing again. They were desperate for revenge and it was a pretty close contest, really nip and tuck but whenever they went in front, they just sat back off us and they were playing with fire because we had big threats. Word on the street is that they changed their defence after that game to become more aggressive. We moved the ball nicely in the first half and they just let us flow through our attacking patterns. Rhys Priestland sent Jonathan Davies over for a try in the first half with a lovely offload out of the tackle.

At half-time, Shaun Edwards was on to me about Ireland scrum-half Conor Murray, who it was felt was having a bit too much space, so I was told to keep an eye on that and shut him down. Later in the game George North barged through their midfield and he threw an outrageous offload to Jonathan to score. Things then got a bit tricky when Bradley Davies got a yellow card for lifting one of their players out of a ruck, off the ball, and dropping him on his head. Now this pissed me off afterwards. It was far worse than what Sam Warburton did at the World Cup and yet Bradley only got a yellow. I'm not calling for Bradley to get a red card here but where was the consistency?

Anyway, George went over for a good try late on and Leigh Halfpenny kicked a match-winning penalty to get us over the line. To be honest, we got very lucky with that last penalty. Stephen Ferris was done for a tip tackle on Ian Evans. If it had gone against us, we'd have been fuming with it. But it went in our favour so happy days. It was far from comfortable but there was just a calmness about us that day and we knew that we could get the better of them if we just stuck to our processes.

That confidence came from how we'd prepared and performed at the Rugby World Cup. We knew we were a good side at this point and there wasn't much that fazed us. The great thing about that day was Andy Powell's reaction. In the last play, I've spun it back to Rhys Priestland, who's booted the ball into the crowd and the ref blows up. Andy was an unused replacement that day but by the time the ball has landed in the crowd, Powelly has sprinted a full 60 metres – you can see it on the highlights online – to celebrate and congratulate the boys.

That is why he was so important to the team. The boys acknowledge that sort of stuff and it says a lot about him. I was chuffed to pick up the man of the match award that day and just really continue my form from the World Cup. One other thing I remember about that day is that, for some reason, Rob Howley wanted me to say something in the team meeting before we got on the bus. Players never speak in that meeting and I wasn't the biggest talker anyway. I just wanted to get my performance right. Looking back, I think Rob was probably trying to develop me as a leader. I never voiced my thoughts and always led by my actions on the field.

The Scotland game was pretty straightforward really, Alex Cuthbert scored a good try, Halfpenny got two, with me sending him over for his second. I held off Mike Blair for Leigh's second and then slipped him a naughty offload out the back of my hand for him to run in an easy try. This was another one of those occasions where I didn't get the credit I deserved from the commentators. It was totally overlooked! We won the game 27-13, which set us up for the Triple Crown against England two weeks later.

I remember starting that game well and putting George through a gap, which settled me down a bit because you always went to start well. There were a couple of penalties in the first half and we trailed 9-6 at half time. Early in the second period, Priestland gets charged down and is then sin binned with the game on a knife-edge.

Owen Farrell kicked another penalty that put England six points ahead and the game was in real danger of slipping away from us. When you go a man down, teams generally concede seven to 10 points. It's all about galvanising yourself and each other but also maintaining a calm head. My plan then was to just get us down in their half and kill the game a little bit, slow everything down, keep the ball and just run the clock down. You can't play without your fly-half, so I wanted us to just chill out, no panic and see out the 10 minutes with as little drama as possible.

We didn't give any points away in that period. I didn't get any praise for that and, in fact, I got a fair bit of stick because people were saying I should have been playing with more tempo and that I was killing our attack. But there's a process that you have to go through when you go a man down. You have to be smart with the ball, even if it's not what everyone wants to see. I did get praise from one guy, though, and to be honest it was probably the last person on Earth I expected it from. After that Six Nations I was on a night out in Cardiff when Welsh footballer Craig Bellamy came up to me and said: "Mike, can I have two seconds of your time please?" So I said: "Yes, of course" but in the back of my mind I'm thinking: 'What's this all about? Have I said something about him? Have I done something to upset him?' We wander over to a quiet corner of the bar and he says: "I just wanted to say, the way you controlled that 10 minutes when Priestland went off against England was superb."

My jaw nearly hit the floor. It was the last thing I was expecting him to come out with but, fair play, for him to have picked that up was impressive. We had a few drinks after that and it was good fun meeting him. Anyway, back to Twickers. Scott Williams ripped the ball off Courtney Lawes and scored that wonder try to put us in front but Halfpenny was the star of that show. In the last minute, England were camped on our line looking for a score to level the match.

We're defending a ruck 15 metres in from the left hand touchline and Halfers is defending second man out from the ruck. England spin it to the far side where David Strettle charges at the line. By the time they get the ball out there, Halfpenny has sprinted across, running past a number of our players, to make the initial hit on Strettle before Jon Davies and North finished the job. It was astonishing defending and it won us that match.

After the game, me and Jamie Roberts had to go and do a Q&A in hospitality with Will Carling, where you answer a few questions and get a nice little fee. Jamie had gone off early in the match with an injury and hobbled into the function on crutches. I was devastated for him because I knew, as we stood there in that room, that we were going to beat Italy and France, win the Grand Slam and that he was going to miss out on that. He gave me some terminology, some doctor nonsense about his meniscus. It sounded like he was going to be out for months so I really felt sorry for him.

Then Monday comes around and we arrive at the training pitch for our first session to find Jamie doing flat-out sprints with the physios. So I'm pretty confused by this given what I'd heard on Saturday night and he went on to start against Italy, score a try and then start against France. He got a fair bit of stick for that. He earned himself the nickname Lazarus, which still follows him around to this day. Although we didn't really cut loose until the second half, we got past Italy without too much trouble. Sergio Parisse lived offside and got away with it because he's Sergio Parisse, although the guy is world class to be fair. Lazarus and Cuthy scored the tries and we were on for the Grand Slam decider against France.

At this point in my life I was actually living at the Vale Resort. So when all the players were going home on the days off, I was stuck in the hotel. I was 29, single and bored out of my mind when all the boys went home. Earlier in the tournament I was around my mate's house and I noticed this girl on his Facebook page, so I asked who she was and it turned out she was good mates with his missus. So I asked him to sort me out with a date. I'd arranged to meet her in London on the day off before what ended up being a Grand Slam decider, it was the Wednesday before the game. We went to a steak restaurant, the food was lovely, we were having a great time and I started joining her on the wine.

I don't know what came over me and I'd almost never drunk this close to such a big game before. The only other instances were when I had a few beers with the boys after the 2005 Grand Slam and had to play for Llanelli the following day, and that time I got away with it after the postponed Boxing Day game in 2010. This, though, was an entirely different kettle of fish. I ended up having seven or eight glasses of wine, nothing too wild but given the circumstances and the fact we were two days out from a Grand Slam game, I should never have done it. I don't know what I was thinking, whether it was the pressure, being cooped up in the hotel all the time, Dutch courage.

Whatever it was, it shouldn't have happened. I got back to the Vale that night and was there for training the following morning. Nobody found out, which is good because if that had got back to the management, there's no way I'd have been playing on the Saturday and who knows what might have happened to my career after that.

I can tell the story now because we went on to beat France and win the Grand Slam but that was a momentary lapse in judgement. Had that date taken place in Cardiff, I'd almost certainly have been caught. Someone would have taken a picture, it would have been in the newspapers, the coaches would have walked in and sat on the table next to me. Something would have happened. But the difference was, because I was in London, I was anonymous. It makes me think back over all the compromising situations I found myself in during nights out in Cardiff.

If I'd never gone out in Cardiff after a match and always gone to London, for example, how much of this nonsense would I have saved myself from? In all probability, quite a bit. As a result, the public perception of me would have been completely different. I'm still the same guy, though. But I got judged because I made a handful of mistakes throughout my career in a place where I was always under the microscope and then my reputation ran away with itself.

There was so much riding on the game for us, a Grand Slam and another Six Nations title, but the fact it was France up last did add a little bit more spice. Obviously, a few months before they had been responsible for the greatest disappointment of my career so, yeah, I really wanted to win that one. The game itself was a bit scrappy but, again, we were the better side. I think France probably looked down their noses at us after the semi-final so it was good to get that one over the line.

Dan Lydiate was absolutely exceptional that day. He was absolutely everywhere, chopping down French attackers all over the pitch. It has to be his best performance in a Wales shirt, or at least in the top three. That was my second Grand Slam and it was hugely important to me. You're remembered for the amount of trophies and Grand Slams you win. My thinking was that if you want to be in the same conversation as the great Gareth Edwards then you have to win Grand Slams.

People always talk about how many Grand Slams Rafa Nadal has won, how many majors Tiger Woods has won – it's all about winning the big trophies. Otherwise, you're no different to anyone else. After the match we were at the function and because all the boys had gone off to meet their girlfriends or their families, I felt like we hadn't really had a moment together, as a squad, to enjoy it all. I went over to Warby and said: "We've done something amazing here, we need to at least get together for a drink, let's get everyone to the bar, just the boys." We'd just won a Grand Slam and I think it's important to make sure you enjoy those moments because you'll never get them back and they pass you by in the blink of an eye.

Even if it's just standing next to each other, talking about what your mates did during the game, the tackle they made, the try they scored and all that stuff. That was the old school in me coming through. It's from my days with Whitland. Chatting in the bar after games was one of the highlights of the day because that's where you really strengthen your relationships with team-mates, get to know each other's personalities and understand each other more. I loved listening to their stories and telling my own. It's such an important part of rugby and any other walk of life, really. So we all went and had a drink at the bar together. Eventually I invited the French boys over and it wasn't awkward at all, they joined in and we all started singing songs together.

I was trying to convince Dimitri Szarzewski to sing Hymne de la Peña Baiona – the Bayonne song – despite the fact he never played for the club. That is such a fond memory for me. I started every game in that campaign with Priestland at fly-half and we had a good relationship on and off the field. He was super talented, very skilful. I played inside him on his first-ever start for Wales, which was in a pre-World Cup match at Twickenham.

Winning Again

After the anthems we had a bit of a chat and I just told him to enjoy the occasion, that he deserved to be there and that he was a class player. He went on to play very well at the Rugby World Cup and was very calm around that time, especially for such a young bloke. He played with a freedom but things changed a little bit and there was enormous pressure placed on his shoulders. A few years later in a game against Australia in Cardiff he replaced Dan Biggar and some fans booed as he came onto the field. That was out of order. He was treated badly and nobody deserves that. I've got a lot of time for Rhys. He's come through all that now and has been playing some brilliant stuff in the last few years, proving his doubters wrong.

Anyway, there was much to celebrate after that Grand Slam because we'd put a few things right after the World Cup and reacted in the right manner. The following day a bunch of us went out in Cowbridge to keep the party going and the *Wales on Sunday* newspaper had given me a five out of 10 in the ratings. The boys had got hold of a copy and were waving it in my face. I didn't mind getting stick in the press.

My approach to that was that one day nobody would want to talk about me so I just got on with it. I had such a strong mindset at that time, so much confidence in what I was bringing to the team, that I couldn't have cared less about the criticism. Everyone gets it sometimes, Warby got it quite a bit around then, but I would happily have taken the blame for every defeat or every bad performance because I was able to just shrug it off and get on with it. However, all that being said, how can you get a five out of 10 after winning a Grand Slam? Nonsense.

The day after all the celebrations I had to travel back to Bayonne and, in all truth, I hadn't slept much and was still feeling pretty merry from the night before. I was bored stiff in a car on the way up to London to catch my flight and I was just scrolling on Twitter only to notice a tweet that had been sent by a journalist named Isabelle Ithurburu, who was married to the head coach of Stade Francais at the time.

I can't explain why I did what I did next but I wasn't thinking straight and replied to her Tweet, which was completely unrelated, saying: "Allez Bayonne! Best team in France! #areyousingle" She promptly replied: "No, married and very happy."

Still under the influence, I decided to respond with: "Are you sure? #77caps" accompanied by an old picture of me wearing nothing but a towel. I wasn't actually trying to come on to her, I was just having a laugh. That caused a bit of a stir. I was on the cover of magazines, opposition players would run past me and say: "Are you sure?" And the boys thought it was hilarious. When I walked back into the Bayonne dressing room for the first time, the place absolutely erupted. The boys were going mental, not because I'd won the Grand Slam but because of this exchange on Twitter. Fortunately she saw the funny side of it as well.

A few years later they broke up and I messaged her to say that I hoped her ex-husband knew I was only joking. She replied saying that it was all good and she thought it was funny too. Then I thought to myself: 'We seem to be on good terms here.' So I decided to ask if she fancied going for a drink, to which she promptly replied: "No." And that was that. Fair enough.

The summer tour that year was rough. We went down to Australia and lost all three Test matches by a combined 11 points. They kicked late penalties in both the second and third matches to win the game. It was brutal. What you have to give Gats credit for, though, is that the year before a Lions tour, Wales would always be the team touring that country.

The boys went to South Africa in 2008 but I missed out through injury, we went to Australia in 2012 and then they went to New Zealand in 2016. People always used to focus on the fact that they could get a head start on things from a logistical standpoint. We could almost scope out all the hotels and training facilities and that would be reported back to Gats, who was on his sabbatical ahead of the Lions tour by this point. Also the fact that Howley, who was attack coach, could also get a close-up look at the opposition was regularly talked about. What went under the radar a little bit is that I think the Welsh players got an advantage from going out there the year before as well because it gave us a chance to get used to the crowds, the conditions, the atmospheres and, of course, the opposition. That was very clever of Gats.

After the second Test I got a bit annoyed. Richard Hibbard had come off the bench and given away the penalty that resulted in us losing the game. Shit happens, he didn't mean to do it, we move on. But Howley comes up to me that evening and says: "Some of the boys don't think Hibbs should play for Wales again after that penalty, what do you reckon?" Now I don't know if he was being truthful or if he was just testing my character but I hope it was the latter because that's a stinking attitude. I told Howley straight: "Anyone saying that he should never play for Wales again because that's a disgrace." You have to win as a team and lose as a team. Hibbs went on to become a bit of a cult hero and was outstanding on the Lions tour the following year.

We made a bit of a fuss about the way we failed to close that game out. We all watched the last 10 minutes back and it was absolutely brutal but all that did was create more tension. The impact of this exercise was the total opposite of what the coaches intended. We basically sat there and watched all our mistakes back. All that did was reinforce negative thoughts.

It was all well and good watching it back from a tactical standpoint but, really, we were just reviewing how we'd blown it in the final moments. What we really needed to be doing there was having conversations about the psychological side of things and addressing why we weren't able to execute properly under that particular pressure. I don't think we really addressed the issue we seemed to be having because we lost the final Test in fairly similar circumstances.

On that occasion, Berrick Barnes kicked a penalty in the last 10 minutes and we lost by a point. It was our seventh defeat in a row against Australia. We had the ability to beat Australia but around this time we struggled to finish off games, particularly against Southern Hemisphere, sides and that was all mental as far as I'm concerned. We weren't equipped with the tools to deal with the pressure and there are many ways we could have gone about it. Of course, you only learn these things as you become more experienced but it's just things like writing down goals, becoming comfortable with your weaknesses so that you can address them, using the losses to drive you on. It was a mental block and Wales' losing run against the Wallabies extended to 13 matches until they finally won in 2018.

We were slow out of the blocks in the 2013 Six Nations. We had a tendency to play poorly in the first game of campaigns and it was because the step up from regional level to international level is just so big. Gats always wanted around 42 minutes of ball-in-play time, which is very high. He wanted us to run teams off the pitch, tire them out and then take advantage in the final 20 minutes.

Winning Again

The ball-in-play time was nowhere near that figure at regional level, so the physical demands were completely different. What frustrated me a bit was Gats and all the coaches knew this, the press always used to bring up the fact that we were slow starters, but we never really addressed it effectively. They used to beast us with fitness sessions but we were lacking that match intensity. There is no substitute for playing. I'd have much rather we play a flat-out in-house game in the fortnight before the first match of a campaign just to get us up to speed with the level of physical exertion required.

Yes you run the risk of injuries but that is a hazard of the job and that risk will always be there. Gatland wasn't involved in this campaign at all because he was on his sabbatical with the Lions. He never took charge of a training session or anything. But Howley was well aware of our slow starts as well.

Anyway, this particular defeat to Ireland came down to our preparation. I never felt threatened by Ireland during my time with Wales. I felt like we had more skilful players, more threats and were better defensively. But it's not always about that. Whenever we lost to them I always felt it was because we got our preparation wrong and this was another one of those occasions. We were terrible and they took a 30-3 lead after 43 minutes. We were getting pumped. Absolutely pumped. I take responsibility for their second try. We were just inside our own half and it felt like we were in No Man's Land. We didn't know whether to attack or kick, there was no real structure, just ambiguity. I dithered around with the pass and Dan Biggar got charged down which led to Cian Healy scoring. I should have probably taken control and kicked it away myself. Dan might have taken all day to kick it but that's a different story!

We fought back well to score three tries and make it look respectable but it wasn't a good performance and we all knew it. If you assess that performance alongside the one we put in on the last day of the tournament against England, we look like two different teams. I kept my head down that night and went to my brother's house. I wanted to have a few beers but wanted it behind closed doors so I didn't have the stress of a night out, with camera phones lurking around every corner. Plus it wouldn't have been a great look if I'd been spotted out in Cardiff after that performance so I decided to try and lay low.

I ended up having a few too many beers and it got to the point where I felt like I was going to be sick. Panic stations. The toilet in his house was upstairs but I wasn't confident of making it in time so I legged it out the front of his house, in the middle of Penarth, and spewed my guts up on the street. The next day is when the paranoia set in: 'What if someone saw me? What if they took a picture?' Those are the kind of things you end up worrying about when you're in the public eye. You feel like everyone is watching you all the time. Fortunately, there were no camera phones around this time otherwise I'd probably have been on the front of the following day's newspaper... again.

After the game I went through the process of taking responsibility and blaming myself for the defeat, like I always did. The coaches weren't really aware of this because it was all internal, so I largely kept it to myself. On the outside I probably gave off the impression that I didn't care but the reality was that I cared more than anyone. I took that defeat hard.

After the kick up the arse from the Irish, I was ready to fly into the French, who were next up. We'd lost eight games in a row since the 2012 Six Nations – a run that included defeats to Ireland, New Zealand, Samoa, Argentina and four at the hands of Australia – and we hadn't won in Paris for eight years. So they were having it. It wasn't a classic for the neutral and we cancelled each other out a little bit but I actually deem it one of my best performances in a Wales jersey. I kicked really well, which is so important away from home, I made a few breaks, I was aggressive, big, strong, dynamic – all the buzzwords the coaches used to drill into me. We were busting our balls, getting around the corner and executing this game plan but everyone was knackered. It was a real arm wrestle and we were drawing 3-3 at half time. I get into the dressing room and I'm absolutely blowing out of my arse.

What I need in that situation is two or three minutes to just bring the heart rate down and relax. But as soon as my backside touches the bloody bench in the dressing room, Howley's in my ear trying to hit me with instructions. There's usually a policy at half-time where players have two minutes to themselves to calm down and gather their emotions and thoughts. But Rob's into me straight away: "Make sure we keep sticking to the game plan, get the forwards around the corner because we're stretchi-." I cut him off.

"Rob, please, go away for two minutes will you?" I said. It was the last thing I needed at that moment and, besides, I had a better feel for how the game was going and the flow of it because I was out in the middle, I knew the game plan so it was all good. I took the kick-off in my 22 and made this 60-metre break right up the middle of the Stade de France, one of my greatest ever breaks.

I think the BBC must have deleted it from their archives because I haven't seen it since! I then bounced French fly-half Freddie Michalak, the smallest guy on the field. He had it! There were 80,000 home fans baying for my head. I was loving it. I felt like I'd set the tone of the second half, did what was expected of me in the remainder of my time on the field and I was feeling pretty good about myself. The confidence was back. The game is famous for being the day that George North's dad ran on the field to celebrate with him after he scored a try in the 71st minute to put us ahead. It was a huge win for the group and a huge win for Howley. Everyone was under pressure because of the losing streak we were on and it was a big relief to end that. Howley had been getting some real stick in the press for the defeats, people were saying that we were struggling because Gats, who was away with the Lions, wasn't there and things like that.

Really, though, the players had to take responsibility for the run we were on. Either way, it was great to be back winning again. We'd had a few in the post-match function and everyone was feeling good. As I got back on the bus, Howley was sat at the front, so I decided to grab him a headlock and say: "Well done Howlers, you're still in a job!" He took it well, it was just banter. But it didn't stop there. We had a couple of beers that night and I was still a bit merry coming down for breakfast in the morning. Howley was on the same table as me and I was giving him shit because he'd replaced me after 70 minutes: "Well done Howlers, took off your star player, I was having a storming game… great coach you are!" Andrew Coombs, who was in his first campaign, was sat next to me thinking: 'What the hell is going on here?' It was banter but I was half serious as well, to be honest.

Again, I think he took it well. But I was only to make those sorts of comments and have a bit of fun because we were winning. I would never take that tone if we'd lost. And if I'd made those comments somewhere near the end of my career they'd have probably booted me out of the squad! But it was good for morale and I kept delivering on the pitch so there was no harm in it. The weather was horrendous in Rome for the next match up against Italy but we got over the line with a good showing. We won the game 26-9 and ended up in some nightclub in Rome.

I never really liked clubbing but nobody was really grabbing the bull by the horns and everyone was just generally milling around in their own little groups, not really doing anything. So I seized the initiative and bought this big bottle of vodka to try and get the boys going a bit. I was a senior guy at this point and felt it was my duty! Dan Biggar tried stopping me and saying: "Mike don't do that, we'll all chip in now!" But I dismissed him with: "No, no, I've been making money a lot longer than you boys so I'll buy this!" That racked up a fair bit. Me and Dan always joke about that to this day. I've got a lot of time for Dan. We played a lot of rugby together at the Ospreys, where we won the league, and with Wales. He's an incredible guy and an absolute winner, the sort of bloke you want alongside you when you take the field. But away from the pitch he's a great laugh too.

Things got interesting that night when Romain Poite, who refereed the match, came into the club. It was carnage. Some of the boys had dragged him over to our little section and suddenly they're ripping his top off and swinging him around by his arms and legs in the middle of this club! I don't know why nobody stopped to think that this probably wasn't the best idea but he was loving it! It was all fun and games but the next morning I was flying back to France to link up with Bayonne during the fallow week while the rest of the boys flew back to Wales.

Me and Romain ended up on the same flight back and I'm walking towards him in the airport, not quite sure how this is going to go. I wave very sheepishly and muster a quiet: "Ahh bonjour. Ça va?" He laughed and said: "Mike, Mike – you boys are crazy eh?" I just chuckled back and went to find a quiet corner of the departure lounge to hide in. Next up we ground out a victory over Scotland at Murrayfield and by now I think my game was evolving. I was maturing into a player that understood what patience meant, which wasn't exactly a strong suit of mine back in the day. Halfpenny kicked seven penalties that day, it was that kind of game. But if that was the way we had to win it, then so be it.

That game wasn't about trying to score every time we touched the ball, it was about putting us in the right areas of the field to just build pressure and win penalties. During this Six Nations I was far more comfortable with my role, I was happy to just be the one controlling games and for other people to be scoring. I was hitting a real peak. After the game I was sat in the changing room at Murrayfield and the thought of going out that night had not even entered my head, given how much was riding on the game the following week, because we could still win the tournament. To my surprise, Howley made the call pretty early that we could go out but there would be a curfew. All the players had to be back in the hotel by midnight. I was genuinely shocked, I was sat there thinking: 'Crikey, that's a big call.' So we get back to the hotel after the post-match function and he pulls us into a room to fire a final warning: "If there's any nonsense tonight boys, you're not playing next week." All this sort of stuff. But, in a room full of about 25 players, he's looking straight at me as he says it. That pissed me off. Anyway, we go out, no dramas and we're back in the hotel for 11:30pm. So a few of us had a quiet beer in my room. I was sharing with James Hook and Taulupe Faletau was there. So we had a beer and we were feeling a bit peckish so we had some burgers delivered on room service. The following morning I'm down in reception on time, fresh-faced, ready to go, paid my room bill and now I'm waiting to board the bus to the airport. Here comes Howley, who has gone to the reception to get a copy of the bill and he's waving it in my face: "Who had the burgers last night?" He says.

I reply: "Burgers? What are you on about? Are you serious here?"

To which he says: "Yeah, I want to know." This carries on as we get onto the coach and then when I board the flight, he's sat at the front and says: "Who was in your room last night?"

Sticking to my guns, I said: "Listen, I was hungry and I was thirsty, I'm not telling you who was in the room. End of."

Next thing Paul James comes up to me, who looks after the fines, and says Howley wants me to pay a £250 fine. I got on well with Paul and told him: "Paul, I'm not paying that, it's a fucking joke." So that wound me up before the build-up to England had even started!

I was fired up even more when I got back to my house that afternoon. A sports psychologist would probably tell you I was getting my mental preparation wrong, getting excited a little bit too early, but I couldn't help it. The day after we beat Scotland, after the Howley interrogation, I was back home watching the Italy v England match on the TV. With about 15 minutes to go in the game, the commentators were already saying things like: "England will be going down to Cardiff with their sights set on a Grand Slam next week." I was sat there thinking to myself: 'You arrogant bastards.'

England had played pretty poorly in the match, they hadn't scored a try and were winning by seven points thanks to six penalties from Toby Flood. Italy still had a great chance of winning at that point so that wound me up. I was bouncing off the walls in my living room. England held on to win the game 18-11 but we still had a chance of winning the title because they'd played very average rugby in Rome.

If they'd blown Italy away by 40 points, we'd have had no chance of winning the title. As things landed, we needed to beat them by eight points in Cardiff on the final weekend to deny them a Grand Slam and win the title ourselves. I couldn't wait for Monday.

Every week I'd search for something that annoyed me about the opposition, that would spark me into life. Those commentators had given me the spark I needed. I was focused and riled up. The night before the game I was sitting around with a few of the boys and I told them we were going to win because we had Kiwi Steve Walsh refereeing the match. Mr Walsh liked to go out and enjoy himself as much as the next guy so I said to the boys: "There's no way he's going to referee a game that we lose because he'll go out for a couple of pints in Cardiff and have a shit night."

Obviously I was joking but I just wanted to show the boys I was confident. If you're surrounded by confident people, that rubs off on you and I was just trying to get into the boys' heads really. But let's face it, it wasn't Steve Walsh's fault England lost that game. We were outstanding. Anyone who played in that match will remember the anthem before the game for the rest of their lives. It's always special to play at the Millennium Stadium but I've never experienced anything like the wall of noise that greeted us onto the pitch that day.

Before games, the away side always takes the field first before the anthems and, that day, we kept England waiting. I don't remember being told it was pre-planned but they were out there a good few minutes before we turned up. They were left to just stand there in the dark because the stadium lights had been turned down ready for our arrival. Meanwhile, the crowd was going absolutely mental. They were completely shell-shocked by it. Did it make a difference?

Well, put it this way, two years later there was a bit of an incident in the tunnel before the match because they refused to take the field before we did. It was like a Mexican stand-off. Those little one percents and how you feel before matches are so important. Anyway, back to 2013. I knew it was so important to get the crowd going early on because it would get us up for it and influence the referee. So I took a quick tap the first chance I got and it worked. As I took the ball into contact, though, I got knocked in the head. I wasn't dazed or anything but it just sharpened my focus, for some reason. I wasn't worried about the points difference, it was just a laser focus on the next job and trying to build a score to win the match.

They just couldn't live with us. Me and Dan controlled things nicely, we got George on the ball a lot, the pack were absolutely outstanding and we all remember the tries. Personally, I felt like I was close to my form in 2011. I made more tackles than any other Welshman in that match and made the most metres. I don't know how the hell I didn't win man of the match to be honest but I suppose Justin Tipuric played alright! The last 20 minutes of that game were unbelievable because everyone in the ground knew we'd won the Six Nations, stuffed England and dashed their dreams of a Grand Slam. Could it be any more perfect? It's not very often you can enjoy the last quarter of a game like that against England.

A few of the boys were already planning where we were going on the night out before the game had even finished but it was great to be able to just stop and take the whole moment in. It was an unbelievable experience. Even after that match I was still wound up about the English commentary on the Italy game six days earlier. I was shaking hands with their players one-by-one thinking: 'Have that! Thanks for coming! Have that!' But I suppose it wasn't their fault. I just wanted a reason to dislike them because it got me going. I was still so pumped up. I could have played another 80 minutes. I was angry, aggressive. Next thing, I'm doing a live interview with S4C – a Welsh language TV channel – pretty soon after the match. These are always a bit dangerous as a player because your blood is still running hot and it's easy to say the wrong thing. I, of course, was still pumped up and in Welsh I finished one answer by basically saying: "And they can piss off back over the bridge now." I did apologise as soon as I said it but that's how pumped I was.

After we'd had the trophy presented and done the lap of honour, we're all back in the changing room and these are special moments too because it's the first time you're in private with your team-mates and you can really let your hair down. We all gather and just before Howley is about to speak, I jump in with: "Right boys, hands up, who had the burgers last week?"

It gave the boys a laugh. Occasionally after matches, Prince William will also come down to the changing room to meet the players. He's the Welsh Rugby Union's patron so he came down from time to time and this was one such occasion. I was on cloud nine at the time so when he came around to me, with a cheeky grin on my face, I said: "When you get the big job now, you've got to make me a Sir, alright?"

To which he replied: "Yeah, yeah okay!" Let's hope he doesn't forget. Sir Mike has got a lovely ring to it. This wasn't the first time our paths had crossed. I first met Prince William at Boodles Boxing Ball in London in 2008. I was there with Lee Bryne and absolutely nobody knew us there. As a joke, I went up to a photographer and said: "Apparently Mike Phillips is in here tonight." And his response was: "Who?" Fair play, he did me there. Half way through the night, myself and Lee are minding our own business by the bar when some random guy approaches us and says: "He's seen you're here and Prince William will be coming up to chat to you in a moment." Sure enough, he came up to us shortly after and started having a chat and asked why we were there. My response was: "I'm just looking for a girl with a rich dad." Which gave him a laugh. Every time I met him after that he was always the same – engaged in what you're saying, asking questions, just brilliant.

Anyway, back to Cardiff. In the after-match function, Andy Farrell, who had been named as Lions defence coach by this point, came up to shake my hand and congratulated me on my performance. I could tell by his body language and the way he was that he was impressed by the defensive side of my game. It's always good to know that you've impressed a Lions coach.

We had a good night out in Tiger Tiger in Cardiff after that win but there were no real issues to come from it. Everyone just had a good time and celebrated the win.

That was a great group of players. We had such a good atmosphere in the camp for that Six Nations. Always singing on the bus and having a good time, just enjoying ourselves, and I think that's why we played some really good rugby. Mark Jones, the former winger who was cutting his teeth as a coach at this point, was in the camp to gain some experience and develop. His nickname is 'Boycey'. If we'd won and boys were flying, we'd used to have these silly chants on the bus where we'd pick out members of the backroom team and sing about them. So we'd pick out people like team doctor Geoff Davies and legendary physio Mark Davies – who everyone knows as 'Carcass' – and sing: "Carcass is a legend! Carcass is a legend! Na na na na, na na na na!" Then it's: "Geoff is on millions! Geoff is on millions! Na na na na, na na na na!" Then came the kicker: "Boycey is on nothing! Boycey is on nothing! Na na na na, na na na na!" The bus would crack up laughing and there would just be general banter flying around. Those are some of the best moments of your career, putting your body through hell for 80 minutes with your mates and then enjoying each other's company afterwards.

After our big night out, I was straight back to France because there were absolutely no days off as far as they were concerned over there. They were paying me and they do not give a damn about Wales at all. Fair enough. So whereas some of the boys who were playing at the regions could carry on going on the piss for a few days, I was back in training on Monday. A good example of that came later, when I was at Racing Metro.

After one international camp, we were straight back in on the Monday as per usual and I was stood next to Jamie Roberts, who'd travelled back with me the day before. Jamie approaches Laurent Travers, a man not likely to take shit from anyone, and says to him in his pigeon French: "Me, errr, no plaquage today?"

Which is basically Jamie saying he's not doing any contact in this session. I was loving it but had to bite my lip to stop myself laughing because I knew how it would go down. Travers obviously had none of it and we trained flat out. I think World Rugby need to really step in a little bit when it comes to this sort of stuff, though. I know the clubs pay the wages and all that but when you're seeing all the concussions and contact injuries in the game nowadays, I just think the players need a bit more care. There should be a mandatory rest period of a few days for all players after an international window.

But the rugby kept coming thick and fast. To be honest, though, I didn't care at the time. I was back on cloud nine, loving my rugby and enjoying life. With back-to-back Six Nations wins under the belt, the Lions tour was calling and I couldn't wait to pull on that jersey once again.

9

A Lion For Life

I was in a great place mentally heading into the 2013 Lions. Things had just snowballed throughout 2012 and 2013. I was ready to absolutely rip into the Wallabies and make up for what had happened in 2009. A lot was made about how a few of the Welsh boys played their way onto the Lions tour that year after our performances during the Six Nations. It was in the back of my mind that it was a Lions year, of course it was, but it really wasn't a big issue for me. In 2009, I was ticking off all my scrum-half rivals as I played against them, assessing whether I'd outplayed them and invariably the answer was yes. But in 2013 I wasn't even thinking about the likes of Ben Youngs, Conor Murray and Greig Laidlaw because I felt I was nailed on. I didn't give a moment's thought to how I'd played against my rivals. Why would I?

There was absolutely no doubt in my mind, in any shape or form, that I'd be on the Lions tour. Again, I hope this doesn't come across as arrogance, but I just had absolute belief in my ability at the time and I had every reason to feel that way. I'd played well on the '09 tour, battled injury in 2010, bossed the

2011 World Cup, won a Grand Slam in 2012 and then felt my form was good as we won the Six Nations in 2013.

There was also no doubt in my mind that I was Wales' No.1 scrum-half and that gave me the freedom to play well. Sometimes it's nice to have pressure on you for your spot but it's also good to know that you have ownership of the jersey and it can bring the best out of you in different ways. As I was heading onto the bus after beating England, I walked past a few of the boys who were speaking to the media and shouted back: "See you on the Lions tour boys!" Which gives you a good indication of how I felt we'd done.

When it was time to meet up in London, for some reason all the Welsh boys had a big 52-seater bus to travel up. There were a lot of us on that trip but not enough to warrant a 52-seater! There was a great vibe on the bus, though, and I gave the boys a little pep talk: "Right boys, let's stick together, don't speak to anyone else!" It was just banter and we were all in a really good headspace.

We spent a week training in Ireland before the tour. It was a really tough camp fitness-wise but I felt like a million dollars physically. When you first meet up with the Lions it's also important to get plenty of team bonding in as well because that's when you make genuine connections. During that week at Carton House I went out and got absolutely hammered with Paul O'Connell.

Every single member of the squad and management went out into Dublin, we hired out a bar and got wrecked and that was the night I told Gats he'd only got the Lions top job because of me. It was reminiscent of my comment to him after the England game in 2008 and, again, I think he kinda loved it. Anyway, it comes to the end of the night, me and Paul have been drinking buddies and we're both in a bit of a state.

It's my second tour, Paul's third and we're loving it. The bus comes to pick us up and we're all getting on. Now anyone who has played rugby at any level will know there is a hierarchy here. Experienced guys at the back, rookies at the front. It works like that in amateur rugby and it works like that with the Lions. Or at least it did when I was there. It was my second tour, I'd bossed the first one so I'm heading for the back few rows.

I was never going for the back row because even I knew that I wasn't quite worthy of that, I'm thinking one or two rows from the back. That's probably where I fit in. Imagine my surprise then, when I boarded the bus to see Owen Farrell – on his first Lions tour – and Stuart Hogg – not only a rookie but the youngest man on the trip – sat in the back row. I can't let this slide. So I go: "Hoggy! Who the hell are you? Never heard of you. Get your arse down the front."

Farrell, whose old man Andy was defence coach, had it next: "Faz, you're only here because your dad is coaching now fuck off down the front!"

Had I been a little brash? Maybe. But Paul came to defuse the situation with: "To be fair lads, he's only saying what we're all thinking."

Not long after the bus got going, though, we had to stop for Paul to get off and have a little moment. It was like being a kid again. But as I keep saying, those nights are important.

The next day at training I grabbed a ball and went to do a little warm-up. I did some lengths just passing the ball with Paul and then we stopped to do some stretching. We were both a little worse for wear and, after a big exhale, he says: "Jaysus Phillsy! I haven't been that drunk since I was 18."

Apparently it was my fault but I don't remember pinning him to the ground and forcing booze down his neck!

Before we arrived in Australia, we stopped off in Hong Kong to play a match against the Barbarians. It was all for the sponsors, really. When we got there, the Lions did this big gala dinner, which was very corporate and is the kind of thing they do to keep the backers happy. My mate just so happened to be at this dinner and someone asked Gatland about how to build a culture within a Lions team and get them to bond.

His reply was: "We basically get a room, put a load of beer in there and throw Mike Phillips in the middle." Which I loved to be honest. But then he was asked if any of the players had broken protocol in the first few weeks of camp and he says: "Yeah one guy has actually, we set a curfew for midnight and he strolled into the hotel at 2:00am with a bottle of champagne under one arm and a woman under the other. It was Mike Phillips and when I confronted him he said: 'Whatever Gats, I got you this job.'"

He said this in front of about 300 people and it was total bollocks! I did tell him that I'd got him the Lions job but it was in very different circumstances. I let it slide because it was fairly harmless but it was untrue and he was just playing on my reputation for the sake of a good story. It was one of those tales that he probably whipped out in his after-dinner speaking because it got a good reaction. Why let the truth get in the way of a good story?

About three days before the game against the Baabaas, the boys were given the green light to have a beer if they wanted to. It was pretty chilled out and you could basically do whatever you wanted. I knew I was starting so I did have my head on a little bit. I only had one or two beers because the game was literally around the corner. Andy Farrell came over to me and said: "Fair play Mike, I've already seen both sides of you on this tour and we're not even in Australia yet – tonight we've got serious Mike and I've seen the wild one!"

The traffic in Hong Kong was an absolute disaster and we were stuck in it for hours on the way to the ground for the game.

Apparently the guys who had gone ahead to set the dressing room up for us and stuff had reported back that traffic was fine and they got there in no time. So we left a little later than scheduled but hadn't considered the fact that we were going to be travelling in rush hour. We literally got to the stadium 30 minutes before kick-off, which was less than ideal.

Paul gave a really good pre-match team talk, as he always did, in the few minutes before we went out to face the Barbarians and mentioned me. We're all in the huddle and in the middle of his team talk he looks at me and says: "Phillsy, drive us around the fucking pitch now. I'll play for you all day, I swear to fucking God I will, so drive us around the fucking pitch."

And that was the last thing he said before we went out onto the pitch. When someone of his standing in the game says something like that to you, it means a hell of a lot. He was the best captain I ever had. He ticked every single box. He was the ultimate professional but he could switch off, he's got a great sense of humour and I knew I had his respect.

The heat and humidity was horrendous for that game in Hong Kong, some of the toughest conditions I think any of us had played in. They had massive fans on the side of the pitch to try and keep the players cool but it didn't do much, to be honest. I was very happy with my performance in general that night but there was a problem.

Around the half-hour mark I shrug off Sergio Parisse, break through and score a try. As I'm on my way to the line, my old Bayonne team-mate Joe Rokocoko comes steaming across to make a cover tackle. He takes me down pretty hard but I still manage to stretch out and score. I get up and straight away it's apparent that something's not right with my knee. I'm not in any great pain but it feels unstable. I played on but I knew straight away there was an issue.

Just after I scored the try I had a run-in with Neil Jenkins, who was bringing the water on and delivering messages from the coaches box. I love Jenks and we've got a great relationship. We used to always have silly little ding-dongs though. It was never nasty and we always had a laugh about it but we had words every now and then. Being one of the greatest kickers of all time, naturally, he was a great kicking coach and he still has that role with Wales now.

He'd always run on with the water bottles during games and shout at me for one reason or another: "Mike! Sort your box kicks out!" Was one of his favourites. I'd be all in a huff after he criticised my kicking because it's stating the obvious, I know when I've kicked poorly. I'd be there thinking: 'Come on Neil, give me something else.' He'd then try and give me a water bottle in the huddle and I'd turn away and throw my hand up, all dismissive as if I didn't want any. But then I'd sneak around behind him and grab one out of the bottle carrier without him noticing. So childish! To be fair, though, he also always praised me when my kicking was on point or if I'd nailed a box kick from a tight angle. He's been kicking coach with the Lions a number of times as well and he was there in 2013. After my try, the humidity was taking its toll. All the boys were blowing. It was savage.

Now, I'm all about efficiency, as we explored during my barney with Rob Howley in 2009. I always used to stand on the right hand side of the field for kick-off returns and I would always shout to the centre on the other side of the field to play scrum-half for the first phase if the ball went over there. My thinking was you could have Usain Bolt at scrum-half but it's still going to take a while for him to get over to the breakdown, so why wait? If our centre can't pass the ball out of a ruck then we've got big problems. I was blowing out of my arse, plus I knew I had a problem with my knee.

The kick-off went to the other side of the field, I watched the ball and I just could not move. Absolutely fucked. So I told the centre on the far side of the field to play scrum-half. At the next break in play, Jenks comes running on with his water and shouts at me: "Mike! Get to the breakdown!" I was in a bit of a tizz at this point and couldn't think fast enough about what to say back so just went with: "It's not my job!" To which Jenks, looking fairly bemused, quite rightly replied: "Mike! You're the fucking scrum-half!" He had a point.

We laughed our heads off after the game about it. Jenks was one of my heroes growing up – I was at Wembley in 1999 when he kicked the winning conversion against England – and I got to play a little bit with him at the very start of my Welsh career. I played with him on my debut and I always remind him about the fact I put him through a gap. I also played inside him on his last-ever game for Wales, which was a really special experience.

Anyway, back to Hong Kong. I scored again in the second half and I spotted Roks coming across again but this time he wasn't able to get near me so I pointed to where I was going to dive because that's what he always used to do. It was the only time in my career that I was able to get one over on him so I wasn't going to miss that chance! Every time I'd played against him before – Sevens, Wales under-21s and the senior team – he'd cut us to pieces.

I was pleased to win man of the match. The night before the game I got into the lift at the hotel with a woman who was working for the Lions and she had a massive magnum of champagne with her, which caught my eye. So I asked: "What's that all about?" And she explained that it was for the player that won man of the match in the game.

Me being me, I replied: "You might as well give me that now then." I saw her again the day after the game and I just shrugged my shoulders and laughed: "See, I told you!"

I might have looked like the same old Mike, cracking jokes the day after the game, but in the back of my mind I knew something wasn't right. As a player, you know your body. You know the difference between something that you can run off and something that's a genuine problem. Every time I have had that sort of pain, it required an operation. I felt like it could go at any moment. The thought of training concerned me because I was worried it would go and put me out of the tour.

Although, I barely trained at all for the first few weeks in Australia. We arrived in Perth the following day and by the time we got there my knee was like a balloon. I was lying on the treatment table and all the physios were huddled in the corner having a quiet conversation, obviously trying to stop me from hearing what they were saying. I wasn't getting good vibes at all. We gave it a few days to settle down but I wasn't taking part in training, I was icing my knee constantly. I was on the back foot straight away. It was hell. I wasn't taking part in training, I wasn't out there on the field with the boys and that's what gives you confidence when it comes to the big matches, knowing that you've done all the training and hard work.

I missed the first two games in Australia, which really dented my confidence. I was at my best when I was able to get a run of games. That's when I felt unstoppable but I was stuck in the stands watching the boys go out and win. I didn't really feel like

I was contributing at all. I wasn't able to go out and have a beer with the boys because alcohol would have hampered my recovery so I couldn't get to know the boys particularly well either. I was putting a brave face on but I was in a really dark place.

In a rugby environment, it was the lowest I'd ever been. We didn't have a sports psychologist with us on that tour and I felt like I really needed someone to talk to. I was pissed off with everything but mainly myself because I barely ever got injured and somehow felt like it was my own fault that this had happened at just the wrong time. I didn't know how to handle the situation that I was going through. Professional athletes are perfectionists and if one little thing is off then it has a big impact. I knew everything wasn't perfect and that was a real problem.

It pissed me off that Gats never came and had a chat with me during this time. I was his No.1 scrum-half heading into the trip, we'd always had a good relationship up until this point and I feel like he could have just come and spoken to me, even if it was just to gauge where my head was at. I think this is where our relationship started to take a turn for the worst. He was distancing himself from me a little bit and I didn't get it. It's an old school way of coaching.

You've got to be communicating with players, asking them questions – especially when they're struggling. I was in a really negative frame of mind and that made me question why nobody was really checking in on me. Don't get me wrong, the physios were great and they did a hell of a job to get me back out there, but I needed more support.

There was just this waterfall of doubt that was cascading down over me and I started questioning other things in my life. One night something popped up on my phone that Aimee, my ex, had been photographed with some new bloke. Suddenly I'm wondering if I did the right thing by ending that. Why was I thinking like that? I knew I was happy to move on but because I was in a dark place I started second guessing myself. It wasn't great.

When I did get out on the field, I refused to let them strap my knee up. I hated strapping. If they did one, I'd have wanted them to do the other one. I felt like it was quite restricting and it was a mental thing for me as well. I also didn't want the opposition knowing that there was a weakness.

My first appearance in Australia was against the Combined Country XV in Newcastle. They were a side made up of fringe professionals and amateur rugby players and we thumped them 64-0. It was a pretty straightforward night and I got to stretch my legs for the first time, which was nice but it wasn't the most enthralling game to be involved in.

The game is mainly remembered for a young Stuart Hogg stepping in and playing fly-half as opposed to his usual position at full-back. Hoggy did brilliantly and got man of the match that night but he was still relatively fresh-faced back then.

The next game was against the Waratahs four days later. This was going to be one week out from the first Test and it was largely expected that Gats would pick something close to his Test side to give us a runout together and then plenty of recovery before facing the Wallabies. I was sitting in the team room before the side was announced to face the Waratahs. Hoggy sits next to me and says: "Oh, I don't think I'm going to be playing in this game because I've just played back-to-back games."

Back then I didn't really know him very well and I looked at him thinking: 'No mate, this is the big boy shit now. You're here to play against the midweek teams!' All jokes aside, I was also thinking: 'Fair play, he's obviously got the right attitude, a brilliant mindset.' I admired the way he was approaching things at such a young age and it's no surprise to me that he's gone on to become an outstanding rugby player and has achieved a hell of a lot.

At some point on the tour the boys decided to fine me for wearing the wrong clothes. I'm not even sure it was a legit fine but I think they just wanted to get me for something because I hadn't been going out. If you got fined you had to roll a dice and each number corresponded to a fine. It was things like; make your own way home from training or call your club coach and explain why you should be captain next season.

I was bricking it about that. Can you imagine me having to ring Bayonne and start explaining why I should be captain? A few of the boys did have to do that. There's a video of Simon Zebo doing the rounds online and it was absolutely hilarious.

Anyway, my fine ended up being that I had to dance for one minute with no music. Myself, Dan Lydiate and Hoggy had to do it at an airport. I was absolutely bricking myself. All the squad were huddled around and I hated it.

It was more embarrassing for me than any of the other fines would have been. I can't dance and I was also extremely low on confidence anyway because of everything that went wrong. You'd never guess this if you watch the Lions DVD because all you see is me smiling and having a good time. Just goes to show that you never know what's going on beneath the surface. I decided to try and be funny and went for the old David Brent dance from The Office. It was a case of making a fool of yourself and moving on.

The 2009 tour to South Africa was a massive stride forward for me because I'd announced myself to the world and proved that I belonged at the top level. But the one thing I didn't get out of that tour, of course, was the series victory. So the tour to Australia was huge, absolutely massive for me. I knew that the Wallabies were there for the taking, I knew we were going to win and I was desperate to be part of it.

To put my name on that plaque for future Lions scrum-halves to look at when they were getting ready to wear the jersey. That meant everything to me and I was determined to make it happen. Despite my injury, I was still pretty confident of playing in the first Test because you get a feel for these things. If you're playing in the Saturday team in the build-up to the Test series, there's a good chance you're going to be picked in the first Test and that's what was happening with me.

However, one of my biggest regrets is playing in that Test match. I felt like the team needed me and that, even if I wasn't at my best, I was still better than anyone else. That was my mentality. But I should have pulled myself out.

If you ever watch footage of the first Test you can tell there is something wrong with me during the anthems. Look at my body language ahead of the 2009 series. My chest is out, my head is up and I'm ready to kill someone. During the anthems in 2013, my posture is slumped, my head is down and my foot is hanging off the floor to take the weight off my injured leg. All I'm thinking about, before one of the biggest games of my life, is my knee. I'm not thinking about Will Genia or the game plan, I vividly remember thinking to myself: 'If I can just get through this then I can get through anything.' Was that brave or was it stupid? I don't know. It winds me up to this day that I wasn't able to put my best foot forward on that tour.

Looking back I should have put my hand up and said I wasn't right but who in their right mind is going to give up their chance of playing for the Lions? I was desperate to make history. Sometimes players need to be saved from themselves and this is probably one of those moments. The coaches must have seen that I wasn't performing to my ability, they were getting reports from the physios telling them about my knee. They should have pulled me up on it. I shouldn't have played in that match.

If you need any evidence of that, look at Australia's first try. Genia takes a quick tap, turns me inside out and then runs away from me before sending Israel Folau over to score. I couldn't run properly. I wasn't myself. I was a completely different player to the one that had finished the Six Nations earlier that year. It still breaks me.

I was gutted after the first Test because I thought I played terribly. I went straight back to the hotel and watched the game back. That's how paranoid I was. It felt like everything I'd done was the wrong thing. I felt sluggish. As I watched it back in the hotel, I remember thinking that I hadn't actually done as badly as I first thought but I knew I was only operating at about 60 percent. I wasn't able to do the things I usually could and that frustrated me. I wasn't as powerful or as sharp as I normally am. The main thing, though, was that we won 23-21. George North and Alex Cuthbert scored two absolute worldies and Leigh Halfpenny kicked us to victory. The Aussies had a chance with the last kick of the game but Kurtley Beale slipped as he went to strike the ball and missed. A slice of fortune? Perhaps, but you need that sometimes.

In the week leading up to the second Test, me and Rob Howley crossed paths in the hotel corridor. He told me that I wasn't going to be in the side. I made the point that it was a huge game and that I wanted to be involved. I thought we were about to win the Test series and felt like they were denying me the chance of being involved. He said the coaches knew I was carrying an injury and told me to just get myself right for the third Test.

I didn't argue with the decision but that didn't mean I approved. My ego was fighting it a little bit because I wanted to be out there but deep down I saw where they were coming from.

Paul O'Connell had fractured his arm in two places towards the end of the first Test. His tour was over. So neither of us were involved in Melbourne and we were sitting next to each other on the bus on the way to watch the boys play.

As we were driving to the stadium we were looking out at the fans and they were all chanting, holding their pints, loving life as we drove past them. He said something like: "Look at all these guys enjoying themselves." We had a conversation about how much pressure we are under sometimes as players and how nice it would be to not have that and be out there with the fans with no stress. How good would it be to just be there to enjoy the entertainment and support the team? It went to show that nobody is immune to pressure.

Paul is one of the greatest players of his generation and he felt it too. Sometimes you have that vulnerability as players but playing professional sport also gives you an unimaginable high. You have to look at that pressure as a privilege because you can't replicate the feeling of being out there with a whole country – our sometimes four countries – behind you. Then the euphoria you get from winning – there's nothing like it. That's why you dedicate your life to it.

I didn't enjoy watching the second Test at all. Ben Youngs started and if he had played well there is not a doubt in my mind he'd have started the third Test. I like Ben, he's a great guy, but he made a few errors that night and it worked in my favour.

The game itself was tense throughout and it was mainly Christian Leali'ifano and Leigh Halfpenny trading penalties for the majority of things until Adam Ashley-Cooper scored late on. Halfers had a kick to win it from inside his own half in the last minute but it fell just short. He was completely distraught afterwards. Personally, my emotions were all over the place as well. That whole weekend was a bit of a nightmare.

As a non-playing member of the squad, it's not really your place to say too much in that situation but we walked down to the changing rooms and went around tapping boys on the head. There was a lot of disappointment around but it motivated me to make sure I was part of the final Test because it was all to play for.

After the second Test, Gats decided to take the squad to Noosa, which is a beautiful resort area on the Sunshine Coast in Queensland. The whole idea was just to give everyone on the tour a chance to relax and recharge the batteries. It was a good idea really because I think everyone needs that opportunity to just switch off, especially after such an intense few weeks. The boys were allowed out on the piss but, again, I didn't go with them.

That was really tough. They were going off and doing different activities during the day as well but I was just stuck in the hotel, icing my knee. I was with the physios all day every day. I really wasn't enjoying things at this point but I felt that if I could salvage something from the tour, then it would be playing and winning in the final Test, becoming a winning Lion. That was all I had driving me at this point.

Any time you tour with the Lions it's a special experience and a large part of that is the fans. Lions supporters are unbelievable. They travel in their thousands, sing all the songs and really make it feel like a home game on certain occasions. The tour is nothing without the supporters. I felt sorry for the Lions boys that toured in 2021 with no fans in the stadium. Of course, safety must come first and I totally understand why fans weren't allowed into the grounds, but it was tough not to feel for the players. This is the pinnacle of their careers. The atmosphere looked flat, the rugby wasn't fantastic and there were no standout moments, like when George North lifted Israel Folau up in 2013, or when the Lions scored that unbelievable try against New Zealand in 2017.

It all felt a little bit weird for me and I'm sure it did for them too. Supporters add so much to the occasion, they create that pressure, that edge. When you're in a full house, you know you have to perform and I'd have probably struggled to play well in empty stadiums because I thrived on that. The fans make those Lions trips and it hit me in the last week of the trip to Australia. I was out with my parents having a bit of down time and there were just red jerseys everywhere. I was getting recognised and a few fans were coming up to me for pictures. So you'd have a bit of a chat, take a picture and then move on.

My mother was so funny with it all because she wasn't really used to it. She started giving me a lecture: "Michael, why don't you talk to them a bit more?" And I had to say to her: "Mam, there are about 200 Lions fans around, it'll take us all day to get down the street!" She is the kind of person who, if someone comes up, she wants to start a conversation and starts asking where they're from and all this. I think she was blown away that she was meeting Welsh people in Australia! My mother, bless her, used to go through it a bit whenever I played.

She used to get so nervous, sometimes she couldn't watch and she'd have to go for a walk. I'd often speak to her after we found out the team and tell her I was playing. Sometimes she'd say: "Oh, why don't you let someone else play." As if I was picking the team! She also used to get a bit annoyed by comments people would make or negative things that got written about me. That sort of stuff used to go over my head but now that I'm a parent, I completely understand where she was coming from. My parents came on both Lions tours to South Africa and Australia and I was really proud of that. Travelling was a big deal for them and I was so happy for them to get the experiences of, not only going to those places, but to see their son representing the Lions there.

The man who was picking the team on that tour, Gats, made some absolutely huge calls ahead of that third Test. The infamous one is dropping Brian O'Driscoll, a Lions legend, from the side and putting in Jonathan Davies.

I remember being by the ping pong table in the team room early in the week of that final Test and I knew something was up. I'd just finished dishing out another lesson – standard – and I spotted Brian pull Paul O'Connell to the side for a chat. They were stood five or six yards away having a quiet conversation. I couldn't hear what was being said but I didn't need to, their body language said it all. Paul had a look of disbelief on his face and Brian had disappointment etched all over his.

Gats had given a big speech about BOD the week before. It felt like he spoke about him for about an hour in a team meeting, saying things like: "We're here for Brian… we need to get the victory for Brian." He was really bigging it up and Brian is obviously a legend. I don't think there was anything malicious in it from Gats' point of view, I think it was one of those last-minute calls that coaches make. Either way, it was a massive decision.

Fair play, though, he did it and it worked out. Jonathan was on fire at the time. He was young, strong and fast. It wasn't like Foxy was an inferior player. A bit of a sickener for Brian is that he'd passed up the opportunity to go out that week. Gats gave the boys a bit of time off to freshen up when we arrived in Noosa and they hit the beers.

I didn't go because I was worried about my injury and Brian didn't go because he wanted to freshen himself up ready for the third Test. I think he regrets passing up the chance to have a few cold ones now. We've spoken a lot in this book about things that go on under the surface and Brian, as a former Lions captain, will have known that he couldn't throw his toys out of the pram. But deep down I think he probably wanted to go mental at that point.

He never let it show, though, he was backing the boys 100 percent that week and extremely professional. Usually I was confident over selection but that is one that I was a bit nervous about. I didn't really know what the coaches were going to do, so it was a relief to get picked. One of the things I remember from the team run is Jamie Roberts spotting a TV camera coming towards our huddle and deciding to give us a big speech! Johnny Sexton also had a massive go at Richard Hibbard for being out of position during one of the run-throughs. He went a bit over the top, to be honest. Hibbs just kept his head down and got on with things. Johnny had that edge to him. I saw him scrapping with players in training at Racing Metro on a number of occasions, he's had a go at me a few times as well but that day in Australia it brought a bit of intensity to the session and maybe that was a good thing going into the match.

I was rooming with Halfpenny at this point on the tour and I always wondered why they put me with him because we're different characters. I did wonder whether it might be because they thought I could be a bit of a calming influence on him but I wasn't convinced they were that forward-thinking. Leigh is an absolutely lovely guy but he can be very intense.

On the night of the game you could hear all the Lions fans outside and he was sitting on the bed with his headphones on taking deep breaths, the total opposite to me. I'm walking around the room, cutting my hair and just relaxing. But that's what worked for him. Leigh is a great guy but he puts a lot of pressure on himself.

I remember after we lost the third Test against Australia in 2012, I was obviously gutted but I looked at him and it just hit him so hard because he'd missed a kick during the match and we lost by two points. Again, as I keep saying though, it's never one individual's fault. I put my personal disappointment to one side in the changing rooms that day and it was all about trying to help him. He was in a different world of pain altogether. I just wanted to help put things in perspective for him. We had a big heart-to-heart once. I'm not going to go into too many details because that stuff should stay between me and him but basically he was finding it difficult to switch off.

During one campaign, we were just chilling out on a Wednesday night and he asked what I'd been up to the previous weekend. I just explained that I'd been down west to see the family and his response was: "When do you start getting your head on for the game then?"

I said: "The game's on Saturday, Leigh!" I used to build steadily up to matches throughout the week. Whether it was Wales or the Lions, we always used to have a backs meeting the night before a match where we'd discuss what we were going to bring to the game individually. It was a psychological thing really. I was always intense but was quite relaxed in the way I put things across in those meetings. Leigh would be on pins. His legs would be twitching and he was ready for kick-off there and then. He was already in the moment.

A Lion For Life

He got very intense in the days before a game and I used to try and get him to just enjoy it, which I think he did, but everyone is different. Sometimes I just felt like I needed to put my arm around him. He was unbelievable on that 2013 tour, bossed the Tests and got man of the series. So as far as I was concerned, he could do whatever he wanted to get himself ready. He went on to kick 21 points and set up two tries in the final Test. When he does switch off, he's also great fun. We met up at the Monaco Grand Prix once, I've met up with him a few times in Dubai and he's got a lovely family.

I felt like I contributed a little bit more in Sydney but it still wasn't my greatest stuff. The forwards did most of the hard work. Adam Jones absolutely dominated and the game was over after 30 minutes really. The forwards gave us an incredible platform. We led 19-10 at half time and then cut loose in the final 20 to absolutely hammer them 41-16. The overwhelming emotion was just relief. I knew I hadn't played to my absolute potential but I was just trying to tell myself that at least I'd played a part in the Tests and we'd won.

At the end of the day, I must have played alright because we won the two Tests that I started and I can be happy with that.

It was on my CV and I'd achieved what I'd set out to even if I wasn't happy with how it all went down. It was nice for all the boys that played in 2009 to get the win. We all felt the hurt in South Africa and this went some way to easing that particular pain. Daniel Craig, who'd bought us a load of champagne in 2009, came into the dressing room after the match and the boys put the James Bond theme song on.

I was a bit starstruck to be fair but he loves his rugby. I said very little to him, just: "Lovely to meet you, congratulations for everything that you've achieved." That was about it. He was a very modest guy and very cool – he is James Bond at the end of the day! There was champagne flying everywhere and it really was party time.

We enjoyed ourselves after that one, hitting it hard for three days straight. After the game I remember drinking in a hot tub with Tommy Bowe and a few of the lads. The morning after the game, me and Leigh decided to turn up to a breakfast meeting in the Australia tops that we'd swapped with their boys. Leigh and Kurtley Beale are a similar size so his fitted alright but I'm twice the size of Genia so I looked a hell of a state. That day we'd organised to hit a beach bar that was rammed with Lions fans. Hoggy was ready to leave the hotel in nothing but a pair of speedos but Paul O'Connell said: "Nah we can't have that, there's going to be cameras everywhere!" That was a great session though. We just kept going.

The airline who we were flying home with had set up a check-in desk in our hotel to make things swift when we got to the airport and I went down to drop my bags off and sort all that out. The woman at the desk says: "I"m sorry sir but you're going to have to stop drinking. I can smell the alcohol." I hadn't even had a drink that day, which gives you an indication of how much we'd gone for it in the few days before. We still had a good crack on the flight home, though, until they stopped serving us booze.

When I got back from Australia I was on one hell of a comedown. It was rock-bottom territory. After the emotional chaos that my knee had caused, the euphoria of winning a Lions Test series and then three days on the piss, I was ready to shut the curtains and curl up in a ball for about a week. The trouble was, the day after I returned to Wales I was due to be best man at my best friend Bleddyn's wedding.

We go a long way back and used to carve up as half-back partners for Whitland youth. Trouble was, all my confidence had deserted me and the speech I gave at his wedding was horrendous. I don't know what I was saying. In Oz, we'd been to this zoo where they told us that a male crocodile goes underneath a female crocodile and blows bubbles to let her know it's on. So I made a note of that.

Then we went to see the koala bears, we're holding them and they're all cute but then they tell us: "The koala bear is savage, he's a womaniser, a real horrible bugger!" So these two things stuck with me and I decided to drop them into my best man speech. I basically told Bledd to be the crocodile and not the koala bear. It was a total disaster. I haven't been asked to be a best man since.

When things started to get back to normal, I met up with a specialist for him to examine my knee. It had settled down with a little break but it needed an assessment. He felt that I needed an operation there and then or I wouldn't be able to last the season. He also told me that, in his opinion, I only had two more years of rugby left in me. That annoyed me. I didn't need him telling me how long I had left in the game. My mindset was that I'll be the one who determined that. I never had the surgery and managed to keep playing for another three years because it settled down on its own but it caused me all sorts of problems on the tour.

That was the end of my involvement with the Lions but I'd made friends for life.

At the 2019 Rugby World Cup in Japan, I met up with Brian O'Driscoll for a few beers and spent a lot of time with Paul O'Connell because we were both working for ITV. It felt like there was someone's birthday on the crew every bloody day on that trip and we were going out for a few beers regularly. One morning at breakfast I felt a bit rubbish and wanted to sweat it out of my system. So I asked if he fancied going to the gym in the hotel just for a gentle half-hour run or something and next thing I know he's planning a full-on session as if we're back on the Lions tour. I was like: "Mate, chill out, I'm not trying to make a comeback!" So we met in the gym about half an hour later – he was there early – and I went to go into a different room just to have a look around and he stopped me: "No, no we can't go in there."

So I say: "Why not?"

"Jonny Wilkinson is there and he's absolutely beasting himself so if we go in there, then we're going to have to absolutely beast ourselves too!" he replies.

We ended up giving ourselves a bit of a pasting anyway. Not quite the gentle jog I was after. That's just the intensity of the guy though, even now. During my career, I always prided myself on performing well when it came to fitness testing but O'Connell and Wilkinson were on a different level. They still work their socks off now. Years after retiring, they're still determined to push their bodies. It's incredible really. We had some good crack at the 2019 World Cup and we were able to finally watch games together and enjoy them like the fans, with no pressure on us.

After I got back from the Lions tour in 2013, I learned about the story of Cai Jones, a 13-year-old lad who had passed away in his sleep on Christmas morning the previous year. At the time, Cai's passing was attributed to sudden arrhythmic death syndrome, which is when a person dies following a cardiac arrest and no obvious cause can be found. His story was brought to my attention by my mother, who had read about it in the *Carmarthen Journal*. The report also said that he wanted to be the next Mike Phillips. I was heartbroken as my mum was telling me all this. The story really hit home. It gave me an instant sense of perspective as well.

Mentally, I was all over the place after the Lions tour, but were my problems really that great? I was back in France so there was a limit to what I could do but I got my mum to pass on a load of my Wales kit to help with the fundraising effort. When I eventually got back to Wales, I went to visit Cai's parents, Nicola and David, at their home. It was an incredibly humbling experience. They'd been through unimaginable pain. It made me think about what was important in life. Rugby meant a great deal to me but it is not the be all and end all.

10

99 Problems

After the way Warren Gatland was with me on the Lions tour in 2013, I began to suspect that things might also now be different when he returned as Wales boss. I was right to be suspicious.

They made me starting scrum-half for the 2014 Six Nations but I could tell things were delicately balanced. We beat Italy on the opening weekend without too many dramas and Rhys Webb came on to replace me in the 67th minute. Nobody really pulled up any trees but we got the job done and we moved on.

The build-up to the Ireland game didn't exactly go too smoothly for me. A few days before the match, I was doing bench press in the gym with the old Cardiff Blues back-rower Dan Baugh, who is now a strength and conditioning coach, spotting me. As I've gone to push out a rep, I felt my pectoral muscle pull. So I've shouted: "It's gone!" Whilst trying not to drop this weight on my sternum. Dan thinks I'm just struggling with the rep, so he's shouting back: "Push! Push!" And I was like: "No! I've pulled a muscle!"

After that, I spent a lot of the week training on my own and I would only join up with the boys for the light stuff. I had to do a fitness test on the morning of the game and it was a bit like the Lions tour the previous year, it just all messes with your head. I should have probably put my hand up and said I wasn't right but I dug in. I didn't play well, the pack got dominated, it was a wet day, they kicked well and strangled us a bit.

By the time Paddy Jackson went over to score in the 78th minute, we were well and truly beaten. But as Jackson went over the line, Liam Williams went across to try and make the tackle. As he's getting up off the floor, I saw Rob Kearney push him back down, which left me less than impressed. My head went and I ran in from a distance to stick up for Liam really. But given we were minutes away from losing the game 26-3, it wasn't a good look. It was nothing too serious, just a bit of pushing and shoving. Referee Wayne Barnes showed me a yellow card to really rub salt into the wounds. To be honest, I should have kicked something off in the first five or 10 minutes because it was pretty dismal stuff.

The morning after the match, I got into a bit of a barney with Gethin Jenkins. It all went back to the build-up in the week. On the Thursday, I joined up with the boys for a bit of a team run and it was a poor session. Balls were being dropped, we weren't slick at all.

Heads were down, it was just one of those days when everyone was just five percent off it. Gethin has a bit of a go, trying to spark something: "The standards today have not been good enough. We've got a huge game away from home coming up against a top class side. Get your heads on!" But, to be honest, it felt to me like he was aiming some of it specifically at me. In the back of my mind, I'm thinking: 'Hang on mate, I'm digging in here.' I was really trying to push the pain of my pectoral injury to the back of my mind and do my best for the team, so that pissed me off.

In truth, Gethin was well within his rights to have a go and you need the experienced players to do that if sessions are going poorly. I just took it personally because the injury was messing with my head. Then after the match we were told to drink in the hotel but about 10 of us ventured out into Dublin. That had started to get on my nerves as well, it felt like we were being treated like schoolchildren and by now I was in my 30s. It felt like there was no respect anymore and if you keep people penned in, that's when it can kick off.

By this point in my career, we were so restricted in the things we could and couldn't do. Generally, everything in the week was so structured, including the game plan. The environment didn't really leave a lot of room for creativity. We were being told we had to be in the gym at 8:00am on the dot, for example, whereas the All Blacks would tell players it didn't matter what time they came to the gym as long as their work was done before 11:30am. There's a subtle difference in that and some players respond better to having that little bit of leeway. Of course, there has to be a schedule but sometimes you need that little bit of flexibility because it leaves room for some creativity and with that comes growth. Without that, you become robotic.

Anyway, the morning after the Ireland game I was a bit worse for wear. I saw Gethin on a laptop in the team room and I said to him: "What are you looking at there Geth, all the penalties you gave away yesterday is it?"

Apparently, it was too soon for jokes. He was not best pleased and got up in my face: "Right. Outside. Now." Obviously we didn't go outside and I didn't have any dramas with him. He's an absolute legend, one of Wales' greatest ever players and there was no bad blood at all. Emotions were just running a little bit high after the previous day's defeat. The coaches made a bigger deal out of it though. Gats didn't like it. Keep in mind this was the same guy who let Gav leave a World Cup training camp to film his own reality TV show but now he wanted to make a fuss about this? He was believing his own hype by this point and I think he wanted to show me who was boss. Either way, it didn't really help my cause going forward. I got quite annoyed that Geth had taken it so seriously, went straight to my room, packed my bag and was going to get my own flight home. A lot of things were building up, the injury, the yellow card, the performance, the way Gats was now behaving towards me.

I just got a bit fed up. I got into a taxi outside the hotel and drove 200 yards down the road before I saw sense and told him to stop. Nobody knows about that... until now. I had a bit of a word with myself and walked back to the hotel before getting straight on the bus. That would have been the end of my Wales career right there had I gone through with it. I'm glad I saw sense because that's not the correct way to carry yourself.

On the journey home, one of the boys pointed out to me that Niall Horan had been Tweeting about me during the match. Now I knew who One Direction were at the time, of course I did, but I couldn't have told you the names of all the band members. Niall's message, which was sent out to his millions of followers, read: "Mike Phillips is like a child throwing his toys out of the pram! His attitude is terrible, looks like a right arrogant idiot." How very rude of him. By the time I found his Tweet on my phone, a few of the boys had huddled around me and were egging me on to respond.

So I replied: "Come down to training in the week big boy. Bring the rest of The Beatles with you."

It was a world class comeback. It wasn't confrontational, it was just a bit of banter. He's got something like 40 million Twitter followers and I think I got about 40,000 off the back of that little exchange. My phone went absolutely crazy after I sent that tweet.

For about a year afterwards I had his fans sending me messages telling me to leave him alone. It was absolutely bonkers. Later that year, I was in New York around Christmas time and I had a text from Johnny Sexton, my team-mate at Racing Metro. He told me that Niall was in the city as well and that we should meet up. So I got his number and we caught up. We met in an Irish bar initially and sat next to the window at the front.

A few minutes later, his bodyguard came in and told us to sit further back because there were girls gathering out the front going mental for him. My mind was blown by just how many people were following him around. It was unbelievable. But he is so down to earth, a really top guy. We were in his car going to the next pub and we drove past Madison Square Gardens and he stopped the car so we could have a picture out the front as if we were going to have a fight. He loves his rugby and his golf so we had a lot to talk about. We still give each other a bit of abuse on WhatsApp from time to time but it's all friendly. I was doing some work with a charity called Follow Your Dreams back around the time we met up. Through that work, I met a young girl named Amy Johnston, who was my No.1 fan. Niall was brilliant and helped me arrange for Amy and some of the other kids to go backstage and meet the band when they performed in Cardiff. That sums him up. Top bloke.

But putting the Twitter banter to one side, we had some problems to deal with on the rugby front. When you look back now, that defeat was the start of a bit of a lull for a lot of the boys. We'd had a really successful period over the last two seasons with a lot of boys going on the 2013 Lions tour. How do you keep that going? It's tough. Did we have the right edge about us at that time? Probably not. We didn't have that desperation and you need it 100 percent of the time at that level, otherwise you get found out. Then coaches start looking for fall guys and I was right in the firing line. It was the start of the end for me.

I knew Rhys Webb was coming through at this point. He was young and very sharp, he had a spark about him, which was great and he was what every young buck should be. He was a very good trainer, very professional. Gareth Davies was starting to come through as well and I was comfortable with that. Everyone has their shelf life.

I'd been in the camp since 2003 and, to be honest, I kind of felt like it was about time someone came through. I'd held the position down for the best part of six years. Rhys started the next two games in that Six Nations against France and England. I could feel them starting to push me out a little bit. I didn't kick off about it because I accepted the situation for what it was. We lost that game at Twickenham and Gethin got yellow carded for a couple of scrum penalties in the 53rd minute. It was immediately after I came on and Owen Farrell kicked a penalty to put them 11 points in front.

I always tell people I never lost a competitive match that I started at Twickenham because I don't count this one. I was good, but 11 points down, 14 men and 25 minutes to go? That's a tall order against a side like England. When Gethin went off, he sent the message up to Gats in the coaches box that he didn't want to go back on because he felt the referee, Romain Poite, had it in for him. In the post-match debrief, Gats praised Gethin and spoke about how it was an outstanding decision, with Geth putting the team before himself. I viewed the situation a little differently and was surprised to see Gatland not only addressing it positively, but also raising it in front of the team. Again, I never had an issue with Geth. He was an absolute world-class operator and looked after the boys as well. When we were in a camp ahead of the 2015 World Cup in Qatar, we all had to go to a local rugby club for a barbecue, which we never minded doing under normal circumstances. But we'd been working tirelessly in the heat and I remember boys were almost passing out at this rugby club.

The seating wasn't great and boys were having to sit on the floor in some cases. Given what we'd been putting our bodies through, it was ridiculous. Fair play, Gethin gave Gats and Alan Phillips a piece of his mind about it, telling them we shouldn't have been there. I wasn't within earshot of what was being said but I was admiring Geth because he was just looking out for the boys and that's what you want from your leaders. So I've got no problems with him, it just so happens that he's involved a fair bit here. I was looking at this situation thinking to myself that he could do no wrong. Meanwhile, it felt like I couldn't do anything right in the eyes of the coaches.

Rhys picked up an injury in that defeat to England, so I was given the start for the last game against Scotland. We smashed them by 50 points. It's the game famous for Stuart Hogg's early red card for a late, high hit on Dan Biggar. To be honest, that made it an easy afternoon for us.

Deep down, I felt like that 2014 Six Nations could have been a case of me owning the No.9 jersey for the last time with Rhys coming off the bench. Myself and the coaches could have had mature conversations about it and made a plan but they never spoke to me. I was never made aware of what their intentions were for me and Rhys. I always felt like I had a good relationship with Gats for the majority of my career, even if things were a bit bumpy with Howley. We'd achieved a lot together, I'd worked tirelessly to help the team win trophies and make that era a successful one. Because of that, I felt like they owed me the decency of just talking me through what was happening.

All they did was give me the silent treatment. I'd seen them do this before. It happened with Martyn Williams, Stephen Jones and Dwayne Peel. Gats was pretty blunt with all of them when it came to the end and we were about to witness the treatment they dished out to Adam Jones. It doesn't take much to just pull someone for a quiet conversation but they let me figure it out for myself.

After the Six Nations in 2014, we were all heading out for a few beers and Gats pulled me to the side and basically told me that if there were any shenanigans that night, I was going to be in trouble. Again, I was in my 30s by now. Did he really need to be talking to me like that? He was doing it because me and Gethin had argued but that happens in that environment. Boys are scrapping in training all the time and it's quickly forgotten about. Me and Gethin didn't have any beef. That was unnecessary from Gats and, looking back, was a sign that our relationship had broken down.

Rhys had an injury and missed the summer tour that year to South Africa. I started both Tests but I didn't really view it as a big opportunity to prove a point because I knew the coaches could be pretty stubborn when they made their mind up about a player. They thought my legs had gone and I was never going to change their mind about that. The first Test was a shocker. We lost 38-16 and, to be fair, Howley said we were too soft and I agreed with him. The Springboks will push you to the floor when you're getting up, they'll bully you and we were far too nice. The generation of players we had at the time were whiter than white.

We didn't have many boys who would push an opponent's head into the floor when they were getting up. Which is fine, but when you're playing South Africa in their own backyard, you have to be a little bit more streetwise and have that edge about you. We were too honest. During the first Test in Durban, Willie le Roux caused carnage. He scored a try, cut us to pieces and got man of the match. Despite how poorly we'd played, I was actually feeling pretty good about how my preparation had gone and I was in good shape. So, before the second Test, Shaun Edwards pulled me to one side and gave me an unenviable task.

"Mike," he says. "We want you to man-mark Willie le Roux."

I'm thinking to myself: 'Man-mark Willie le Roux?' I had my roles in the side – where I stood to defend lineouts, scrums, when I could jump out of the line and all that sort of stuff. I'd never man-marked someone before.

"We want you to follow him," Shaun continues. "Wherever he goes in the back field, you go with him."

It was no easy job but this is why I loved Shaun. He always thought outside the box and it worked. Le Roux didn't score a try in that second Test and we had much more of a chance because of it. We played well that day but just completely blew it, again. Liam Williams gets a lot of stick for the penalty try in the last few seconds of the match but it wasn't my style to blame individuals. He was pretty upset about that in the changing room so I tried to console him a little bit. It was just another one of those tough moments that players go through sometimes. He's come out the other side of it and is doing pretty well for himself.

The trip is memorable for me for a reason other than the rugby. When we were out there, I bought a diamond with the intention of saving it for an engagement ring that I could use when I eventually plucked up the courage to propose to my girlfriend. I got the ring made up and she's wearing it today.

One thing that really pissed me off on that trip, though, was the way they treated Adam Jones. Nobody needs me to tell them how much of a legend Adam is and what a great servant he was for Welsh rugby. For me, he was the best player in our team at times and I don't think we'd have won the tournaments we did without him. He was vastly underrated. In that first Test, which was his 100th Test match by the way, they substituted him after 31 minutes with the Springboks leading 21-6. They blamed Adam for two of the tries South Africa had scored but the reality was that very few of us were playing well.

The coaches didn't need to do that to him, they could have at least let it get to half-time. I was furious about it, after everything he'd done for them and his country. They should have given him a proper send-off in Cardiff. They should have let him wave goodbye before a home game – even if he wasn't playing. The fans would have gone nuts and think about the impact it would have had on the younger players in the squad, they'd have been looking at it thinking: 'This is what I can achieve if I work hard enough.' But no, they yanked him off after half an hour in Durban and that was that. I was disgusted by it.

After Adam had gone, I recall being in training and overhearing Gats making a comment about Adam in front of other players. I think Adam had made a comment in the press but Gats shouldn't have been saying stuff in front of other boys like that. Given the way my international career was about to go and the way they were about to treat me, I wish I'd let him know what I thought about it.

Webby had started the year really well and by the time the 2015 Six Nations came around, he was their number one choice. He was scoring a lot of tries and was looking sharp. Sometimes you just have to see the facts for what they are. He forced his way in and started the first game against England, scoring a try after seven minutes. As far as I was concerned, the writing was on the wall.

In the game against Scotland, he made a couple of wrong decisions with regards to the game plan. We were playing very structured rugby – as we did for the majority of Gatland's reign – and if the scrum-half goes the wrong way once, then it can throw the whole thing off. They were only little errors, and it was fair enough because he was still relatively new on the scene. If you didn't know what you were looking for, you probably wouldn't even notice them. Anyway, I came on for the last six minutes to see the game out and we were winning by 10 points until they scored with a minute to go. So I slowed everything right down, just to manage the clock. I took as much time as I could get away with at the base of rucks and we won the game by three points.

In the video review session the following week, Howley didn't mention a single mistake that Rhys had made with regards to the game plan but absolutely hammered me for the way I played in the final six minutes. It was shocking, really, and none of the stuff he said was making any sense. It was genuinely baffling. He said I should have kept the tempo in the game and kept playing to score more tries but all we had to do was see the game out. I seriously regret not giving it back to him. Looking back, the main reason I didn't let rip then – and when they treated Adam shoddily the previous summer – is because I knew I was approaching 100 caps.

I know that's a selfish way of looking at things but I wanted to hit that milestone, so causing trouble at this stage wasn't in my best interests. But by now, the only time the coaches really spoke to me was to pick holes in my game. The communication had completely stopped. I didn't feel like they even wanted me around. I didn't enjoy it at all. It was horrible. I came off the bench three times in the 2015 Six Nations and did okay but I could see where it was all going. I'd seen them do this before. When you're out, you're out.

They should have said to me: "Mike, thank you, you've been great for us but would you mind now mentoring Webby and Gareth Davies?" I could have watched clips with them, gone through the game plan, explained where they need to be defending and stuff like that. I'd been an international rugby player for 12 years at this point, surely I could have been of use to them in that regard. But they shut me out, which I thought was a poor use of my knowledge.

Me and Howley clashed quite a lot in my career – just in case you haven't been paying attention – but, in the early days, we would have a bit of fun after our bust-ups. We usually sorted things out. But by the time the training camp for the 2015 Rugby World Cup came around, the relationship had turned a little bit more sinister. He'd have a go and there'd be no fun after it. Throughout my career, I lost patience with him a fair bit. He would just constantly scream and shout in training sessions, sometimes at younger players.

A lot of the time, it was completely unnecessary, just over the odd dropped pass and things like that. It wasn't helpful when the boys are trying to create this positive environment and it's no wonder I lost it with him because he might have been able to shout at the younger boys coming through but I wasn't going to take it, especially if I felt like he didn't have a point. I was one of four scrum-halves named in the wider squad along with Webby, Gareth Davies and Lloyd Williams. This was my fourth World Cup training camp. I had a lot of miles on the clock, I'd played a lot of rugby. We went to Fiesch, a sleepy little village in the Swiss Alps, to do some training at altitude. It was fairly brutal stuff but I was managing with the workload, even if I did feel like they didn't really want me there at that stage. The one thing I really disagreed with was that, around that time, I found out that I'd been dropped from the starting spot in the newspapers. I thought the coaches should be giving players the courtesy of telling them to their face. So, fair enough, Howley was about to do that. While we were in Switzerland, everyone in the squad was having a one-on-one meeting with the coaches. It was the first time it had ever happened. I was called into a meeting and I could sense something was up because of all the cold shoulder treatment I was getting. All the coaches were in this meeting and Rob hits me with: "We don't think you're the same player you were before you went to France, we think your form has gone."

My response to that was simple: "How do you work that out? I've won a Grand Slam, a Six Nations title and a Lions Test series since I moved to France."

There was no comeback to that one. I might have won that little tussle but I knew they were about to get rid of me. Again, looking back, I should have gone apeshit in this meeting and ripped the arsehole out of everyone in the room. But again, I was on 98 Test caps, including my five for the Lions, and I kept my cool. If they'd just said: "Look, Mike, clearly you're old…" I'd have accepted that. Just say it like it is. Don't come up with this nonsense about my form going when I've just helped you win trophies. I just kept my head down and got on with the training. Next up we went to Qatar for a heat camp. That was no cakewalk either. We were blitzing three sessions a day. There was one fitness drill we used to do called runways. You basically have to hit the deck, get up and run a fairly long distance.

In the first camp, I'll admit that I was way off the pace but by the time we got to Qatar, I was flying in these fitness tests because I'd worked my arse off. I'm not saying I was keeping up with Rhys and Gareth but I wasn't far off and I was feeling sharp. At the end of the day, they are both six and eight years younger than me but what I had over them was that experience, and by now I understood the bigger picture and how I fitted into it. At that point, Gats actually came up to me for the first time in months to acknowledge my efforts. I was tidy enough to him but I sit here now and wish I'd had a bit of a go at him for the way it was being handled. I think he would probably have respected that in a funny way.

Sometimes he liked players biting back. Perhaps he felt I wasn't fighting for my position but I knew in the back of my mind that I was losing the battle. The fire that had burned inside me since the day I first pulled on a Wales shirt was going out.

After Qatar, we played Ireland in a warm-up match. They picked me at scrum-half and James Hook at 10 but it was an extremely inexperienced side, with six boys making their debut. As soon as I saw the team, I knew what they were doing. I went into the game knowing it would be the last time I'd play for Wales. I hoped they might give me a 100th cap but, deep down, I knew. We'd done almost no preparation on the rugby side of things, so there was never going to be any fluidity in the performance. They'll never admit this but my honest opinion is that they set us up to fail.

They needed an excuse to get rid of people like me, Hooky and Richard Hibbard. They wanted to make it easy for themselves and, to be honest, I'd had enough of being in the environment and putting up with the shit. There was no respect anymore. Predictably, Ireland thumped us 35-21 and then it was a case of waiting for them to tell me I wasn't going to be in the squad.

After the match, I remember seeing Hooky with his family. I think James probably knew that it was going to be his last cap as well. He'd also had his issues with the coaches. But at least he had his son, Harrison, with him on his final cap. That was pretty cool for him.

In that moment, I thought to myself: 'At least Harrison has seen his dad play for Wales.' That's when I realised that my children were never going to see me play for my country. I wasn't even married at the time. That cut me up a little bit. Usually after Test matches, the whole team goes back to the Vale together on the bus but for that match, they allowed players to park their cars at the stadium and drive home if they wanted to. I didn't really agree with that because there was no togetherness. I was one of about 10 players that got on the bus and went back to the Vale. As we're driving through Canton, Gats stops the bus and makes the driver get off to buy some beers in an off-licence.

I thought to myself: 'This is a bit mental... but at least he's buying us some beers.' I was mistaken. Enough beers were bought for the management group but not the handful of players that were also on the bus with them. Again, I came very close to kicking off.

With the utmost respect, the other players who were on the bus that day weren't my close mates, the boys I'd been playing with for the best part of a decade. Those boys hadn't been on the scene very long so I hadn't made that sort of connection with them. It was a bit of a lonely journey back to the Vale and when we got there, everyone just jumped in their cars and went home. I thought to myself: 'Really? Is this how my Wales career comes to an end?'

For me, rugby was all about going through something together, as a group, and then having that moment together afterwards. It just didn't happen that day. The week after the Ireland game, they took us to North Wales for a bit more training.

They had a bit of a go at us in the team meeting because of the performance. Gats opened the floor to anyone who had something they wanted to say but I didn't play particularly well, so didn't feel like I was in a position to speak. A few weeks later, they put out a much stronger side to play Ireland again in Dublin and won a closer match 16-10. I wasn't involved. Two days after that match I received an email telling me that I hadn't made the squad for the upcoming World Cup.

An email.

After all those games and all those trophies. I wish I was joking. Let's face it, there is no nice way to be dropped and I probably wouldn't have been thrilled regardless of how the news was broken to me. But they'd had plenty of time to pull me to one side and tell me to my face that I wasn't going to be picked in the squad but no, I had an email. I know I wasn't the easiest player to deal with sometimes but after everything I'd given to the jersey, I felt like I deserved to have that conversation. Wales' most-capped scrum-half and I was never thanked for my services. People may disagree but I felt like it was out of order.

Remember how Steve Hansen told me I wasn't going to the World Cup in 2003? I hadn't even won anything for him but he still found the time to have a chat with me. It was chalk and cheese. I was ready for it all to end and I'd made peace with it. And I understand that Gats was only making decisions that he felt gave Wales the best opportunity to win a World Cup. I can't knock him for that. But it was handled poorly. I lost some respect for the coaches that day.

I was back with Racing when Rhys suffered a horrible injury in the final warm-up game for the tournament against Italy. Even though he was the guy who'd taken my shirt, I felt awful for him, of course I did. I never had any personal beef with Rhys and he'd worked bloody hard to get to where he was. You never want to see another player go through that kind of thing but, obviously, Wales now needed a replacement. I soon had team manager Alan Phillips on the phone.

He phrased things very interestingly. It wasn't a case of: "Mike, we're calling you up, pack your bags." He said: "Mike, do you want to come back?" That told me that he knew I'd been treated poorly. Thumper will have known what the coaches had done in the camps leading up to the tournament, how they'd ignored me and pushed me out. He'd have seen it and been privy to the private conversations Howley and Gats had about me.

I think they were expecting me to tell them to shove it up their arse. The thought did cross my mind after the way things had gone, especially the email situation. But I would have regretted it for the rest of my life had I turned them down. Regardless of what I thought of the coaches, it was still a Wales call-up and I never took those for granted. I also looked at the fixture list and saw the game against Uruguay and the short turnaround between the England and Fiji games in the group stages.

I thought there was a chance that I'd get on in those games and get my 100th cap. So I thanked Thumper and played it well in the press. I said all the right things, talked the coaches up but in my head I was desperate to go nuts, set fire to the whole thing. I think they were expecting me to explode in the press and say the wrong things but I kept my feelings to myself, despite how much I really wanted to tell the truth. I'd have been well within my rights to have a go but it probably would have gone against me. If you look at some of the best tennis players in the world – the likes of Roger Federer, Novak Djokovic, Serena Williams – they've all lost their cool in press conferences and minimal fuss is made. But if I'd done it, I've no doubt it wouldn't have ended well for me.

For the first time in my life, I played the politics a little bit!

Going back into the camp was a bit strange. The vibe was different. As I alluded to earlier, we all got on but I didn't have many close mates in the side. I almost felt like I didn't belong anymore. There weren't many people around who hadn't come through an academy system somewhere. It was cold.

Before the second group match against England, Tom Jones – the legendary Welsh singer – came into the team hotel to present the players with their jerseys. I wasn't involved in the matchday 23 but I was still excited to get the opportunity to meet Tom Jones! As the meeting time was approaching, me and a few of the other boys who were not picked made our way over to the room only to be confronted by Thumper at the door: "Sorry boys, matchday squad only." They wouldn't let us in.

They would spout all this stuff about togetherness and family in the press when, in reality, this is what was going on.

I was shocked. Absolutely shocked. It all felt a bit petty and unnecessary. It also made no sense whatsoever. I was experienced enough by now to just brush it off but I can't believe the coaches didn't consider the psychology of it all. You've got to make extra effort to ensure the squad players not in the 23 feel involved and part of it all. Otherwise, they are the ones that, in some environments, can start causing problems. Those non-23 boys might have to come on in the next big game. These things can make a big difference. The boys did well to get out of the group at that World Cup but I didn't feature against Uruguay or Fiji and, at that point, I knew I wasn't going to play unless there was an injury. For them to not give me my 100th cap felt like the final 'fuck you' from the coaching staff. I was good enough for 99 caps but now I can't get 15 minutes against Uruguay?

I knew I wasn't the same player and I was ready to go but that felt personal. Eventually the boys got knocked out in the quarter-final by South Africa and then I left the Wales camp for the last time.

After that World Cup I thought it was the end for Gats and the coaching staff. We'd reached the semi-final in 2011, we still had largely the same squad but the players were vastly more experienced now, had gone on a Lions tour and were more developed. Yes we had a few injuries but to only reach the quarter-final, to me, felt like going backwards. New Zealand wouldn't have accepted that.

We'd brought the team on in the four years previous, we'd changed the mentality of fans and raised the levels of expectations. Reaching a quarter-final is no longer good enough in Wales and I see that as a positive. We should be expecting more from ourselves. We didn't win a trophy for six years after the 2013 Six Nations and I just struggled to see where we were going. We'd gone from a team that played wonderful free-flowing rugby in 2011 to a side that couldn't score against 13 men in the Australia game in 2015. We never really got on top in the quarter-final against South Africa either, it always felt like they'd win it in the end. When the pressure came on, in the big games, Gats would tighten the game plan up a little bit and we'd resort back to relying heavily on a kicking game, despite the fact we had largely the same team that had carved up between 2011 and 2013. He felt the pressure more than anyone at times. It didn't help that he was taking a sabbatical every four years to go and do the Lions, either. As soon as they came calling, he was off. There was no putting Wales first or anything like that. He was gone. I think it lacked respect.

I regret the way I approached the final year or so of my career in some ways. I saw the century appearing on the horizon and I became a little too focused on hitting that milestone rather than concentrating on being the best I can be every day. But I was a bit older and that was the goal I'd set myself.

Really, my target should have been to just keep improving and adding value to myself. Alun Wyn Jones is the perfect example of that and it feels like he's going to go on for another 10 years. He deserves every accolade he gets and is a perfect example.

Being an international rugby player for over a decade was a bit like being in school when you're a kid. You never think it's going to end. You get into the flow of it and you just think you're never going to leave. But when the end comes, it comes sharply. You get old very quickly in professional sport. At least that's how it felt to me.

I was never told that they were going to stop selecting me but when you're left out of a squad for the first time, you sense what's happening. Despite the way my relationship had broken down with the coaches, it was still a huge decision to retire from the international game and take the decision out of their hands but it was a fairly straightforward process. You put out a statement, do an interview or two and that's pretty much it.

Suddenly you're no longer an international rugby player. Gats left me a voicemail after it was made official but I've not really spoken to most of the coaches since I called it a day. I thought that was a bit of a cop out from Warren. We should have had a conversation. The one guy I have kept in touch with is Shaun Edwards. He always checks in on me and that relationship has continued but that's the only one. I wish Shaun all the best with the rest of his career, even now that he is with France!

Me and Gats were at a hospitality function a few years ago but barely said a word to each other. It was sad because at one point we got on really well. When he first came in, there was no ego with Gats but my honest opinion is that he began to enjoy the fame. He's done very well for himself over the years and he deserves credit for that. But at one point I think he said a few things in the press that were a bit unnecessary because he enjoyed making headlines.

As the years have gone by and I've reflected on the whole thing, I look back with a huge sense of pride at what I achieved with Wales and the Lions. If someone had come up to me as a nine-year-old and told me about all the things I'd accomplish, I'd have been chuffed and that's what you have to remember. I don't have massive regrets about not reaching 100 caps.

It would have been nice but I knew the time was right to walk away. The passion just wasn't the same. But the main thing for me was that I'd gotten everything out of my body, I'd given everything I had to the shirt, proven a lot of people wrong and played some of the best rugby of my life alongside my mates. That's what I'll remember when I look back on my international career; the trophies and the good times.

11

All Good Things...

There's no hard and fast rule for retiring and there are no wrong answers. Each player is different and will do what is best for them. Some players will go on for as long as they possibly can, they just can't walk away from it. I took a slightly different approach. I never wanted to become that old guy who couldn't quite do it like he used to. I didn't want to be the bloke who youngsters could just run around and get the better of. I hated the idea of coming up against some kid, who has grown up watching me on the TV, and him thinking: 'Is this it? I thought Mike Phillips was special.' If you get to that stage, you've hung around for too long. So I thought long and hard about my next move when I knew my time was up in Paris. I was 33 at the time, my international career was over, could I have just called it a day at the end of the 2015/16 season? It was certainly something I looked at.

I put a string of seven or eight good performances together in my last season in France, which helped us get to the top of the league. It put me in the shop window a little bit and I thought it might prove to any coaches that might have doubts over my age that I could still cut it. When it started to look like nothing was going to come from Racing, my agent came over to Paris to stay with me and discuss my next move

"Right, what are the plans for next year then?" I said, expecting him to reel off a list of potential moves, pretty much rubbing my hands together.

His reply was: "Well, there's always the chômage." Not what I was after. The chômage is basically France's version of unemployment benefits for professionals. You get something like €7,000 per month for 23 months whilst doing absolutely nothing. I was playing out of my skin for one of the biggest clubs in Europe, we were top of the league, I'd been on two Lions tours and he was telling me my only option was to go on France's version of the dole! In all seriousness, we had to have a proper discussion about my future.

Whilst I thought I wanted to continue, I was no spring chicken and my body had been through a lot. I could have gone on the chômage for two years and earned the equivalent of a one-year contract. So it was a case of 'do I want to put my body through another year?'.

Around that time, if I lost a game on a Saturday, I'd be ringing my agent on a Monday and talking about how much I hate rugby but then come Friday I was like a different person. That's what he was putting up with. Sometimes you can't walk until Tuesday, your head is all over the shop. Then later in the week I felt like I could play for another three years. All rugby players – and I guess athletes in general – are a little bit bipolar to a certain extent.

One minute you're on top of the world, the next minute you're down in the dumps. Players have to live with a defeat for the entire week and forensically analyse every mistake you made. Did I really want to put my body through another season, especially seeing as I could pick up €7,000 per month for doing nothing? I thought about it. But I wasn't ready to walk away. I was finishing the season really strongly with Racing and, after a long discussion with my agent, I felt I had more to give. I was very conscious of hanging around too long but I just felt I had a little bit more to squeeze out of my body.

After ruling out the chômage, Sale came sniffing around. There wasn't much else on the table at the time and it became an attractive proposition. It was another league to experience and there was the offer of being the starting scrum-half. It's a big club in a great part of the UK. I did my research and spoke to a few former players who all spoke highly of the club, so I signed on a one-year deal to empty the tank and see how much more I could give. I certainly hadn't decided that it would be my last year in rugby at that time but my answer would come pretty quickly.

Sale was old school, the gym was old school, the values were old school. It suited me in many ways. When the weather turned really bad, we used to go and train in Manchester City's facilities. It was a different level altogether but it was pretty cool to be sharing an environment with them. I became good mates with Bacary Sagna, who was playing for Manchester City at the time. Our wives knew each other and we spent a lot of time together. Bacary is a great guy and he would often invite me to his box, and I went to watch a few games at the Etihad Stadium.

He'd come down to watch me play for Sale as well. We used to spend a lot of time with his family. Bacary and his wife Ludivine have two kids – Elias and Kais. I loved the name Elias so much and that's why myself and my wife decided to name our son Elias.

All Good Things...

There was a good bunch of youngsters at the club. They got up to all sorts and found a bit of mischief, a bit like me in my younger days but I'd calmed down by this point.

Guys like Mike Haley and Will Addison were a great laugh. I'd join them for a few beers and they'd used to say: "Come on, we want to see the real Mike!" I used to get that all the time but just used to smoke bomb and go home all the time, just leave without saying goodbye, disappear without a trace. I was leaving the youngsters to have their fun at this stage, making better decisions. We had a good team bonding trip to the Grand National that year but I ducked out early and got a taxi back to Hale, where I was living at the time. I was home by about 8pm and I was expecting a pat on the back and a 'well done' for coming home at a reasonable hour. I still got a bit of stick from my partner, so I might as well have stayed out!

The Curry brothers were starting to emerge around the time I was there. They'd turn up to training in their Vauxhall Corsa and make the older boys tea. It's been great to see Tom go on and play for the Lions and Ben play for England. They've matured into top class players and they're great blokes too. Paul Deacon – the former rugby league player – was attack coach at the time and he was one of the best I worked with. I learned a hell of a lot from him – even at that stage in my career – in such a short space of time. He was all about using good decoy runners to manipulate defences and create space, as you might expect given his background.

He was all about sticking the first and second defenders. We focused so much on engaging those two players in the defensive line and I'd never really done that before but it made so much sense. If you don't stick those first two defenders, then there is no point in spinning the ball wide because there will be no space to attack, everyone can drift off. Mike Forshaw was the defence coach and he was another great bloke. They were a perfect example of the impact that just being good blokes can have. I didn't need a great deal of coaching at this stage in my career but I knew they were great guys and it made me want to fight for them.

One of the best things about the club, though, was the kitman. These guys are always the heartbeat of the club and I've been lucky enough to work with some legendary kitmen down there years. There was obviously 'Rala' – Patrick O'Reilly – who was Ireland's old kitman and also worked for the Lions. He's been on four Lions tours now and is a bit of a cult hero with a wicked sense of humour.

Anyone who has watched the Lions documentaries will be familiar with him. But the best one I ever had was at Sale. He was a Scottish guy called Robbie Dickson and he's been at the club for the best part of 50 years. At the Sharks there was an initiation process after you'd played your first game for the club. Most teams make you sing a song, some teams give you a drinking challenge. I don't really know how to explain this one but here goes.

Dicko would stand on a bucket in the middle of the changing rooms and pull his pants down. You'd have to go on all fours in front of him, not getting too close I should add, and then everyone sings Flower of Scotland.

Not strange enough for you? I've got more.

One day we had the great Manchester United manager Sir Alex Ferguson come in to give us a bit of a pep talk, probably the greatest coach or manager in the history of any sport. So Sir Alex gives his speech, which was very interesting. He spoke about getting to know the players as people and understanding their backgrounds. He felt players who came from tough backgrounds would fight for you and fight for the jersey a bit more. He didn't give too much away but when someone like Sir Alex Ferguson speaks, you hang on every word.

As his chat was winding down, all the boys start shouting Dicko's name. We all knew what was coming next. Fair play, he grabs a stool, plonks it down right next to Fergie, stands on it and drops his trousers. With that, the entire room belts out the Scottish national anthem. I was looking around the room thinking 'this is brilliant'. It was just proper old school rugby nonsense. It's probably not right and it's definitely not something you could get away with if you worked in an office but that's rugby for you. Fergie didn't didn't know what to make of it all. I don't think he'd ever seen anything like it. On a serious note, his talk was great.

He spoke about how they used to select players who had demonstrated that they were willing to fight for the jersey. It really resonated with me but Dicko's antics were just as memorable for different reasons.

The season got off to a bit of a ropey start. We lost against Newcastle in the first game, missing a kick to win it at the end. Had we snuck that, we could have kicked on but it put us on the back foot. We started to get a few injuries as well, so one day, director of rugby Steve Diamond gives this speech where he basically says nobody is allowed to get injured anymore

"I've had enough of it!" Steve barked.

The following week against Gloucester, I felt my pec pull. I was very aware of the fact that I'd just arrived, on decent money and with a big reputation, so I played through it. I couldn't do a press-up for weeks but it seemed to get better as the season went on. I should never have played through it really. It was pretty bad and I was ducking out of weights sessions just to avoid putting any stress on it. I pushed through but it still gives me problems today occasionally.

I really liked Steve. He's proper old school – there's a theme here with Sale – and we got on really well. He understood me, understood what made me tick and knew how to communicate with me. I wish I'd gone there when I was a bit younger because at this point I wasn't able to walk for two days after matches. I was really emptying the tank one last time.

The people at Sale were very down to earth and there was a lovely atmosphere at the club. I was living in Hale, which is a lovely little suburb of Manchester, and it was a really enjoyable season. Lou Reed – one of Welsh rugby's biggest characters – was there at the time. He's a big old second row and is absolutely hilarious. He wasn't getting picked at one point and so we went for a coffee one day for him to get a few things off his chest. He was moaning about not being picked – which, to be honest, I think he was half happy about. So I said to him: "Kick it off in training then, start swinging some punches – Steve will love that, he's old school."

Lou looks at me through his glasses and says: "Mike, If I hit someone, they're not getting back up mate." We had some great laughs that year and having him around made my final year even more enjoyable.

The best Lou Reed story, and the one that will give you an insight into what a funny bloke he was, revolves around a Boxing Day derby. He was playing for the Scarlets against the Ospreys and when the first scrum hit, he shouted: "Hands up who had turkey yesterday boys!" Just a hell of a boy. During our time together at Sale, we played Toulon away. The club took everyone on this trip and it was a hell of a social gathering for the non-playing squad. First thing to mention here is that Lou is a hell of a singer. The boys had ended up in this nice restaurant and were egging him on to belt out a song, so he did, smashed it and everyone in the place loved it.

Everywhere they went, they were getting into Lou trying to get him to sing songs. The following week we were doing some training but Lou wasn't involved. One of the locks got an injury so the boys were calling over for Lou to come on from the sidelines. He ran onto the pitch and as he was running past me he goes: "What's up? They want me to sing another bloody song, do they?" He's just always up for a laugh and those characters are so important in a squad.

I had a really good run after Christmas, featuring regularly and playing well. That was huge for me because I was still adding value to the side and contributing in a positive way. I was starting to think that I could possibly go on for another year but deep down I knew it was coming to an end. I might have been playing well but I couldn't do the things that I used to be able to do. If I couldn't be the best version of myself then I knew my time was up.

My body was in pieces by this point. I wasn't taking a full part in the training week and sometimes I'd struggle to walk for three days after matches and, in truth, I wasn't quite the same. The fire in my belly wasn't burning quite as bright anymore and that was the real sign that it was time to call it day. I signed a one-year contract and that was probably a sign as well. If I was serious about playing on for longer I'd have pushed for a longer deal but I didn't.

I announced that I would be retiring from the game at the end of the season on April 11 but, in truth, I'd made a decision long before that. It was a case of seeing what I had left in the tank and I realised quite soon that it would be my last year.

My last game for Sale was at home against Bath. I was really happy with the way I played that day, I put in a good performance and I was glad to be going out like that. I controlled the game well, made a few breaks and was happy with my efforts. We won as well, which topped it all off. If I'd played poorly and we'd lost, that would have probably annoyed me forever, so it was good to finish like that.

I got a lovely standing ovation from the crowd when I left the field because by then everyone knew it was my last game. I was just really content with my decision and everything I'd achieved and, again, it was nice to be going out on good terms with the club. Steve spoke really nicely about me in the press and it was all very positive. At the time I was doing a bit of coaching for the Senghenydd Women's team as part of a series for S4C. I said to Orchard, the production company, that it might be an idea to come and follow me for my last 24 hours in rugby.

So I had a film crew with me the night before the game and the day of my final match. I had a load of mates travel up from Whitland Cricket Club to watch the match and all the family were there. Amy from Follow Your Dreams came up to watch the match with her parents as well. It was a really nice occasion. I got a bit emotional. How can you not? I'd been a professional rugby player for the best part of 16 years. It was pretty much all I ever knew. But I knew I was making the right decision. That night me and all the boys went into Hale and had a great night celebrating.

A few months after retiring, I was spending my days just chilling out, enjoying the weather in Dubai, and figuring out what my next move would be. Then in November 2017, I got a phone call from my old half-back partner Stephen Jones. He was attack coach at the Scarlets back then. I was on loudspeaker and Wayne Pivac, head coach at the time, was there. They'd had some injuries and Gareth Davies and Aled Davies were away with Wales, so they asked if I wanted to link up with them on their mini tour of South Africa and sit on the bench for two games. I wasn't sure to be honest but I thought, having started at the Scarlets all those years ago, it would be a nice way to finish.

They rang me on a Monday and I went straight to the gym for the first time in ages and absolutely beasted myself. I travelled on the Wednesday, got there on the Thursday and we were playing on the Sunday. When I got there, Steve sat me down in the team room and put this sheet of paper in front of me to talk me through the moves. A few of the backroom staff were milling around and Steve's running me through all these plays and I just jump in and explain: "Steve, sorry but I'm not the man I was mate! I'm just going to play it as I see it!" Steve laughed. He basically told me to train as much or as little as I wanted. It was a good insight into Steve as a coach.

I wasn't in great shape so my thought process was to not go looking for contact. All I wanted to do was just pass and do the basics well enough. I was on the bench against the Southern Kings, it was a beautiful day, dry ball. I was thinking that if I could get on for the last 10 minutes, that would be great and I could go big if I wasn't going to be on for that long.

Early in the match, starting scrum-half Jonathan Evans rolled his ankle. I was sat on the bench absolutely devastated by this. Fair play, he managed to get through until half-time, then I came on and we conceded a try within a minute of me being on the field. Things were looking pretty grim at that point and I was thinking: 'Shit, come on now.' So we sorted things out and came back from 23-10 down to win 34-30 and claim a bonus point.

Pivac and Steve were over the moon, I loved it and it was great. We had a good few drinks after that first game.

I was rooming with one of the young wingers and he said to me one night: "I'm just going FaceTime my missus because it's her birthday."

So I said: "Ahh tidy, wish her happy birthday from me, how old is she?"

He goes: "She's 17."

I'm thinking to myself: 'Bloody hell!' He was only 18 or something but there I was at the age of 34. That made me feel old! I felt like I should have been sat in the corner with my pipe and slippers on.

Because of the injury Jonathan Evans had suffered, suddenly I was the only fit scrum-half on the trip, which was a bit of a problem. So they managed to rope in a young South African guy named Herschel Jantjies. I thought he was just some guy who was third choice for his club, looking for a game. Next thing, I see him scoring tries for South Africa and winning the World Cup! It was brilliant, I was chuffed when I saw him on that stage just a few years later. It was also good to see that he was paying attention during those few training sessions we had together in Bloemfontein!

It was really interesting to work with Pivac, who is now Wales coach, a little bit as well. He was great. I really like the way he looks at the game. He's all about creating space, scoring tries and being positive. I think he'll go on to be a very successful Wales coach. He'll have a big impact on Welsh rugby. I obviously hope he helps us win the World Cup but even if he doesn't, he'll still have a huge influence on the game in Wales just because of the style of play he wants to employ. Hopefully that'll trickle down.

On the Tuesday before the second game, we'd gone out to a restaurant and as we get back to the hotel, Pivac and Steve ask me to join them for a beer in the bar. Now I knew I was starting on Saturday so I was like: "Whoa now boys, I'm starting Saturday, better not!" But they talked me into it, not that I needed much convincing!

I really enjoyed playing with James Davies, Jonathan's younger brother, in the second game of the trip against the Cheetahs. We're all from the same village, so it was great to play alongside him. It was interesting to see the way the other boys looked up to him in the dressing room, even though he was still relatively young. He's a great player and he should have had far more Wales caps and received the call-up long before he did. They had this perception that he was a bit of a rogue but he was winning back-to-back man of the match awards and Gats kept overlooking him. James won a silver medal in the sevens at the 2016 Rio Olympics, which is an absolutely phenomenal achievement and just goes to show how talented he is. Jonathan, though, has had a phenomenal career.

It was clear from a young age that he was going to be success-ful. He's gone on multiple Lions tours, got man of the series in 2017 and has now captained Wales a couple of times. It's no surprise. Jon came through with the new wave of ultra-professional youngsters but he struck the right balance, in my opinion. He was always up for a good time and enjoyed himself without going overboard. We all went to Bancyfelin Primary School, which has produced an impressive number of outstanding rugby players, when you consider there were only about 50 kids there when I was around.

The legendary Delme Thomas, who helped Wales win a Grand Slam in 1971, captained Llanelli to a famous win over the All Blacks in 1972 and went on three Lions tours, came from the village. He was actually a hero of mine growing up because there was a big picture of him on the wall in school that I used to look up to virtually everyday. My dad's big claim to fame is that he played with Delme when they were younger.

Apparently Delme deems his greatest achievement to be playing with the father of Mike Phillips! I've been lucky enough to have a number of conversations with Delme and I would always get blown away by him. He's a complete legend. He used to tell stories about the Lions tours, when all they'd get given is a blazer and a tie. They'd have to take all their own training gear and things like this. It was a completely different ball game to these days. Players get showered in kit, free boots and all sorts now. Charles Lynn Davies, who earned a few caps in the mid-1900s was a Bancyfelin boy. There's Wayne Evans, who played over 200 regional games and my cousin Aled Thomas, who won the Sevens World Cup with Wales.

Anyway, the game comes around and the Cheetahs are better opposition than the Kings so we were down a few points. I decided, for some stupid reason, to try and take a quick tap. I bounced one of their players, got tackled and placed the ball back. Suddenly I could barely move. I was absolutely spent. If I needed confirmation that I'd made the right decision in retiring the previous season, that was it.

They brought Jantjies on and in the end we picked up a losing bonus point, which, given the circumstances, wasn't a terrible outcome. The boys came second in the league that year. I think my runners-up medal must have got lost on its way to Dubai! After the second game I shook hands and rode off into the sunset. I flew home business class on my tod, sipping on champagne listening to 80s and 90s music, singing to myself and loving life!

I've been thinking recently about how different my career might look if I knew what I know now back when I was just starting out. If I was as mature as I am now, if I knew the pitfalls that come with being in the public eye and was a little bit more switched on. It's impossible to know the answer but if I didn't have that side to me, the edge, the part of me that didn't care what people thought, would I have been the same player?

Probably not and, in turn, it's unlikely I'd have achieved as much as I did. This is true for every walk of life but when you're 20, you don't know half as much as you think you do. When you're 30, you know 10 times more than you knew when you were 20. When you're 40, times it by 100. That's just life. You make mistakes but that's how you learn, how you grow. I look back and think: 'Crikey! I was a bit nuts sometimes.' But that's who I was and it got me 99 Test caps, three Six Nations titles, two Lions tours and made me the most-capped scrum-half in Welsh rugby's history. Decent shift. If I could give one piece of advice to a 17-year-old version of myself, though, it would be to just be more aware of who you're with and where you are when you decide to let off some steam. Everybody needs to let their hair down sometimes, it's only natural. But if you're a Welsh rugby player, Cardiff ain't the best place to do it, as much fun as it is at the time.

A fortnight after retiring, myself and my partner got married at a small wedding in Paris. When I first sat down to write the guest list, like most couples, it started to get out of control pretty quickly so we kept things really small in the end.

Mike Phillips

We then had our wedding reception on a boat on the River Seine. The only picture we've put out from the day is with our backs to the camera. She works with a lot of people who are in the public eye, so she has an understanding of the pressures that can bring. With me being an ex-professional athlete, she knows there will be people interested in knowing who she is but she prefers the quieter life and would rather be anonymous. Given the public scrutiny I endured during my career, I can see her point!

Before we met, my wife had a plan to open a new branch of her company in Dubai and I liked the sound of that. I knew I could come here as an ex-professional rugby player and be pretty unique because there aren't many of them walking around the Middle East. I felt like there would be plenty of opportunities to make things happen for myself out here as opposed to being one of many in the UK.

So pretty much straight after I retired, we upped sticks and moved over. I'd only recently made her follow me to the north-west of England for a year and the weather there is not the best in the winter, so it was only fair that I went along with Dubai! I've absolutely loved living here from the moment we arrived. Don't get me wrong, I really enjoy going back to Wales but then I can't wait to return to Dubai.

You can be anonymous here, nobody knows you and you've got to make things happen for yourself. You've got to build relationships and do some networking. The weather is always good, which helps! I feel really settled here now. Since arriving, I've been searching for what I want to throw myself into next.

I've dabbled in a few different areas; property, coaching, the media, business development. I'm still searching but instead of having to divide up my energy between a few different areas,

I've decided that I need to find what I'm going to do next and give it 100 percent of my energy. Just like my rugby career. It's taken me some time to get stuck into the next chapter of my life. I think the WRU could have been doing more for players when they were coming to the end of their careers. It's pleasing to see the Welsh Rugby Players' Association doing some work to get players on courses and preparing for life after rugby but I never really had that. Maybe I could have been more proactive but I didn't know where to start. It felt a little bit like I was a piece of meat and when they were done with me, that was it.

There is something to be said for what Saracens were trying to do. I'm not condoning breaking the salary cap or anything like that and ultimately they were found guilty of wrongdoing. But essentially they were attempting to get players into businesses and safeguard their futures after rugby. Is that such a bad thing? Of course you have to do it within the rules but, from where I'm standing, they were doing more to look after their players than most. Boys don't get paid enough as it is for what they put their bodies through.

If the Principality Stadium sells out, the WRU will make somewhere in the region of £6.5 million from one game. At one point in my career, I played every minute of the Six Nations and was paid £15,000 after tax. I understand the WRU provide funding for the grassroots game and have to pay the regions for access to players but people are making money and the players deserve to be looked after.

My wife is an events planner, which keeps her incredibly busy. Towards the end of my playing career, we were on the Amalfi Coast and, through her, I met Puff Daddy on his yacht. That was an experience and a half. Jimmy Iovine – who created Beats with Dr. Dre – was also there.

After spending some time with them, the only thing going through my head was that I just have to work harder at the things I'm going to do in retirement. Puff Daddy was constantly busy and taking calls, he was always hustling and to see the way he operated blew my mind and opened my eyes in so many ways. He had this aura about him, it was massively inspiring to see his work ethic first hand.

All of his mates were really welcoming too and I remember going out for food one night in this unbelievable restaurant. I was mesmerised by their anecdotes and life experiences. I've also attended events that my wife has arranged. She's done a lot of high-end events for a lot of very successful people. It's just a different world to what I'm used to.

I'll be walking around with my head in the clouds just innocently asking: "So, err, how much does this yacht cost then?" And she'll be kicking me under the table, giving me the death stare. She's very good at what she does and I'm incredibly proud of the things she has achieved in her own career. I don't spend too much time in her world but when I do it becomes apparent that all these incredibly successful people are just normal human beings, the only difference is they work harder than anyone else and that has had an impact on me.

It's funny how the world works but my wife actually did some work with a Cardiff Blues player back when I was at the region. Back then, she'd just set up her events company with a friend. They acquired a small office in Paris with two desks. They're sat opposite each other and it was a case of: 'Right, what now?' They knew a guy who was hosting a cocktail party and inviting a load of clients, so they convinced him to let them brand it as their launch party. It all went well, there were loads of people there, and then a few days later a fax came through from Adidas.

They wanted my wife and her friend to organise the launch of their massive new store on the Champs-Élysées. They were absolutely buzzing, reading this fax line by line as it was coming through on the machine. Then there were massive meetings about how they were going to launch it and the Adidas representatives started saying things like: "Oh my god, he's coming, I can't believe he's coming!" My wife asked who they were talking about and the response came back: "We've got Jonah Lomu coming to open the store." I must have been busy that day.

Anyway, my wife didn't have a clue who Lomu was but went along with it all and he attended their launch party while we were team-mates at the Blues. Talk about six degrees of separation and all that. This was about eight or nine years before we finally met.

Our wedding was an amazing day, one of the happiest of my life and only eclipsed by the birth of our sons Elias in 2018 and Zayn in 2020. I'd wanted to be a father for such a long time and it's just incredible. There's no better feeling than when your child comes running up to you for a hug, better than anything I experienced during my career.

I love the responsibility that comes with being a father. I'm a bit of a soft touch when it comes to them, my wife is a bit stricter! I find it difficult to say no to them but I'm pretty good at instilling a bit of discipline into them as well. It would have been great if they'd been around to see me play but my highlights are on repeat on the TV so I think they get it – hours of entertainment. No Peppa Pig in this house! In all seriousness, neither of them are old enough to realise what I did for a living just yet. The other day, I was trying to put one of my Lions jerseys on my oldest and he was saying: "No, no daddy, I want Lion King top."

I was trying to tell him: "No, daddy was Lion King! This is a Lions top, daddy played for the Lions."

He wasn't having any of it, so I had to take the Lions top off him and get the Lion King one. The other day, I told him again that I was the Lion King and he replied: "No, I'm Lion King!" Maybe one day, son.

When they are old enough to get it, I hope they're proud of what their dad achieved. I'd love to take them to a game in Cardiff. Just get a ticket like a normal punter and sit in the stands.

Let them experience the roar of the crowd, see the flames and the fireworks before kick-off as the players run out onto the field. I've got many special memories in that stadium but sharing that moment with my boys would top them all.

My father used to take me to Stradey Park and the Arms Park to watch the big matches. I remember walking around the outside of the stadiums and peaking through the gaps to see the pitch and the crowd and then getting to experience that atmosphere. Those moments grip you as a youngster, they inspire you and they're really fond memories. There is plenty of time for all that, though.

Right now it's a really special time in their lives, seeing them grow and develop every day and I'm trying to savour it all. I get asked a lot whether or not I want them to be rugby players when they grow up. They've got some options because my wife has both French and Moroccan heritage.

If they're bang average, they can play for France and if they're world class like their old man, they can play for Wales! If not, there's always Morocco. Jokes aside, I won't be putting any pressure on them. I want them to find their own passion and their own path.

For 16 years I was living the dream, working every day to become the best scrum-half in the world. Now, though, it's no longer about me. My only goal is to be the best possible father to my kids and husband to my wife. Nothing else matters.

Do I miss the game? Not one bit.

I'm really content with my life right now, I enjoy every day and the future looks bright.